Under the Apple Tree

Under the Apple Tree

God's provision for love, sex, and marriage

Dr. Jon McNeff

XULON PRESS

Xulon Press
2301 Lucien Way #415
Maitland, FL 32751
407.339.4217
www.xulonpress.com

Unless otherwise indicated, Scripture quotations taken from the
New American Standard Bible (NASB). Copyright © 1960, 1962,
1963, 1968, 1971, 1972, 1973, 1975, 1977, 1995 by The Lockman
Foundation. Used by permission. All rights reserved.

Printed in the United States of America.

Paperback ISBN-13: 978-1-6628-0549-3
Hardcover ISBN-13: 978-1-6628-0653-7
eBook ISBN-13: 978-1-6628-0550-9

TABLE OF CONTENTS

SECTION ONE: FALLING IN LOVE

How does God bring couples together?

What should I look for in a man?

What should I look for in a woman?

SECTION TWO: TYING THE KNOT

What are the guidelines for dating and courtship?

How do you handle pre-marital doubt?

What's the purpose of a wedding?

ENDORSEMENTS

J on McNeff's study in the Song of Solomon is solidly biblical, being built on years of exegetical experience where the reader is brought into the text and the world of 10th century BC. But it is not overly so because of the decades of work that reveals a pastor's heart driven to take the text into people's lives for hope and help. Not only does one gain a better understanding of the background and flow of the book, but he learns God's Word on biblical romance and marriage.

An important read for any serious student of the Song of Solomon, and a useful tool in the hands of those helping others understand God's Word and ways for relationships. As a biblical counselor, this commentary will serve me well in helping others grow and change in their marriages.

Chris Bruynzeel
Sr. Associate Pastor
Bethany Bible Church
Thousand Oaks, CA

I've known Jon McNeff for over 25 years. We've partnered in many, many counseling situations over the years. Jon's book is like his counseling: Professional and personal, doctrinal and practical, thoughtful and organized. You'll get a ton of great practical wisdom from this book that will enhance both your newly married years as well as your later years.

Steve Mawhorter
Pastor of Adult Ministries
NorthCreek Church
Walnut Creek, CA

In a day where there is so much confusion about gender and what constitutes a true marriage, *Under the Apple Tree* by Jon McNeff is a refreshing book that looks at God's true purpose and design for marriage. With great insight from the biblical text and the added perspective and wisdom from nearly fifty years of marriage, McNeff walks the reader through the Song of Solomon, tackling various topics, including dating, the wedding, the realities and troubles of married life, and staying in love. Not only is this a wonderful resource for those desiring to get married and those newly married, but it is also an encouragement for those of us who have been married for decades.

Phillip Foley
Lead Pastor
Community Bible Church
Vallejo, California

ACKNOWLEDGEMENTS

The contents of this book were first delivered as a sermon series to the congregation of NorthCreek Church in Walnut Creek, California in 2016. Their encouragement and feedback was fundamental in shaping the direction of this book. I wish every pastor could have the experience of leading a church like this.

There are many people who contributed their friendship, example, critiques, advice, editorial skills, and feedback on the issue of marriage for this book. I want to thank each of them who have spent much time and effort in reading various drafts of this book and offering their feedback.

Your family can always tell if you are lying and I've had five members of my family read through the manuscript. They have not only checked for authenticity, they have applied their editorial skills and insights throughout the process. In addition to my wife Anne, I have three brothers who read through the manuscript and offered their insights. Dave and Mike McNeff are both pastors, and Jim McNeff is a career law enforcement officer and managing editor of *Law Officer*. My sister-in-law, Sandie McNeff, served over thirty years as a legal assistant. I also profited greatly from the editorial skills of

Lois Gonzenbach, Sue Christy, and pastor Chris Bruynzeel. I am deeply in debt to all of them for their theological knowledge, editorial skills, and life experience that challenged and focused my thinking on a number of issues.

DEDICATION

This book is dedicated first of all to my wife Anne. Her commitment to the Lord and her love for an imperfect husband has been a steady stream of encouragement as a faithful partner through almost fifty years of marriage. I married up when I married her.

How thankful I am for the fruit of that relationship that has brought our children and their spouses into our lives. Casey and Brent Moutier, Lindsey and Nick Christy, and Pete and Lindsey McNeff, are a constant source of joy as we see them building their own family trees in the next generation through Riley, Bailey, and Sydney Moutier, Caleb, Micah, Jude, Seth, and Grace Christy, and Hallie and Colten McNeff.

I also want to dedicate this book to the memory of my parents, Allan and Twyla McNeff. Their simple devotion to the Lord and their love for each other shaped my life in a profound way.

PREFACE

M arriage is one of God's best ideas, second only to Redemption itself! God created us in his image – male and female – wired to be attracted to one another to become ONE for mutual completion emotionally, intellectually, physically, and spiritually, in a lifelong exclusive relationship, making Marriages and Families the core of society and the basic building blocks of communities and nations.

The depths of human personhood in God's design is indescribable, making the potential of the meaning and fulfillment in a marriage equally indescribable. On the other hand, when the dysfunction of our fallen nature is unleashed, marriage can be the most miserable experience on earth. That's why books like this that reveal God's design and intention for marriage are so desperately needed in our day.

As their Youth Pastor, I was privileged to observe Jon and Anne's courtship and honored to officiate at their wedding on August 12, 1972. I wished I could have given a warrantee when I tied their "knot", but Jon and Anne had to forge their own warranty by seriously following God's teaching on marriage.

Jon's down-to-earth writing style draws us into his skillful exposition of The Song of Solomon, revealing deep insight and valuable practical application for newly-weds as well as those who have accumulated decades of wedding anniversaries. Our fallen world subjects all marriages to the storms of life, but only those who sink their roots deeply into God's Truth and Character find the strength to not only survive but THRIVE. Jon and Anne's marriage has proven to have that kind of strength, especially when God led them through the "valley of the shadow of death" when they tragically lost their precious three-year-old son, Charlie, in 1982.

The best recommendation to read this book is not from me, but from how the countenances of Jon and Anne, now in their retirement years, exude joy and energy from a deeply fulfilling marriage bond, resulting in a beautiful family raised, while pastoring God's people for forty eight years.

Adjust your recliner – or prop up your pillows in bed – for a soul nurturing and marriage enriching experience.

Gratefully,

Wayne Bibelheimer
Pastoral Care – Senior Adults
Quail Lakes Baptist Church

EXPLANATORY NOTES

Almaty, Kazakhstan is the home of the apple. In fact, the former name of Almaty was "Alma-Ata" which means "father of apples." I've been to Almaty many times and have seen the vast apple orchards where apples once grew wild. The genome of the apple has been traced back to the Tien Shan forest outside Almaty to prove that this area is the cradle of all of the large and tasty Fuji, Honey Crisp, and Red Delicious apples available today.

It might seem strange to tie the title of a book on marriage to apples, but in the Song of Solomon, the apple tree is referred to twice by a young shepherd girl who became King Solomon's wife. In Chapter 2 she compared Solomon to an apple tree, saying, "In his shade I took great delight and sat down." She continued, "his fruit was sweet," indicating she reveled in the shade of his provision and protection.

In Chapter 8, both Solomon and his wife are under the apple tree enjoying the shade of protection and provision from their parents who brought them into the world. This is the picture our world needs. Despite many attacks, marriage remains God's provision for mankind and the best chance we have for achieving the best things life has to offer.

THE STORY

The story of the Song of Solomon is relatively simple. There are five canticles or brief songs in the book. They depict the romance of a country girl who lived in the hill country near the Sea of Galilee. She met Solomon, the young king of Israel, while he was in the area checking on some of his flocks of sheep. They were mutually attracted to each other, and their relationship blossomed into marriage. Soon after the marriage they had a misunderstanding. Their reconciliation and affirmation of marriage occupies the remainder of the book.

The narrative moves from meeting to courtship to wedding to married life. This is done through a series of flashbacks, remembrances and bits of conversation that toggle back and forth between Solomon and the young woman.

THE INTERPRETATION

The various interpretive methods of the Song of Solomon are all over the map. No doubt this is driven by the form of Hebrew poetry that is used throughout the book and the lack of historical landmarks to guide us.

The allegorical method

The *allegorical* method of interpretation is used by many. This means that when you read something it really represents some kind of deeper, hidden meaning. The passage in question doesn't contain any factual or historically valid record of the past. It's only an extended metaphor used as a literary device.

Those who apply this interpretive method say the Song of Solomon is not a true historical account of two lovers. They symbolize something else. Most who hold this interpretive model see the book as a picture of Christ's love for the church. They say the *"beloved"* is the church and Solomon is a picture of Christ.

Roman Catholic scholars take the allegorical method a step further. For example, they say the words in Song of Solomon 4:7, "You are all fair, my love; there is no flaw in you," are speaking of the Immaculate Conception of the Virgin Mary. They also hold that "Your navel is as rounded bowl that never lacks mixed wine" in Song of Solomon 7:2 refers to the baptismal font.

This is a flawed approach that stretches the bounds of belief. It's very hard to explain the explicit language, physical passion, cautious meetings, and the wedding caravan as mere allegories of Christ's love for the church. There is nothing that would lead us to believe that the people and events of the Song of Solomon are allegories for something else.

Song of Solomon as a type of New Testament truth

Others view the Song of Solomon as a *type* of New Testament truth. A *type* means that something you see in the Old Testament is a *type* of something in the New Testament. But when the New Testament doesn't make any direct connection, we need to be careful about saying the Old Testament passage is a *type* of something in the New Testament.

There is a distinct *absence* of certain words in the book that would provide a tie to the New Testament. For instance, similar to Esther, there is no mention of God. The word *Lord* is used only once. There is also no mention of words associated with worship like *high place, throne, mercy-seat, temple, altar, offering, sacrifice,* or *priest.* Theological terms like *evil, faith, truth covenant, sin, wisdom, grace, mercy, justice, save, holy, wicked, blessing, worship, heaven,* and *Law* are also absent.

With such a lack of any key theological words, it's virtually impossible to make a case for using either the allegory or type method to interpret the Song of Solomon. They must be rejected as valid interpretive models.

Interpretive extremes

A basic rule of biblical interpretation, is "when the first sense makes sense, seek no other sense." In other words, stick with the most natural reading of the text. An objective person reading the Song of Solomon at first glance would think that they are reading a love story between a man and a woman. This is true but it can lead to two erroneous extremes.

The first is the oversexualization of the content. Some interpreters find an explicit sexual reference seemingly in every other verse. This makes the couple seem like sex-starved teenagers who can't keep their hands off one another. This does not fit the character of a book inspired by God on the subject of sex and marriage, or the character of Solomon and his bride.

But this is not a steamy romance novel, despite the sexual inferences and pictures in the book. And we certainly can tell that the couple has a normal physical attraction to one another. But their expressions of intimate love are seen through the eyes of mature marital reflection in a manner that doesn't violate a sense of social decency and proper restraint.

The other interpretive extreme is to ignore the sexual allusions or pretend that they are something else. This is a major flaw of the "Christ and the church" interpretation. Taking this approach distorts the text and ignores the obvious physical nature of the love between a husband and his wife.

The most natural interpretation

The proper balance is to recognize the sexual language is there and celebrate it as a gift from God for husbands and wives. In fact, it fits in with other passages of Scripture that describe sexual content in a way that doesn't awaken voyeuristic interest, such as the creation account in Genesis 2.

God created sex. In this tawdry age it is refreshing to study the one book that he devoted to this wonderful provision for mankind without making it something sleazy or prudish. Edward Young describes it this way:

> The Song does celebrate the dignity and purity of human love. This is a fact that has not always been sufficiently stressed. The Song, therefore, is didactic and moral in its purpose. It comes to us in this world of sin, where lust and passion are on every hand, where fierce temptations assail us and try to turn us aside from the God-given standard of

marriage. And it reminds us in particularly beautiful fashion, how pure and noble true love is.[1]

Solomon's Lovesong

The Song of Solomon is set in the form of a love song about King Solomon and a young shepherd girl who became his wife. It has all the heart and emotion of a contemporary song that brings nostalgic feelings to any couple. You can see that in the very first words of the book.

Solomon writes, "The Song of Songs, which is Solomon's," meaning, "THE Song of Solomon – the one surpassing all the others." The Hebrew word for *song* "refers not to singing intended solely for aesthetic effect but to the musical performance of address to God formulated in fixed language, usually of praise."[2] The Song of Solomon is literally Solomon's formal song of praise to God in thankfulness for his wife.

1 Kings 4:32 indicates Solomon wrote three thousand proverbs and over a thousand songs. But *this one* stands out above all the others in his mind. The construction of the phrase "Song of Songs" is the same as that of the phrases "Holy of Holies" and "vanity of vanities" in the Old Testament. It's a superlative that emphasizes superiority.

That explains the high Jewish attitude toward the book. Rabbi Akiba, a leading rabbi of the Bar Cochba Revolt (132–135 A.D.) stated, "No day in the whole history of the world

---

[1] Edward J. Young, *An Introduction to the Old Testament* (1949; repr., Grand Rapids, Michigan: Wm. B. Eerdmans Publishing Co., 1989), 336.

[2] Ernst Jenni , ed., and Claus Westermann, ed., and Mark E. Biddle, trans., *Theological Lexicon of the Old Testament (English, Hebrew, Aramaic and German Edition)* (Peabody, MA: Hendrickson Publishers, 1997), 1320.

is worth so much as that in which the Song of Songs was given: for all the writings are holy, but the Song of Songs is the Holy of Holies" (Mesilla 7a).[3] In another place Rabbi Akiba said, "The whole world attained its supreme value only on the day when the Song of Songs was given to Israel" (Mishnah Yadaim 3:5).[4]

Despite the high esteem for the book, the Song of Solomon was forbidden to be read by anyone under thirty because of its erotic content, a clue that the Jews regarded the book as literal instruction on marriage and not an allegory or type of something else. But once a man reached thirty the *Midrash Rabbah* points out that, "Had any other man composed them, it would have been incumbent on you to incline your ear and to listen to them; all the more since Solomon composed them. Had he composed them out of his own mind, it would have been incumbent on you to incline your ear and listen to them; all the more then since he composed them in the Holy Spirit."[5]

THE CHARACTERS IN THE BOOK

Solomon

It's very clear from the very first verse that the author of Song of Solomon is Solomon. There is no reason to take this as a euphemism for someone else. He is referred to as "king"

---

[3] Dr. Arnold G. Fruchtenbaum, *Biblical Lovemaking: A Study of the Song of Solomon* (Tustin, CA: Ariel Ministries Press, 1983), 1.

[4] Ibid.

[5] Ibid.

or "Solomon" five times. This is Solomon, the son of King David who served as the third king of the nation of Israel from 970 BC to 930 BC. Though David had a number of sons, on his deathbed he expressed his explicit desire that Solomon succeed him.

Some people refer to Solomon as the "smartest man in all the world." That may sound like an exaggeration, but 1 Kings 4:29-31, 34 says,

> Now God gave Solomon wisdom and very great discernment and breadth of mind, like the sand that is on the seashore. Solomon's wisdom surpassed the wisdom of all the sons of the east and all the wisdom of Egypt. For he was wiser than all men, than Ethan the Ezrahite, Heman, Calcol and Darda, the sons of Mahol; and his fame was known in all the surrounding nations...Men came from all peoples to hear the wisdom of Solomon, from all the kings of the earth who had heard of his wisdom.

The word for "wisdom" in Scripture is the Hebrew word *hokma*. It is not the mere accumulation of knowledge. "Wisdom" speaks of "a manner of thinking and attitude concerning life's experiences; including matters of general interest and basic morality. These concerns relate to prudence in secular affairs, skills in the arts, moral sensitivity, and experience in the ways of the Lord.[6] Solomon had this

---

[6] Louis Goldberg, "647 חָכַם," ed. R. Laird Harris, Gleason L. Archer Jr., and Bruce K. Waltke, *Theological Wordbook of the Old Testament* (Chicago: Moody Press, 1999), 282.

in abundance. Read through the book of Ecclesiastes where his wisdom is displayed in evaluating the pursuits of man.

Shulammite

The other main character in the book is the unnamed young shepherd girl. Solomon never reveals the identity of the young woman, but we have a clue to her identity in Song of Solomon 6:13 where he addresses her as *"Shulammite."* Most scholars feel her name is a reference to a small town called *Shunem* in the Galilee region near Mt. Gilboa. This could mean that Solomon was addressing her here as *the* Shulammite, referring to her hometown, but you could also make the case that he used this as her name.

We also see that even in English, *Shulammite* resembles the word *Solomon*. Since the word is feminine, it's possible that it's the feminine form of *Solomon,* indicating it could be rendered "Mrs. Solomon." I will refer to her as *Shulammite* or *Mrs. Solomon* throughout the book.

Ultimately her name doesn't matter. It is clear throughout the book that Solomon loves her deeply and she returns his affection. Her character and integrity are what matters most. Old Testament scholars Keil and Delitzsch describe her this way:

> That which attached her to him is not her personal beauty alone, but her beauty animated and heightened by nobility of soul. She is a pattern of simple devotedness, naive simplicity, unaffected modesty, moral purity, and frank prudence, — a

lily of the field, more beautifully adorned than he could claim to be in all his glory. We cannot understand the Song of Songs unless we perceive that it presents before us not only Shulamith's external attractions, but also all the virtues which make her the idea of all that is gentlest and noblest in woman. Her words and her silence, her doing and suffering, her enjoyment and self-denial, her conduct as betrothed, as a bride, and as a wife, her behaviour towards her mother, her younger sister, and her brothers,—all this gives the impression of a beautiful soul in a body formed as it were from the dust of flowers. Solomon raises this child to the rank of queen and becomes beside this queen as a child. The simple one teaches the wise man simplicity; the humble draws the king down to her level; the pure accustoms the impetuous to self-restraint. Following her, he willingly exchanges the bustle and the outward splendour of court life for rural simplicity, wanders gladly over mountain and meadow if he has only her; with her he is content to live in a lowly cottage."[7]

The daughters of Jerusalem

Another group mentioned seven times in the book, is the "daughters of Jerusalem." This probably referred to a group of women in Jerusalem who became friends and confidants

---

[7] Carl Friedrich Keil and Franz Delitzsch, *Commentary on the Old Testament*, vol. 6 (Peabody, MA: Hendrickson, Publishers Inc., 1996), 499–500.

of the bride to be. Some feel that these women were members of Solomon's harem, but that is highly unlikely.

First of all, the Song of Solomon is set when Solomon was a young man and had not fallen to the political pressure to have a harem. Secondly, the ladies are called "the daughters of Jerusalem" which connotes a connection with the city which would not have been true of foreign women. Finally, the content of the conversations they had with Shulammite are typical chatter that might be expressed between young women who are best of friends.

These women probably grew up with Solomon. Perhaps they were the daughters of attendants and workers in the palace. No doubt they had read and heard some of Solomon's poetry and songs. They knew of his love of God. As Shulammite came to the palace and met them they became close confidants and friends.

THE STYLE OF WRITING

The first thing you will notice about the Song of Solomon is it uses very descriptive words and phrases. The second thing you might notice is that it is hard to follow. It's hard to tell who is speaking to whom and what is meant.

That's because the book is a form of Hebrew poetry. But Hebrew poetry is very different from ours. English poetry has meter and rhythm, and it usually rhymes. It's unusual for English poems not to rhyme. I'm sure you've heard this "poem" that proves my point. "Roses are red, violets are blue, some poems rhyme – but this one don't!" We expect our poems to rhyme.

Hebrew poetry isn't like that. It doesn't rhyme. Most often it is arranged by topic or graphic word pictures. Sometimes the poet arranges couplets or verses in alphabetical order with each verse beginning with a successive letter of the Hebrew alphabet.

Solomon uses places and things from his world to picture abstract truths he wants to explain. We must also recognize that some of the strong, graphic language was shared by Shulammite with Solomon after they were married. This allows him to comment on feelings and events with knowledge of what she was thinking at the time.

It's also best to understand that the observations in the book are not mandates or commands. They simply comprise a picture that is instructive. These observations are profitable for everyone, married or unmarried, because we all love a good story that holds up the virtues of marriage in a flawed world.

My son-in-law's wedding ring is a visual picture of a key truth in marriage. It is three gold bands intertwined together in a way that they can't be separated. Even when he is not wearing it, it sort of jangles like three keychains linked together. The ring is a symbol of man, wife, and God in the marriage.

That's a beautiful picture of what we see in Solomon's love song. A man – a woman – and God – all intertwined in the most intimate of earthly relationships in a way that depicts God's love for us. Marriage in the Song of Solomon depicts God's provision of romantic love between a man and a woman enabled by a clear conscience, spiritual meaning, emotional stability, and passing on the best things in life from one generation to the next.

The Big Question

Before we begin looking at the book, there is a question that is lurking behind the scenes in the Song of Solomon. Anyone who knows about Solomon knows that 1 Kings 11:3 says Solomon had "seven hundred wives, princesses, and three hundred concubines."

The obvious question is, "How in the world could this love song to one woman be penned by a man with 700 wives and 300 concubines?" How can this book be seen as a picture of an honorable man and woman displaying the virtues of a godly marriage? Good question.

It sounds rather naïve to think that a man could have 700 wives and 300 concubines without being consumed by his sexual appetites, but there is evidence to suggest this may have been true. The first thing to notice is that these women were political alliances (1 Kings 3:1). In biblical times, it was common for a king to maintain peace by marrying a member of the ruling family of a neighboring nation, even though God expressly forbid this practice (1 Kings 11:2).

But this doesn't mean that Solomon abandoned his commitment to marriage – or his love of God. God was certainly angry with him for disobeying his command against marrying foreigners (1 Kings 11:9-13), but we can see Solomon's commitment to the integrity of marriage in the book of Proverbs, mostly written by Solomon.

Solomon spends all of Proverbs 5 warning his own son about the pitfalls of adultery. In verses 15-18 he instructs his son to "drink water from your own cistern and fresh water from your own well. Should your springs be dispersed abroad,

Streams of water in the streets? Let them be yours alone and not for strangers with you. Let your fountain be blessed and rejoice in the wife of your youth."

So, what happened to Solomon? 1 Kings 11:4 says, "when Solomon was old, his wives turned his heart away after other gods." Despite his love for the wife of his youth Solomon's heart was turned away to the pagan gods worshipped by the many women he married. He first slipped in his spiritual life which led to sexual sin. Like many other men before and after him, it seems that when the voice of the Lord grew dim, the voice of vice became louder.

But that doesn't mean Solomon ended his life that way. Nehemiah 13:26 records, "Did not Solomon king of Israel sin regarding these things? Yet among the many nations there was no king like him, and he was loved by his God, and God made him king over all Israel; nevertheless, the foreign women caused even him to sin." His reputation as a man who sinned yet was loved by God is intact over 500 years later.

The end of the book of Ecclesiastes also contains some of his final thoughts. Ecclesiastes 12:1 says, "Remember also your Creator in the days of your youth, before the evil days come and the years draw near when you will say, 'I have no delight in them . . .'" Solomon certainly committed sexual sin in his later years. But that doesn't detract from the lessons on love, sex, and marriage he expressed in the Song of Solomon.

SECTION ONE

FALLING IN LOVE

"I love you so much, I don't mind that life made me wait so long to find you. The waiting only made the finding sweeter....I live in a permanent Christmas because God gave me you."

— Ronald Reagan

CHAPTER ONE

BOY MEETS GIRL
(Song of Solomon 1:1-8)

West Side Story was ahead of its time. Set in New York city in the 1950s, it's a story about the conflict between a white gang and a Puerto Rican gang. But the deeper theme is the love story between Tony and Maria. Tony had been part of the white gang but had taken a job and wanted to put the ways of the street behind him. Maria was the younger sister of Bernardo, the leader of the Puerto Rican gang.

Officer Krupke did everything he could as the cop on the beat to keep it light between the gangs. One night he invited both sides to a dance. They came – but with leery looks of distrust and apprehension about the other gang who stayed on the other side of the dance floor.

But then the music slows down. The lights dim. The camera zooms in on two people who inadvertently wander to the center of the floor and bump into each other. It's Tony and Maria. Tony's gone! For the next five minutes he sings "Maria! Maria! I've just met a girl named Maria." Girls swoon over this, but guys usually make puking sounds when they hear a song like this in a musical.

When I was young, I had several "serious" girlfriends. There was Janet, and Marsha, and Diane. And then I got to Junior High! In High School I learned what it was to be the *dumpee* as well as the *dumper*. Oooo! Love hurts!

In college a group of my friends formed the BTR club – "Bachelors til the Rapture!" We all thought, "Yup, I'm never gonna get married." Of course, we would never admit the club was formed to protect all of us macho men from another broken heart.

And then one day the music slowed down and the lights dimmed for me. I was a sophomore at Cypress College. I was looking out a darkened window on the third floor of the Fine Arts Building adjusting my tie for a stage production I was in. That's when I saw *her!* She was walking across the parking lot three floors below with a friend. My eyes followed her as she entered the building.

About five minutes later a friend of mine grabbed my hand and dragged me into the hall to introduce me to a girl she had gone to high school with. It was *her!* The girl from the parking lot! Her name was Anne. "Anne! I just met a girl named Anne!" And I immediately resigned my position in the BTR club!

What is that? We might call it simply boy meets girl, but it can turn into something much more than that. God created us to be attracted to a person of the opposite sex in a way that leaves us dumbfounded at some point. If circumstances allow and feelings deepen, we get married.

The Song of Solomon begins with this kind of attraction. The first eight verses are the characteristics of the initial relationship of Solomon and a girl we are going to call Shulammite throughout this book. This is the "getting to know you" part of their story.

PHYSICAL DESIRE

Shulammite's opening line gets right to the point. "May he kiss me with kisses of his mouth" would have almost any guy willing to oblige. But this doesn't fit with the first words a girl would say to a guy, nor does it fit with the way events unfold throughout the book, so it seems best to consider these words as something Shulammite later told her husband that she thought when she first met him.

But they were not just a teeny-bopper's expression that the guy was hot. It was more than that. Shulammite's words convey something deeper than a kiss.

Kissing is an intimate expression. It's more intimate than a handshake or a hug. And this is not a peck on the cheek. It's on the mouth! This is a natural desire when a boy and girl meet, but kissing is a big deal because, as all couples come to realize, a kiss might be innocent for the girl, but for the boy it gets his engine running.

This desire is displayed in thousands of movies. The facial expressions before "the first kiss" are filled with questions and unspoken desires and questions about what will happen after their lips touch. Of course, most modern movies display what comes after in living color as they move from the first kiss right to the bedroom.

Intoxicating love

The context of the kiss Shulammite speaks of is because "your love is better than wine." This expression definitely projects beyond the first kiss. The shift from first person to second person isn't a grammatical problem. She is acknowledging the reason for her desire to be kissed. His love was intoxicating. The kiss she desired wasn't their first kiss or even a casual kiss. She was thinking of a kiss sheltered in love.

Her usage of the particular Hebrew word for "love" gives a clue to what she is thinking. In English we have only one word for love. I might use it to say, "I love pizza," "I love my dog," and "I love my wife." What a range of objects for my affection. But the love described here is not ambiguous.

Unlike English, the biblical languages of Greek and Hebrew are more descriptive. The Hebrew word *dod* is equivalent to *eros* in Greek. It refers to erotic or sexual love. The Hebrew word *ra'eyah* is equivalent to *phileo* in Greek and it points to the natural emotional response of family and friends. The Hebrew word *ahavah* is parallel to the Greek word *agape* and describes the active sense of love as in Christ's love for us.

So which word do you think Shulammite used here? It might surprise you to learn that the word she uses is *dod*, referring to erotic love. The root word means "to cause to boil up." It speaks of the contents of a boiling pot being stirred vigorously.[8] It's also important to note that "it is a plural form with singular meaning and describes all aspects of sexual love."[9]

This type of love is natural and good in the sight of God. After all, He created it. But it is to be applied in marriage. The book of Genesis tells us that God created the male-female attraction when He created Adam and Eve. After creating Adam, He caused a deep sleep to come over him and then He created Eve out of his side.

When Adam woke up and looked at the woman God had created for him in Genesis 2:23, he said, "this is now bone of my bones, and flesh of my flesh; she shall be called woman, because she was taken out of man." "This is now" might be translated as "Whoa!" Adam was stunned by God's provision of a help mate in the form of a beautiful woman.

And God blessed this feeling. In fact, He makes it the basis for the marital relationship. Verse 24 continues, "For this reason a man shall leave his father and his mother, and be joined to his wife; and they shall become one flesh. And the man and his wife were both naked and were not ashamed."

God's creation of marriage accomplishes three basic functions. First, this is God's creation. Marriage is not a social construct. It has not evolved over time. God welded the first man and woman together so that they would not come apart. This is how God intends for every marriage to be.

Second, marriage is complementary. It is not meant to benefit man over woman or the other way around. Men and

---

[8] Carl Friedrich Keil and Franz Delitzsch, *Commentary on the Old Testament*, vol. 6 (Peabody, MA: Hendrickson, 1996), 512.

[9] Graham S. Ogden and Lynell Zogbo, *A Handbook on Song of Songs*, UBS Handbook Series, (New York: United Bible Societies, 1998), 19.

women have equal dignity in marriage. Man is to have leadership in function (as we will see later) but not in value.

Third, the "one flesh" nature of their relationship is intended for their personal joy, for the reproduction of the species, and as a picture of the gospel. Sex reveals God's glory in all these manifestations. That's why Jesus said, "So they are no longer two, but one flesh. What therefore God has joined together, let no man separate" (Matthew 19:6).

Hebrews 13:4 expresses it this way, "Marriage is to be held in honor among all, and the marriage bed is to be undefiled; for fornicators and adulterers God will judge." The word for *bed* is *koite*, from which we get the word *coitus*, or sexual intercourse. God is literally saying here that there is nothing defiled or dirty and inappropriate about sexual intercourse in marriage. It is His design for the joy of the couple, the procreation of the earth, as well as the singular picture of Christ's love for the church.

Mike Mason carefully explains the beauty of marital love in his book *The Mystery of Marriage*. He writes,

> What can equal the surprise of finding out that the one thing above all others which mankind has been most enterprising and proficient in dragging through the dirt turns out in fact to be the most innocent thing in the world? Is there any other activity at all which an adult man and woman may engage in together (apart from worship) that is actually more childlike, more clean and pure,

more natural and wholesome and unequivocally right than is the act of making love?[10]

Shulammite's statement acknowledges that she experienced a physical attraction to Solomon, but that attraction wasn't merely sexual. It was an expression of hope that this man would live up to her highest aspirations of what a kiss should mean in the context of marriage.

Perverted love

But every elevator that goes up also comes down. Though Shulammite doesn't mention it, the opposite of intoxicating love is perverted love. We can see this by noting that *dod* is also used in a negative light in scripture. It's the love of the harlot in a one night stand expressed in Proverbs 7:18; "Come, let us drink our fill of love until morning; Let us delight ourselves with caresses." Ezekiel 23:17 uses it to depict the perversion of religion: "The Babylonians came to her to the bed of love and defiled her with their harlotry."

The equivalent perversion is seen in the New Testament. 1 Corinthians 6:9 tells us that, among other things, fornicators, adulterers, effeminate, and homosexuals will not "inherit the kingdom of God." Likewise, in 1 Thessalonians 4:3 the Apostle Paul explains clearly, "this is the will of God, your sanctification; that is, that you abstain from sexual immorality."

Unfortunately, these distortions and abuses of sex have become symbols of the sewer in every generation since Adam.

---

[10] Mike Mason, *The Mystery of Marriage: As Iron Sharpens Iron* (Portland, Oregon: Multnomah Press, 1985), 121.

It's amazing that the beauty and innocence of marital love that has been blessed by God has become so commonly perverted.

Sex is like a river. It is beautiful and productive when it stays within its banks. But a river can be affected by both drought and flood. The first causes the river to dry up and lose its beauty and productivity, and the second allows it to become a raging torrent that destroys everything in its path. Both are destructive.

Redeeming love

But there is hope. The broader implications of Shulammite's desire for the kiss of love is seen in the New Testament. This is where we find the ultimate expression of love in marriage because marriage is the visible picture of Christ's love for the church. Ephesians 5:25-27 explains, "Husbands, love your wives, just as Christ also loved the church and gave Himself up for her, so that He might sanctify her, having cleansed her by the washing of water with the word, that He might present to Himself the church in all her glory, having no spot or wrinkle or any such thing; but that she would be holy and blameless."

What a powerful picture. The husband's love for his wife is a picture of Christ's love for the church. This began before the earth was created when God decided to take on the form of a man and come to earth in the person known as Jesus Christ (Philippians 2:6-8). While on the earth he lived a perfect life, made himself known to thousands of people through his teaching and miraculous works, and willingly gave up his own life to be unjustly tried by Jewish leaders, and crucified by Roman authorities (John 10:18) in order to take on himself the burden of our sin.

But the transforming glory of those events is that he was physically resurrected from the dead and returned to heaven, proving that he was indeed God and his work on the cross was valid. This brings hope to us since all of mankind has been born into sin, meaning that not one of us is righteous (Romans 3:10), that every one of us has sinned (Romans 3:23), and our mind is actually hostile toward God and unable to obey the law of God (Romans 8:7-8). Our experience tells us this is true.

But John 3:16 tells us, "For God so loved the world, that He gave His only begotten Son, that whoever believes in Him shall not perish, but have eternal life." God had to intervene because man was helpless to do anything about his condition, so Jesus came to seek and to save the lost (Luke 19:10). He didn't come to temporarily heal people, to set up a new government, to solve the economic or educational problems of man, or to offer psychological reformation. He came to bring spiritual regeneration.

When Jesus died on the cross his last words were, "It is finished" (John 19:30). That means there is no need to confess anything to a priest, join any church, pay any amount of money, do any kind of a religious act or ritual, turn over a new leaf, or try our very hardest to get into heaven.

Our part is simply to "repent and believe in the gospel" (Mark 1:15). Repenting means to see our sin and turn one hundred and eighty degrees in the opposite direction. Believing refers to the facts related to the identity of Jesus as

God in the flesh, and His sacrificial work on the cross to pay for sin. Paul tells us that "if you confess with your mouth Jesus as Lord, and believe in your heart that God raised Him from the dead, you will be saved" (Romans 10:9).

This is enacted by faith, which means we place all of our confidence in what Christ has done for us. According to Ephesians 2:8-9, "For by grace you have been saved through faith; and that not of yourselves, it is the gift of God; not as a result of works, so that no one may boast."

Saving faith means knowing the facts, accepting them as true, and acting on them by saying "I do" in a commitment like marriage. Engaged by faith, His redeeming love secures a place in heaven for us (Ephesians 2:6) and gives us the example and power to live in a way that reflects and models what He has done for us.

Justin and Lindsey Holcomb explain, "The gospel is the story of God covering his naked enemies, bringing them to the wedding feast and then marrying them rather than crushing them."[11] Most of us forget this. We think we are pretty good blokes who come off pretty well when compared to the guy down the street.

But God doesn't measure us by the guy down the street. He measures us by His standard which is absolute holiness. The passage in Ephesians 5:25-27 that we saw previously tells us that Christ made us holy by taking all the shame and debt of the bride (us) in exchange for the wealth and royal status of her bridegroom (Jesus).

Michael Reeves and Tim Chester explain it this way:

---

[11] Justin S. & Lindsey A. Holcomb, *Rid of My Disgrace: Hope and Healing for Victims of Sexual Assault* (Wheaton, Illinois: Crossway, 2011), 114.

Christ is full of grace, life, and salvation. The soul
is full of sins, death, and damnation. Now let faith
come between them and sins, death, and damnation will be Christ's, while grace, life, and salvation
will be the soul's; for if Christ is a bridegroom, he
must take upon himself the things which are his
bride's and bestow upon her the things that are his.
If he gives her his body and very self, how shall he
not give her all that is his? And if he takes the body
of the bride, how shall he not take all that is hers?[12]

Marital love cannot be divorced from the gospel.
Repentance, confessions, grace, and forgiveness, are indispensable to married life.

When Shulammite said, "your love is better than wine"
in Song of Solomon 1:2, she would not have been aware
of the New Testament context of love. But the context of
their commitment to integrity, along with our knowledge that
Solomon was a man who feared God and sought to keep his
commandments (Ecclesiastes 12:13,14), indicates Solomon
and Shulammite understood this kind of redeeming love.

That makes them what we might call "Old Testament
Christians." As we look *back* and believe the message of the
cross by faith, so people who lived in the Old Testament times
looked *forward,* and laid hold of the promises of God just like
we do – by faith.

We know this because this is the way Abraham was saved.
In Genesis 15:6. God had just revealed to him that he and

[12] Michael Reeves and Tim Chester, *Why the Reformation Still Matters* (Wheaton,
Illinois: Crossway, 2016), 86.

his wife Sarah would have a son, even though they both were well past child-bearing age, and that his descendants would be as numerous as the stars in heaven. When Abraham heard this, "he believed in the Lord; and He reckoned it to him as righteousness." Paul quoted this same verse in Romans 4:3 to show that we are saved in the same way as Abraham, through faith.

Nothing is more important for a married couple than to understand biblical love in this context. It's what empowers them to love each other in the way God designed. Solomon and Shulammite knew that.

The nose knows

But let's move along. Shulammite moves from her lips to her nose in the next verse. This may seem trivial but it's not. In Song of Solomon 1:3 she said, "Your oils have a pleasing fragrance." Basically, "You smell good!" In the hot desert climate in Israel during Solomon's day, men rarely bathed because water was scarce and precious. But that doesn't mean they were unaware of personal hygiene. In lieu of bathing they used a variety of oils and lotions to keep skin from drying out and to smell good.

Proper grooming and hygiene can be vain and overdone. There are all kinds of soaps, oils, creams, lotions, sprays, and ointments available to all of us to keep our bodies properly groomed and presentable. That's what Solomon did. He combed his hair, brushed his teeth, and put on some foo-foo juice to make himself smell good. And Shulammite noticed!

The Bible doesn't condemn good grooming. Proverbs 27:9 says "Oil and perfume make the heart glad." When Naomi gave Ruth instructions on how to get noticed by Boaz in Ruth 3:3, she told her to "Wash yourself therefore, and anoint yourself and put on your best clothes, and go down to the threshing floor; but do not make yourself known to the man until he has finished eating and drinking."

Neither is there anything wrong with beauty itself. Sarah (Genesis 12:11) and Rebekah (Genesis 24:16) were both called beautiful. Joseph's wife Rachel "was beautiful of form and face" (Genesis 29:17). Likewise, Queen Vashti was called beautiful (Esther 1:11) and her replacement, Queen Esther "was beautiful of form and face" (Esther 2:7). We are also told that Saul, David, and Absalom were all handsome.

Few of us will ever be the king and queen of the prom. But that doesn't mean you shouldn't take care of yourself. You don't have to overdo it but remember that you only get one chance to make a good first impression. If you need some grooming help, ask someone who is well groomed to give you some suggestions.

A GOOD REPUTATION

But Shulammite goes much beyond the physical. This is a great lesson for all of us. The sum total of a person's worth is not found in their looks. Shulammite also notices Solomon's character.

In Song of Solomon 1:3 she continues, "Your name is like purified oil." This is the first of many poetic pictures that is set in ancient times and thus in need of explanation.

The word for *name* is *sem*. It means "to mark or brand." It refers to something that distinguishes one person from another.[13] The picture is much like the old West practice of branding cattle to establish ownership. The word *name* here represents the totality of a person. It's not what they *think* they are, nor how *they want* to be perceived, but rather, what they really *are* deep down inside.

The words *purified oil* referred to the first pressing of the oil from olive trees around Jerusalem and was designated for the lampstand that burned in the Temple day and night. It was intended for Temple use only. Therefore, it was the best oil. It was given to God first. Shulammite is saying "I've seen your brand, and it's the best!" In other words, "You have an excellent reputation."

By the time she reflects this to Solomon she has seen what he is made of. She's been around people who know him. She's met his mom. She has seen his devotion to God and the way he treats the people around him. A reputation is built over a long period of time and destroyed in a second. Time reflected Solomon's reputation.

Shulammite's girlfriends were also aware of his reputation. This prompted the observation, "therefore the maidens love you." The word for maidens is *almah*. It refers to unmarried virgins. It's possible that she had girlfriends around her home, but this probably refers to the "daughters of Jerusalem" that are mentioned frequently throughout the book.

The love of the maidens for Solomon is *ahavah*, not *dod*. The *ahavah* kind of love is not based on feelings or sexual

---

[13] Walter C. Kaiser, "2405 שֵׁם," ed. R. Laird Harris, Gleason L. Archer Jr., and Bruce K. Waltke, *Theological Wordbook of the Old Testament* (Chicago: Moody Press, 1999), 934.

attraction. It is based on doing what is right for the benefit of the person loved. Genesis 22:2 says Abraham loved his son Isaac in this way before he took him up the mountain to sacrifice him. After Naomi and her daughter-in-law Ruth's husbands both died, the ladies returned to Israel destitute and Naomi's friends told her that Ruth loved her in this way (Ruth 4:15).

Solomon also did not have a reputation as a lady's man. If he was, his friends would have known it. There is nothing that kills a good reputation for a man like having a roving eye. How many young women have ignored their friends' warnings of "He'll break your heart," or "He's a player," only to find out the hard way that they were right.

A young man or woman needs to know something about the reputation of the person they are interested in. How do they treat their family and friends? Do they merely go to church or do they talk about their faith openly and honestly? Do they have a good work ethic? Are they more caught up in their things than they are with people?

It's better to know the reputation of the one you're interested in before you marry them because you will inherit their reputation after you're married. Do your investigation now.

Pleasing Conversations

Pop culture today assumes, "boy meets girl and they jump in the sack." Movies flood our senses with gauzy backgrounds and sensual music as the couple inevitably complete the act no matter where they are. The implication is that all women are like a dog in heat and all men are oversexed hardbodies.

(By the way, remove the word "studs" from your vocabulary unless you're a horse trainer.)

Some read this kind of scenario into v. 4, "Draw me after you and let us run together! The king has brought me into his chambers." They see this as a passionate uncontrolled march to Solomon's bedroom. But it's not.

The reasons to reject this interpretation are obvious. First, the word for *chambers* can indeed be used for *bedroom*, as described later in Song of Solomon 3:4 and Joel 2:16. But more often it simply means the inner rooms of the house apart from the outer courtyard. In Genesis 43:30 it's used to describe the place where Joseph went to cry after he met his brothers in Egypt (Genesis 43:30).[14]

Second, we can reject this reasoning because the word is plural. It makes more sense to say Shulammite was invited into the inner rooms of the palace than to his bedrooms (note the plural). Multiple bedrooms doesn't make sense.

Third, in the last part of v. 4 the words "we" and "they" are employed, referring to the daughters of Jerusalem. That hardly sounds like a private sexual encounter. So much for the bedroom theory.

So, what's happening here? She was delighted that Solomon had invited her to "his chambers" to hang out and meet some of his friends. In these conversations she learns what they think about him. In the last part of v. 4 she comments, "We will rejoice in you and be glad; We will extol your love more than wine. Rightly do they love you." She uses both of the words for love that we've seen before. They extol his

---

[14] Ibid., 265.

dod, and they *ahava* him. Are both sentiments possible in the same breath? Apparently so.

It seems the daughters of Jerusalem understood and talked about the virtues of sexual love, but they viewed it in the holy expression of a committed relationship. This is how it should be. God has provided sexual desires to be fulfilled in the context of a mutually committed couple in marriage. But until marriage this desire to be together must be tempered and controlled.

SELF-CONFIDENCE

As Shulammite grows more comfortable chatting with her new girlfriends in Solomon's house she described herself candidly in Song of Solomon 1:5. She said, "I am black but lovely, O daughters of Jerusalem, like the tents of Kedar, like the curtains of Solomon." The "tents of Kedar" referred to a nomadic tribe in northern Arabia that made their tents out of black goat hair. This refers to the dark color of her skin and has nothing to do with race.

Nevertheless, she was very self-conscious. She declared, "Do not stare at me because I am swarthy, for the sun has burned me." No one likes to stand out in a crowd. We like to fit in. When our skin color or our clothes are different than everyone else, we are painfully aware that people are staring at us.

That's the way she felt. She was a country girl, born and bred. But now she was around a bunch of city girls. In comparison with the daughters of Jerusalem she must have felt extremely out of place. These girls seldom ventured out in the hot Near-Eastern sun. Living in Solomon's Jerusalem allowed them to pamper their skin with ointments and lotions and they took pride in their milky white skin.

Shulammite feels the need to explain. She continues in v. 6, "the sun has burned me" making her appear swarthy or tanned. In California where I live, being tan is often associated with surfing, boating, golfing, tennis, and going to the beach. The Coppertone look is a sign of a vibrant, healthy lifestyle.

Not for Shulammite. She tries to make excuses for her looks, explaining in v. 6, "My mother's sons were angry with me; they made me caretaker of the vineyards, but I have not taken care of my own vineyard." She seems to be pleading for empathy and reveals something of the harsh reality of her home life that left her without the time or ability even to take care of herself.

And yet her self-assessment isn't all negative. She exhibits self-confidence in revealing her personal assessment in the first place. In v.5 she also notes, "I am black, but lovely." The word for "lovely" means "beautiful, comely, or suitable."[15] It's almost as if she is saying, "I may be dark, but I'm beautiful, and that's good enough for Solomon!"

This teaches us a critical lesson about relationships. While there is nothing wrong with beauty it is not the most telling component of a relationship. Any woman who dresses provocatively and smiles and giggles at every guy in the room is not a woman to pursue. Just because she is "hot" doesn't automatically mean that she is wife material. If she is emotionally needy or needs to be told how beautiful she is all the

---

[15] Ibid., 541.

BOY MEETS GIRL

time, a young man is best advised to keep looking. Don't be fooled by a beautiful package.

Shulammite may have thought that she wasn't as good looking as the other girls, but it didn't seem to bother Solomon one bit. He looked past the physical appearance, social status, and family background and saw a gem! And she didn't "sell" herself by sex appeal and worrying about physical appearance.

AVOID GOSSIP

The scene appears to shift between vv. 6 and 7. Shulammite is talking with the ladies, but then it seems she makes a direct statement to Solomon which led to a response from him. Later in v. 10 we find that all this happened "while the king was at his table," indicating they were still in the "chambers" she mentioned in v.4.

It sounds as if Shulammite wanted the crowd around them to understand the nature of their relationship. So, in v. 7 she asks Solomon to "Tell me, O you whom my soul loves, where do you pasture your flock, where do you make it lie down at noon? For why should I be like one who veils herself beside the flocks of your companions?"

Shulammite remembers her first encounter with Solomon. He was in Galilee with some of his shepherds. He had noticed her, and they had begun a conversation. She wanted to get to know him, but she didn't want to be known as one of the shepherds "groupies."

The "one who veils herself beside the flocks of your companions" refers to prostitutes who followed shepherds. They were desperate woman who needed money or were looking for a husband in the wrong way. These women would try to entice lonely shepherds sexually by putting a veil over their face to hide their identity and shame. Shulammite refused to be a woman like that.

Instead, she asks to meet him in the light of day whenever he takes a break from his duties. She is not merely looking for a hookup or a one-night stand. She is merely expressing her desire to get to know him. She understood how easily gossip spread and she wanted to avoid it.

What a great principle for meeting someone. Those who depend on their sex appeal to attract a boyfriend may end up getting the kind of guy they are asking for, someone who is only interested in sex. Rejecting sexually suggestive fashions and mannerisms will attract a completely different kind of person. The boy has met the girl. Now what? How do you know what you have at this point? Read on and we'll find out.

*"We make men without chests and expect of them virtue and
enterprise. We laugh at honor and are shocked to find traitors
in our midst. We castrate and bid the geldings be fruitful."*

— C. S. Lewis

CHAPTER TWO

MAN OF YOUR DREAMS

(Song of Solomon 1:8-14)

Have you ever "fallen head over heels in love?" The phrase describes the way many people describe their deep emotion when they meet someone they love. Greeks called it "a temporary case of insanity." Plato called this deep, passionate love the "madness from the gods." American poet and minister Edward Taylor wrote to his beloved that his passion for her was "a golden ball of pure fire."[16]

This even affects religious groups not known for talking about falling in love. The letters of Puritan lawyer John Winthrop to his wife are an especially well-known example of Puritan romanticism. He closed his letters with "I kiss and love thee with the kindest affection," or "I kiss my sweet wife and remain always thy faithful husband." English Puritan

---

[16] Leland Ryken, *Worldly Saints: The Puritans as They Were* (Grand Rapids, MI: Zondervan, 1990), 50.

pastor William Gouge said, "Under love all other duties are comprised: for without it no duty can be well performed ...It is like fire, which is not only hot in itself, but also conveyeth heat into that which is near it."[17]

Falling in love takes two people. But, assuming you know who you are, how do you find the other person? What kind of qualities do you look for in trying to find the man or woman of your dreams?

This section is not exhaustive, but it gives us a look at some of the admirable qualities a mature man and woman possess as they consider marriage. We will look at the qualities for a man first in this chapter, and the woman in the next chapter.

"Real men don't eat quiche," or so we're told. But what is a real man? The model changes somewhat over time, but the epitome of a real man usually involves a guy who is a buff womanizer who charms the ladies and makes the other men jealous.

He's a combination of John Wayne, James Bond (any of them), Denzel Washington, and the Dos Equis "most interesting man in the world." He can hang off the tallest building in the world while fighting a bad guy, drive a car 120 mph – backwards – break any ransomware code, take on the enemy with an AK in both hands, and he gets the girl every time.

This could have been Solomon. He was a king. Later in his life he demonstrated the power to build a military machine, capture the money markets of the world, serve as the design-builder of huge government projects, and write books and poetry in his spare time. He certainly had the power and

---

[17] Ibid.

means to overpower a lowly shepherdess and claim her as his bride.

But that's not the picture we see. Instead, we see a man who exhibits the qualities of a mature man that has nothing to do with the fact that he is the king. These are qualities that a young woman would be wise to assess in a man she is interested in.

HE RESPECTS HER

"Will you still respect me in the morning?" is the rhetorical question asked by a woman negotiating an adult sleepover with privileges. The question is asked humorously to mock anyone who would expect a negative answer. But the answer must be no because the situation isn't about respect, it's about lust and selfishness.

Respecting women is one of the least seen but most admirable qualities in a man. Hearing Shulammite refuse to act like other women who prostituted themselves with the shepherds, Solomon wanted to know this woman better. Shulammite was the rare woman who stood against the sexual mores of her time. Solomon noticed and found that refreshing.

He quickly responded in Song of Solomon 1:8, "If you yourself do not know, most beautiful among women, go forth on the trail of the flock and pasture your young goats by the tents of the shepherds." He didn't want her to follow him like one of the prostitutes who usually followed the shepherds. He wanted to meet her openly at a designated time and place. He respected her virtue and made it clear that he too wanted to proceed with honor and accountability in building their relationship.

Women, let me say this as strongly as I can. A man of integrity does not respect a woman who throws herself at him. A woman who lets a man know that she is sexually available will cause a godly man to run. That's not to say that any man can't be sexually tempted, but a man who wants to maintain sexual purity will act like Joseph did in Genesis 39:12 when Potipher's wife threw herself at him. He ran away so fast that he left his cloak on his way out.

SPEECH LESSONS

It's been said that most men use about 2,000 words a day and 1,900 of them are used up by the time he gets home from work. And if you could record a man's conversations, they usually involve computers, cars, guns, sports, and stocks. In high school we used to say a guy's interests were cash, cars, and cuties.

Ladies, if a man hasn't grown out of that high school stage, learn the word "next." The man to look for is one who at least tries to communicate beyond his occasional grunt or monosyllabic contributions.

Not all men are talkers. I get that. But a sign of maturity is reflected in a man's ability to carry on some sort of appropriate conversation, given certain circumstances.

In the following section, Solomon gives four "speech lessons" that provide a template for what to look for in a guy you want to date. Guys who learn these communication skills will touch the heart of the woman they love.

Mutual possession

There is an abrupt change that occurs between vv. 7 and 8. Earlier we heard Shulammite express some hesitancy about her looks. She said, "I am black but lovely." In v. 9 Solomon answers, "To me, my darling..." Now, I know what some of you men are thinking. "That's for girly men! I'm not good at that kind of mushy talk." But we need to stop and look at this. It's in the Bible.

Solomon was not a girly man. He was a man's man. He was a rancher, a builder, an architect, an equestrian, and a man with strategic leadership abilities. And he was generally regarded as the wisest man alive at the time (1 Kings 3:12).

His comment, "To *me, my* darling" (emphasis mine), pictures relational intimacy. This is not a callous statement that regards a woman as a possession like a piece of furniture. Every woman wants to know that she is in an exclusive relationship with her husband. She is your wife and you are her husband. This isn't constricting or pejorative. This is the essence of marriage.

In the New Testament, the Apostle Paul expounded this same quality in the middle of first century Roman culture that was perhaps more confused than we are. Roman emperors were so vile that Emperor Nero once castrated a teenage boy to live with him as his wife. This came after he had accidentally killed his pregnant wife and her baby when he kicked her in the stomach after she complained about his coming home late from night racing where he lit the track with torches made from the burning bodies of Christians.

Yet, in 1 Corinthians 7:2-4, Paul asserted, "But because of immoralities, each man is to *have his own wife*, and each woman is *to have her own husband*. The husband must fulfill his duty to his wife, and likewise also the wife to her husband. The *wife does not have authority over her own body*, but the husband does; and likewise also *the husband does not have authority over his own body*, but the wife does" (emphasis mine).

A woman may have felt very resistant to commit herself to a man in Nero's Roman Empire. But Paul encourages Christians to view this differently. This is also what Solomon was saying.

We must take the same kind of stance today. When you get married you say "NO" to every other woman and man – forever. This is not merely a nod to our patriarchal past. Marriage is not a socially constructed paradigm from which we must be liberated.

My wife is *mine* and I am *hers*. This is a mutual sharing of passion and dreams that enlivens and protects the covenant of marriage. God made it that way. We cannot let it slip from our grasp just because some "experts" with PhDs feel compelled to share their ignorance with us about relationships.

So, the first "speech lesson" is to express mutual ownership. You will probably use different words, but if you want to touch the heart of the woman you are trying to win, you will do well to let her know that you are looking for a mutually exclusive contract in your marriage. If she bolts, you have lost nothing.

Value

Solomon's second "speech lesson" is seen in *how* he addresses Shulammite. The word used for *darling* is *ra'eyah*. In Chapter 1 we noted that it is equivalent to the Greek word *phileo* and points to the natural emotional response to family and friends. This word is used nine times in the Song of Solomon.

The word *ra'eyah* means "beloved, my love, or darling." It comes from a root word which means "friend, neighbor, associate."[18] The composite used here means "companion, a woman who is the object of a man's love and affection."[19]

One commentator expands on it this way, "The central meaning of the verbal root is to guard, care for, or tend, with the emphasis on the delight and pleasure which attends that responsibility ...action takes precedence over words and the concepts of friendship and companionship are linked with expressed concern for the protection of her well-being."[20]

Rather than a low view of possessing his wife like a piece of furniture, Solomon regards her as a treasure. This demonstrates incredibly high value, not low esteem.

"Darling" means "you are my dearest and closest friend." This is more than "Hey, how ya doin'?" Men and women in

---

[18] R. Laird Harris, "2186 רָעָה," ed. R. Laird Harris, Gleason L. Archer Jr., and Bruce K. Waltke, *Theological Wordbook of the Old Testament* (Chicago: Moody Press, 1999), 853.

[19] William D. Mounce, general editor, *Mounce's Complete Expository Dictionary of Old & New Testament Words* (Grand Rapids, MI: Zondervan, 2006), 1043.

[20] G. Lloyd Carr, *The Song of Solomon: An Introduction and Commentary,* Tyndale Old Testament Commentaries, vol. 19, (1984; repr., Downers Grove, Illinois: InterVarsity Press, 2009), 89-90.

a strong relationship express their feelings, their dreams, their failures, their wishes and desires as they open their hearts and minds to one another.

This communicates value. Someone has said that men are like hunters in their relationship. They devote every expense and effort in bagging their prey, but when they get it, they hang it on the wall and move on.

Men, you must learn how to convince the woman in your life that she is, and always will be, more valuable to you than friends, hobbies, work, your kids, your fancy car, your house, and every other person or thing on the face of the earth. You don't have to beat around the bush in doing this. Just say it in bold, clear statements.

President Ronald Reagan was a master of this. He wrote many romantic notes to his wife Nancy that communicated she was *his darling*. He wrote, "I more than love you. I'm not whole without you. You are life itself to me ... I love you so much, I don't mind that life made me wait so long to find you. The waiting only made the finding sweeter... I live in a permanent Christmas because God gave me you."[21]

Partnership

The third "speech lesson" Solomon communicates is a commitment to partnership. Song of Solomon 1:9 continues, "To me, my darling, you are like my mare among the chariots of Pharaoh." Again, this sounds strange to us. I will go out on a limb here and say that very few modern men have

[21] Nancy Reagan, *I Love You, Ronnie: The Letters From Ronald Reagan to Nancy Reagan* (New York: Random House Trade Paperbacks, 2002). 55, 103.

ever referred to their wife as a horse. But it was different in Solomon's time.

1 Kings 10:26-28 tells us Solomon had fourteen hundred chariots and twelve thousand horsemen. We also know that Pharaoh's chariots were always pulled by a pair of stallions. As is still common today, these magnificent creatures were used for breeding. A good stallion from Egypt could run one hundred fifty shekels, (roughly two years wages).

Yet Solomon says Shulammite was like "my *mare* among the chariots of Pharaoh" (emphasis mine). Why does he specifically compare her to a mare *among* stallions? Stallions are strong and powerful. But they are self-willed and hard to bring to harness. So, chariot teams were led by a "boss mare." When she took off, the stallions followed. Solomon is saying Shulammite is like a fine filly among the stallions.[22]

This doesn't envision a bossy woman who treats everyone as her subordinates. It points to a woman who knows what's appropriate in various situations. She knows how to handle her home, her family, her work, her friends, her neighbors, and her church.

It's too easy for a husband to treat his wife like she is just along for the ride in their marriage. If you want a clean house and three square meals a day, hire a maid and a cook. But, if you want a partnership, you will learn to lean on her unique contributions that make your relationship grow.

---

[22] David Jeremiah, *What the Bible Says About Love, Sex, and Marriage* (New York, NY: FaithWords, 2012), 38.

He compliments her beauty and status

Solomon gives us a final "speech lesson" in v. 10 where he said, "Your cheeks are lovely with ornaments, your neck with strings of beads." What's happening here? Solomon mentions *ornaments* and *beads*. As before, we must understand these poetic terms.

Jewelry revealed a lot about wealth in ancient times. Today we say "diamonds are a girl's best friend" which expresses the same value. Most men understand that their wife loves beautiful pieces of jewelry that are bright and shiny. Unfortunately for most of us, they are also usually expensive.

But jewelry also revealed status. Ancient Egyptians adorned female slaves who served in the king's court with gold, lapis lazuli, silver, turquoise, carnelian, and amethyst.[23] We also know that women of Solomon's times wore ankle jewelry, headbands, pendants, bracelets, scarves, headdresses, sashes, signet rings, nose rings, and jewelry for the arms.[24]

But notice, he's not talking about jewelry when he says, "*Your cheeks* are lovely with ornaments, *your neck* with strings of beads" (emphasis mine). He is talking about her cheeks and neck, *not* the jewelry. This is a reference to her high cheek bones and the creamy texture of her skin. This meant more to her than, "Wow, that's the most beautiful pearl necklace I've ever seen." These comments are a supreme compliment to both her beauty and her status.

---

[23] Miriam Lichtheim, *Ancient Egyptian Literature: The Old and Middle Kingdoms*, vol. 1, (1973; repr., Berkeley: University of California Press, 2006), 152.

[24] Douglas R. Edwards, "Dress and Ornamentation," David Noel Freedman, ed., *The Anchor Yale Bible Dictionary*, vol. 2, (New York: Doubleday, 1992), 235.

Think of how that must have made Shulammite feel! As far as we can tell her father was not in the picture. He was either dead or not involved in her life. And her brothers were angry abusers who demanded her forced labor in the fields.

My point is that this young woman had no man in her life to tell her that she was pretty. There was no Daddy to call her "princess." And she realized that even her girlfriends thought she was *swarthy*. She didn't fit in anywhere.

This might not seem like a big deal to men, but I suspect that every woman you asked would admit that it touches her heart to have the man in her life tell her that she is pretty! There is nothing wrong with that. That's not appealing to the ego of a woman. It is just recognizing the deep-seated desire in the heart of a woman to receive this expression of love from her man.

Listen to the words of Solomon on the subject of compliments elsewhere in Proverbs 12:18 – "There is one who speaks rashly, like the thrusts of a sword; but the tongue of the wise brings healing." Proverbs 15:4 – "A soothing tongue is a tree of life, but perversion in it crushes the spirit." Proverbs 16:24 – "Pleasant words are a honeycomb; sweet to the soul and healing to the bones." Proverbs 18:21 – "Death and life are in the power of the tongue, and those who love it will eat its fruit." Proverbs 21:23 – "he who guards his mouth and his tongue, guards his soul from troubles."

Be careful with your words. Picture a tape recorder strapped around your neck and listen to the tone and choice of words you use. Think of the demeaning nature of the following categories. I'm not trying to be funny or cute. I've actually heard these phrases come from the mouths of husbands:

1. <u>Her weight</u> – Only comment about her weight if you are asked. Never, ever, ever, use words like "fatty," or "wide load."

2. <u>Clothes</u> – Questions like, "Are you going to wear that tent?" "Where'd you get that, the Goodwill store?" don't help at all.

3. <u>Hair</u> – If you ask, "Did you cut your hair with a weed-whacker?" expect a cold response.

4. <u>Habits</u> – Comments like, "You'll be late to your own funeral," or "Do you expect me to eat this?" will only demean her or start a fight.

5. <u>Crude words</u> – Cursing, slang, and references to sexual or bodily functions don't belong in anyone's vocabulary.

6. <u>Name calling</u> – words like "old lady" or sarcastic nicknames don't build respect.

7. <u>Sarcasm</u> – This can be fun, but beware, when overused this gets old and can reveal your true feelings about her.

If you don't learn to compliment her when you are dating, you will probably not grow into the habit after you are married. Don't fall into the trap of thinking that buying jewelry means you don't have to clean up your mouth? Believe me, jewelry is not a viable substitute for words that edify and touch your wife's heart.

John Newton, the hymnwriter, spoke of his wife saying, "I am always a little awkward without you and every room where you are not present looks unfurnished."[25]

Winston Churchill, the Prime Minister of Great Britain during World War II, was at a banquet where he was asked if he could not be himself, who would he choose to be. He took his wife's hand and said, "If I couldn't be who I am, I would most like to be Lady Churchill's second husband."[26]

Most of us need to up our game here. Make a specific effort to change the tone and content of your words. Ask your girlfriend or wife about your speech. Look for opportunities to compliment her. Try saying things like; "You look nice in that blue blouse," "You are a very creative person," "Thanks for being so kind and generous with your time," and "I'm very thankful to be your friend." You don't have to make things up. Find something that deserves an honest compliment and say it. You may be surprised at the response.

He Is Generous

In addition to his "speech lessons," Solomon learned another secret that many men ignore – the giving of gifts. Solomon mentions this in v. 10, "We will make for you ornaments of gold with beads of silver." Notice that "we" is plural, indicating something like, "Everyone thinks you are worthy of gifts."

---

[25] John Pollock, *Amazing Grace: The Dramatic Life Story of John Newton* (San Francisco: Harper & Row, 1981), 165.

[26] James Humes, *Churchill, Speaker of the Century* (Briarcliffe Manor, NY: Stein and Day/Scarborough House, 1980), 29.

Gifts are more than just social protocol. They are signs of respect and admiration. For Solomon they were the natural extension of his love for her. He obviously could afford silver and gold. These "ornaments" were probably earrings, necklaces, and bracelets fashioned out of gold and silver and precious stones. They were very expensive items, but money was not the key.

Regardless of the monetary value, gifts communicate value to the receiver. That doesn't mean that you can get by with merely giving gifts. And expensive gifts don't mean as much if you are depending on the value of the gift to communicate your love. If you tell her, "That necklace cost me a thousand bucks!" it loses its value.

Frankly, I find the giving of gifts to my wife hard to do. It's not because I don't love her. And it's not a monetary issue. The problem is that a good gift takes time and careful thought. Thankfully, my wife is not one who likes a lot of jewelry. And we have both learned that buying clothes for each other doesn't go well either.

So, I've found that the thing that moves her the most are simple well thought out messages on a card or note that convey my feelings. If I combine that with a tangible gift, I know she likes or needs, I've got a winner!

HE GIVES HIS TIME

Falling in love doesn't just happen, it takes time. Verse 12 takes place, "while the king was at his table." The NASB, ESV, KJV, and NIV translate this as "table" or "couch" because of the banquet table or bedroom motif as seen in Song of

Solomon 2:4-6. Others think this refers to the banqueting table on the night before their wedding.

Neither of these ideas fits the scene. The Hebrew word for "at his table" is *mesab.* The basic meaning of the root word "seems to involve the idea of turning or going around" and can also characterize the "the turning of one's mind so as to give attention to thorough investigation."[27] This could simply point to the fact that Solomon was "among his own surroundings."[28] In other words, he was "hanging out" with her.

Spending time together deepens our knowledge of another person and can lead to deeper feelings. This elicited her response of devotion to him seen in vv. 12-14, where she expressed her devotion in poetic pictures that centered around perfume.

Time is at a premium in our jam-packed world. But time communicates value. You value what you give your time to. We try to get around this by saying, "I stress *quality* time over a *quantity* of time." That's baloney! That's like being served a 1 oz. cube of filet mignon. That's unacceptable because when it comes to steak, quality without quantity is like a swimming pool without water.

When you come to the end of your life, you won't regret spending time with your wife and kids, even if it means giving up a promotion or never making partner. If you want them to show up at your funeral you need to pay it forward by the investment of time now.

---

[27] Harris, Archer, and Waltke, *Theological Wordbook of the Old Testament,* 615.

[28] Carr, *Song of Solomon,* 91–92.

He Touches Her Heart

This time was a wise investment for Solomon. As she was spending time with Solomon, Shulammite said in v. 12, "My perfume gave forth its fragrance." It was a very expensive and exclusive perfume, imported in sealed alabaster boxes and reserved for special occasions.

But there's a further component of her response expressed in v.13, "My beloved is to me a pouch of myrrh which lies all night between my breasts." Myrrh is a resinous gum that comes from a South Arabian tree. It is also the special anointing oil used in the temple and was one of the gifts brought by the Magi to baby Jesus. Here it appears to function in a similar fashion to the *"oils"* mentioned for men in Song of Solomon 1:3. Because of the lack of bathing, this perfume served as deodorant for women.

This is not a sexual come-on. Like most women, she wore it between her breasts which was close to her heart. She compares Solomon to the valuable perfume which is close to her heart. Like the constant pleasing fragrance of myrrh, he was close to her heart night and day. This is more a reflection of him than it is of her. The question is, what had he done to get so close to her heart? No doubt it was his speech, his compliments, his gifts, and his time. Smelling the myrrh reminded her of him.

Guys, if you want to find a way to her heart, that's the path. You will touch her heart if you treat the woman in your life the way Solomon treated Shulammite.

HE PROVIDES SECURITY

Shulammite also found rest and security in her time with Solomon. Song of Solomon 1:14 carries this connotation, "My beloved is to me a cluster of henna blossoms in the vineyards of Engedi." Henna is a common shrub found in the lush oasis of Engedi ("place of the wild goats") halfway down the western shore of the Dead Sea. It grows about eight to ten feet high and produces a mass of bluish-yellow flowers. When they are tightly packed, they resemble a cluster of grapes. From the dried leaves of the plant, a dye is produced and applied to hair and nails.[29]

Solomon's father, King David, found refuge in Engedi when Saul was chasing him in 1 Samuel 23:29. No doubt this is because of the streams that flow down from the mountains above and provide refreshment in the hot desert climate. Often when we stop there on tours of Israel it's hard to get people out of the refreshing cool water.

I counseled a couple where the woman said that life with her husband was like riding in the passenger seat of a car while her husband broke the speed limit, ran red lights, took corners on two wheels, and erratically changed lanes without signaling, all while she held onto the baby in her arms and bounced around with no seat belt.

If a woman can't rest and feel secure in the company of a man, then love won't have a chance to grow. A man's calm demeanor, consistent character, commitment to truth, and his confident ability to do and say the right things at

---

[29] Robert Davidson, *Ecclesiastes and the Song of Solomon*, The Daily Study Bible Series (Louisville, KY: Westminster John Knox Press, 1986), 111.

the right time breeds a sense of confidence and trust in the woman he loves.

Love grows where these elements are in evidence. Without them love is smothered beneath callous indifference and self-service. A solid marriage can never be built on those grounds. Women open your eyes and look at these qualities again. Your future depends on it.

"[She had] an appearance without pretense, character without affectation ... a mind without vainglory, intelligence without conceit ... character without limits, immeasurable self-control ... the ornament of all the humble."

— John Chrysostom on Olympias,
a deaconess of Constantinople

CHAPTER THREE

THE WOMAN OF YOUR DREAMS

(Song of Solomon 1:15-2:7)

One of the most iconic locations in the world of sports is the Old Course in St. Andrews, Scotland. Even those who aren't golf aficionados recognize the iconic Swilcan Bridge on the 18th hole. The birthplace of the game of golf draws thousands of people yearly to view this famous golf course by the sea.

But within walking distance of the 18th hole of the Old Course stands the Martyrs Monument, a dramatic reminder of the stark battles that took place on that spot during the Scottish Reformation of the sixteenth century. This struggle that shaped the identity of Scotland also shaped the future of the Protestant Church around the world.

One of the leaders of this movement was John Knox. Knox was a nemesis of Mary, Queen of Scots, and led the Protestant struggle to gain freedom from the Church of England. One of the main issues was the identity of the leader of the Church, King James I of England at the time, or Jesus Christ. The Church said James and Knox said Jesus.

Knox had a daughter named Elizabeth who married a man named John Welch. Following the theology of his father-in-law, Welch was arrested and accused of high treason and imprisoned in London. Elizabeth gained an audience with the king to plead the case of her husband.

This was King James I of Scotland who also inherited the throne of England and become King James VI of England when Queen Elizabeth died with no heirs. He later called scholars to Hampton Court to work on a new English Bible which became the King James Version of the Bible.

Knowing who her husband was, the king asked who her father was. She said, "John Knox." The king replied, "Knox and Welch! The devil never made such a match as that."[30] He then asked how many children Knox had, and Elizabeth replied, "Three lasses," although he also had two sons by his first wife who died. "God be thanked," the king said, raising his hands in joy. "For had they been three lads, I would have had no peace in my three kingdoms."[31]

---

[30] Douglas Bond, *The Mighty Weakness of John Knox*, A Long Line of Godly Men Profile, (Orlando, Florida, Reformation Trust Publishers, 2011), 46-47.

[31] Ibid.

The king told Elizabeth that if she could convince her husband to recognize his authority over the church, he would release him. Elizabeth grabbed the corners of her apron and held it out to the king. "Please your Majesty, I'd rather have his head there!"[32] Some woman! May her tribe increase!

We often miss women like this in our historical accounts. But they are there. That's what makes the Song of Solomon so unusual. Solomon wrote the book and certainly shared his points of view, but it's also true that his wife Shulammite was also a key voice in the book.

The only thing we know about her physical appearance is that she had a good tan and yet the qualities we see in her life would qualify her for any "Woman of your dreams" contest for any thinking man. Let's look at some of her qualifications.

SHE IS NOT EASILY IMPRESSED

As they spent time together in the palace, Solomon continued to compliment her in Song of Solomon 1:15, "How beautiful you are, my darling, how beautiful you are! Your eyes are like doves." This may have been in direct response to her comments in 1:5 where she said she was "black but lovely." She stood out like a drunk at a Sunday School picnic because her tanned look invited the stares of the creamy skinned beauties in the palace court.

So, his remarks about her beauty no doubt fell on a receptive heart. But she didn't play with his emotions. She responded in like kind. In vv. 16-17 she responds, "How handsome you are, my beloved, and so pleasant!" This is intense

---

[32] Ibid.

language that shows a longer dialogue, but it's obvious she felt the same way toward him.

Guys, if a girl doesn't respond to your pursuit then you might need to read the signs and back off. A relationship is not a one-way street. Obviously, every relationship until you find the one to marry will end in one or the other failing to respond to the other person. Don't read this as failure. It's simply time to move on.

But we can see the willing response of Shulammite in her desire to further spend time with him. In vv. 16-17 she continues, "Indeed, our couch is luxuriant! The beams of our houses are cedars, our rafters, cypresses." This is another place where many infer some kind of sexual suggestion, but that's not the case.

The words "couch" and "our houses" sounds as if she's talking about a bedroom but she's not. The word for "couch" indeed means a "bed, divan" of some kind. But notice the type of couch she mentions. It is "luxuriant" which literally means "a green tree," or "trees growing and flourishing."[33] This is not an indoor couch with an arrangement of fancy, fluffy pillows. It's an outdoor "couch" in a green meadow with trees all around.

Furthermore, "the beams of our houses are cedars, our rafters, cypresses," is also a picture of being outside. Trees are not indigenous to the hot, dry climate of Jerusalem. Wood dries out and cracks in that environment. Likewise, *"houses"* is plural, indicating she is not thinking of literal buildings they owned since they weren't even married yet.

---

[33] Wilhelm Gesenius and Samuel Prideaux Tregelles, *Gesenius' Hebrew and Chaldee Lexicon to the Old Testament Scriptures* (Bellingham, WA: Logos Bible Software, 2003), 774.

This is revealing. She's a country girl talking about a walk in the woods, lying on the green grass looking up at the sky through the canopy of cedar and cypress trees.

She obviously knew that Solomon was the king, but she wasn't impressed by his wealth or power. There is nothing here that shows she is trying to get her hooks into him. She simply enjoyed being with him for a walk in the woods.

Most girls would have wanted a ride in his chariot or a tour of the palace. Not Shulammite. She responded to him simply as a man. She expressed her feelings and showed she enjoyed being with *him,* not in the palace, but out in the open air where they could enjoy God's creation.

Guys, the girl you want will not be impressed with your position or your possessions. If she is looking for a guy with a Bimmer, take a walk. If she always wants expensive dinners and exotic dates, watch out. If you marry her, you will be trying to satisfy an insatiable desire for fancy things the rest of your life.

SHE IS HUMBLE

Another verse, another allegory, is the theme of many who read the beginning of Song of Solomon 2:1 where Shulammite states, "I am the rose of Sharon, the lily of the valleys." Both of these phrases are almost always used as a picture of Jesus Christ. But in this context this interpretation is incredibly far-fetched.

The word for "rose" is *habatselet,* but it's not the rose we know. It is a little single stem flower with two clusters of six petalled trumpet-like flowers. These little flowers grew wild in the valley of Sharon which refers to the low-lying coastal plain running from Jaffa to Carmel. Former Prime Minister Ariel Sharon of Israel took his name from this area where he had a ranch.

She is saying, "I'm just a common wildflower you can find anywhere out in the fields." She didn't see herself as a beauty queen. She was a daisy, not an orchid.

Is this false modesty? No, she's already told us she's aware that her skin isn't milky white like the other girls. This is simply a humble girl admitting that there were plenty of girls who were just as pretty as she was. And she expressed no desire to be like the women in the palace or anyone else.

SHE IS NOT OBSESSED WITH BEAUTY

Her response also reveals she is not obsessed with beauty. In this day of beauty aids and fashion experts lighting up the landscape like Times Square on New Year's Eve, it's increasingly hard to find a girl who humbly accepts what God has given her to work with. This humility is actually a sign of the confidence others seek in putting on make-up and following their favorite fashionistas.

We all admire beauty but it's refreshing to meet a beautiful woman who doesn't act like she knows it! Of course, our world doesn't encourage this. We've made multi-billion dollar cosmetic industries out of the vanity of women who paint it on like they're laying asphalt. We hold mass beauty pageants which fuel the folly that a beautiful woman is somehow more valued than those who didn't make the cut.

To women who obsess about their beauty, there are some things to remember. First, God made you the way you are. You can't change your height, color of your eyes, or your face. The more you spend on cosmetic enhancements, the more you demonstrate that you are not happy with the way God made you.

Second, you will reach the pinnacle of your beauty at age seventeen. After that, it's all about maintenance. You will put on weight, your hair will turn gray, and your face will become lined with age. That's the harsh reality of every woman who has ever lived.

Third, while there is nothing wrong with a modicum of beauty enhancements, you can win a beauty contest and still be ugly and insecure on the inside. No beauty aids will change that. Remember the old saying, "Beauty is skin deep, but ugly goes clear to the bone – and keeps on digging!"

Notice Solomon's response in v.2, "Like a lily among the thorns, so is my darling among the maidens." This wise man is saying, "When I look at you all the other women look like weeds!" A godly man values humility over beauty.

Ladies, if a man obsesses about your beauty, and constantly criticizes your hair, your clothes, and your make-up, you will never please him. He doesn't want a real woman. He wants a trophy wife. Get rid of him!

Likewise, look at your own heart. If you are married for fifty years you will wake up next to your husband over 18,250 times. A woman obsessed with her beauty will soon realize that she will not be able to keep up the façade of beauty for all those morning wake-up calls.

Men, if a girl is obsessed with her appearance, beware. You might end up paying for her tummy tucks and botox treatments later on in life. You will never be able to satisfy an insecure woman who gets her sense of worth by looking in the mirror.

A young couple encountered this on their wedding night. She stood in front of the mirror criticizing various parts of her body. Her husband was frustrated. He came over and put his arms around her. "You are criticizing my choice in a woman. From now on, I will be your mirror, and I'm telling you that you look perfect to me." Wise man!

SHE ACCEPTS HIS PROVISION

Shulammite continues revealing her character. In v. 3 she says, "Like an apple tree among the trees of the forest, so is my beloved among the young men. In his shade I took great delight and sat down, and his fruit was sweet to my taste." This is a picture of the sweet fruit and bountiful shade of the apple tree.

A *forest* wasn't cultivated in Jerusalem. Even though Solomon was an accomplished farmer and agronomist, it would have been surprising to find an apple tree in Jerusalem. Furthermore, apples usually grow in tended orchards, not forests. So, what is she saying?

It seems as if she is recognizing the care that was needed in that inhospitable climate to cultivate an apple tree. It took a lot of work to clear the ground, plant the seeds, keep the trees watered, watch for bugs, and prune the trees – all before you even got to the harvest.

Shulammite "took great delight and sat down, and his fruit was sweet to my taste." That is, she rested, secure and respectful in his provision. This was her choice, no one forced these feelings on her. She was thrilled to place herself in the shade of Solomon's tree and partake of the sweetness of his life.

Ecclesiastes 2 lists some of Solomon's accomplishments. He was an agronomist, a prolific composer and author, a builder, a scientist, and a statesman. It would be impossible to enumerate how many people profited from these endeavors. Shulammite recognized she would be the recipient of his bountiful provision.

Few of us will be kings or CEOs or superstars who make the big bucks. But every man with a job who brings home a paycheck week after week and year after year is a productive man and provides sufficient shade for his family in his own environment.

A woman who chafes at the provision of her husband will demean him and detract from the strength of their relationship. Accepting the shade provided by her husband will enable him to lead with confidence. A man will work his hands to the bone to provide for his family. The woman who stands with him and encourages him with her respect and support will do more for her family than griping and complaining about the perceived lack of earning power by her husband.

She Doesn't Want To Change Him

Often a woman wants to change something about her husband after they get married. Not Shulammite. We see this wonderful quality in her statement, "his fruit was sweet to my taste." The word for "sweet" means "to chew." It results in the smacking of the lips when you taste something pleasant. Keil and Delitzsch again help us by commenting,

> The taste becomes then a figure of the soul's power of perception; a man's fruit are his words and works, in which his inward nature expresses itself; and this fruit is sweet to those on whom that in which the peculiar nature of the man reveals itself makes a happy, pleasing impression. But not only does the *person* of the king afford to Shulamith so great delight, he entertains her also with what can and must give her enjoyment.[34]

Her words not only depict respect, they show that she had no desire to change him. Sadly, some men aren't worthy of respect. They have no ambition, no drive, no goals, and little hope for the future. Some men are also drunks or physical brutes who think women are made for sex and nothing else.

This is not who I'm talking about. I'm talking about any man who goes out every day and works hard for his family. God did not intend for man to live in the shade of his wife. A man is to take the leadership in the home, not as an autocratic chauvinist, but in loving headship.

Granted, some guys need to broaden their fashion statement beyond khaki, so a woman could be of great help there. But if a woman isn't basically content with his wardrobe, his

---

[34] Carl Friedrich Keil and Franz Delitzsch, *Commentary on the Old Testament*, vol. 6 (Peabody, MA: Hendrickson, 1996), 528.

job, his salary, or his personality, then it would be better not to marry her! If your girlfriend doesn't respect who you are before you get married, she won't respect you after you get married. She will always compare you to her father, her sister's husband, her first boyfriend, the neighbor, or some other man in her life.

A woman who doesn't respect her husband is a miserable sight. Solomon elaborates in Proverbs 21:19, "It is better to live in a desert land than with a contentious and vexing woman." The word for contentious means "quarrel, dispute, or nagging."[35] Solomon also comments in Proverbs 19:13, "And the contentions of a wife are a constant dripping." That's what happens when there's no respect – and he knows it!

My wife Anne's dad was a graduate of USC. He was a gifted professional man who traveled the nation as a VP for an electric wire and cable company. I was a hick kid from Kansas with ten brothers and sisters heading to seminary when Anne married me. At times I've thought, "What was she thinking?" She might have thought the fruit and shade of my future provision would be pretty limited. But she didn't. And for almost fifty years she has never exhibited any manifestation of being dissatisfied with what I have provided. What a wonderful woman God gave me!

That kind of woman can make a man. Of course, the opposite is also true. I've seen examples in ministry where a woman is not solidly behind her husband, questioning his abilities, his calling, and the church he serves. That kind of woman can destroy a man and his ministry.

---

[35] William Lee Holladay and Ludwig Köhler, *A Concise Hebrew and Aramaic Lexicon of the Old Testament: Based upon the work of Ludwig Koehler and Walter Baumgartner* (1971; repr., Leiden: Brill, 2000), 183.

She Is All In

Marriage is hard enough without being totally committed. A successful marriage must be shared by two people who are all in with no excuses, no reservations, no questions, and no way out. We see this kind of spirit exhibited by Shulammite in Song of Solomon 2:4-6 where we see six successive pictures of their growing commitment to each other. Each step pictures her willingness to enter his world and be introduced as his bride.

The first picture is in v. 4 where she comments, "He has brought me to his banquet hall." Literally, this means "the house of wine." It was probably a large hall used for banquets. It's obvious that Solomon has now brought his bride to Jerusalem so she can meet his family and friends.

Second, she continues, "and his banner over me is love." A banner was a "large military standard." This was often used in the book of Numbers where it referred to a flag or banner set up to designate each tribe. Smaller banners designated clans and families.[36] Each flag or insignia was displayed on a pole, "possibly a family crest to identify each family." A banner was also used in warfare to identify military units.[37]

The banner over Shulammite was *"love."* This was Solomon's public statement for all to see, indicating this was probably some kind of formal engagement party. "Here she

---

[36] Wilhelm Gesenius, Samuel Prideaux Tregelles, trans., *Gesenius' Hebrew and Chaldee Lexicon to the Old Testament Scriptures* (Bellingham, WA: Logos Bible Software, 2003), 189.

[37] Tom Gledhill, *The Message of the Song of Songs: The Lyrics of Love,* "The Bible Speaks Today," (Downers Grove, Illinois: IVP Academic, 1994), 125.

is. I'm staking my claim to her because I love her. This is the one I'm going to marry!"

Now think for a minute about how this would have made a simple country girl feel. Knowing the reservations she's expressed before about her looks, she must have drawn great comfort to hear Solomon's words before all the assembled parties. She's not a field hand anymore. They are out in the public eye and he wants everyone to know she's his bride to be!

The third picture shows she was overwhelmed at being the center of attention. In v. 5 she pleaded, "Sustain me with raisin cakes." She probably uttered this to herself or possibly to some of the women attending her because her choice of words is a little curious.

Some see this as some kind of aphrodisiac. But it is better to view this as simply some kind of hors d'oeurve. It was used this way in 1 Chronicles 16:3 when King David celebrated bringing the Ark into Jerusalem. He hosted a party and served refreshments, giving "to everyone a loaf of bread and a portion of meat and a raisin cake."

In like manner she continued in v. 5, "Refresh me with apples." This seems in line with her desire for something to eat. For Shulammite, the excitement of the moment got to her and she needed something to settle her stomach. She was simply saying, "I need something to eat." In fact, the word for "refresh" means, "to have strength restored by eating or resting."[38] She wasn't used to palace parties where the King introduced her to his court as his bride to be. No wonder her emotions got to her.

---

[38] James Swanson, *Dictionary of Biblical Languages with Semantic Domains: Hebrew (Old Testament)*, 2nd ed., (Oak Harbor: Logos Research Systems, Inc., 2001). n.a.

The fifth picture indicates she needs this refreshment "because I am lovesick." This is not a sexual urge. She used *ahava* to describe her feelings, not *dod*. She is emotionally overcome by the complete dedication of Solomon to her that she feels it physically.

This is the country girl who had been a field hand with the "swarthy" look who had been treated harshly by her brothers in the fields, now being introduced by the king in his banquet hall as his bride to be! She is dizzied by all that is taking place!

Esteemed Old Testament commentators Keil and Delitzsch explain this idea of lovesickness. They comment,

> The subject of the passage here is not the curing of love-sickness, but bodily refreshment: the cry of Shulamith, that she may be made capable of bearing the deep agitation of her physical life, which is the consequence, not of her love-sickness, but of her love-happiness ...hasten to me with that which will revive and refresh me, for I am sick with love.[39]

This picture is also often misinterpreted. She comments in v. 6, "Let his left hand be under my head and his right hand embrace me." Some see sexual positioning in this but that is without merit here. This "embrace" means simply "embracing someone else to show fondness or affection."[40]

---

[39] Keil and Delitzsch, *Commentary on the Old Testament*, vol. 6, 529.

[40] R. Laird Harris, Gleason L. Archer Jr., and Bruce K. Waltke, *Theological Wordbook of the Old Testament* (Chicago: Moody Press, 1999), 259.

Solomon can see he has swept her off her feet. She is shaken and he reaches out to her in a tender embrace. He puts her head on his shoulder and his right hand around her waist and hugs her. This isn't something tawdry. It is a powerful touch from an observant and caring man intended to comfort his young bride to be.

SHE WAS PATIENT

It gets better. This last characteristic we see is the most admirable. In v. 7 we find, "I adjure you, O daughters of Jerusalem, by the gazelles or by the hinds of the field, that you do not arouse or awaken my love until she pleases." This phrase is repeated in Song of Solomon 3:5 and 8:4 where it divides major sections of the book so it must be important.

We can clarify this phrase a bit by noting that most translations correctly note that "my" has been added to the text by putting it in italics. We also note the word "she" is literally "it" in the original Hebrew. Thus, a more literal rendering of the phrase would be, "that you not arouse or awaken love until it pleases." She is talking about her sexual desire, not Solomon.

The word "adjure" means "to swear." In Genesis 31:53 Jacob "swore by the fear of his father Isaac" when he parted company with Laban. When you swore by something, you were calling its power into play.

Shulammite swore "by the gazelles or by the hinds of the field." These were antelope and small female deer. They were beautiful, graceful, fast, and free. Speaking to the "daughters of Jerusalem" she is asking her girlfriends to help her hold her emotions in check until the time is right to express them.

She doesn't want to arouse the power of her sexual desires or her desire to get married until the proper time.

In our culture today this seems as wacky as playing tennis in combat boots. Who needs that! But Shulammite knew nothing of that kind of misguided sentiment. She was committed to preparing for marriage in the right way and at the right time.

Some think she is expressing a desire for constraint on her sexual desire. But again – not so. Remember our two words for *love?* Which do you think she used here? She used *ahava,* not *dod.* It is a feminine noun and here it best depicts a woman's natural emotional desire to get married. That's only natural but it might not be wise.

So, she doesn't want to get married too soon. She wants to act in a responsible way that reflects the dignity and integrity of a godly marriage. She is saying, "Don't let my emotions run away with me like a wild deer until the time is right." There would be a lot less marital heartache in the world if more women (and men!) thought the same way.

She Was Submissive

This suggests another discussion that is appropriate here, and that is the subject of submission. This is potentially as volatile as a hand grenade in our culture, but a brief observation is offered because it is part of God's provision for marriage.

Submission is not explicitly in the text, but Shulammite's respect for Solomon pictures a willing submission to her husband to be. This is seen elsewhere in scripture.

In 1 Timothy 2:13-14 Paul notes the reason a woman is not to teach or exercise authority over a man in the church is because "it was Adam who was first created, and then Eve. And it was not Adam who was deceived, but the woman being deceived, fell into transgression."

What happens when this standard is abridged? Genesis 3:16 reflects part of God's conversation with Adam and Eve after they rebelled against Him in the Garden of Eden. Among other things, He said to Eve, "your desire will be for your husband, and he will rule over you." This sounds sexual when you first read it, but it's not.

The only other time "desire" is used is in Genesis 4:7 right after Cain killed his brother Abel. God said to him, "sin is crouching at the door; and its desire is for you, but you must master it." In this verse desire is used in a negative way. God was telling Cain that his sin wanted to dominate him. If that meaning is transferred to Genesis 3:16, that would indicate the woman will attempt to dominate the man. That is, sin is seeking to overpower you in the same way that the woman's natural desire is to overpower her husband.

This is not God's pattern for human relationships, but it is a common human inclination since the time of Adam and Eve. Submission and authority are God's pattern for every human institution whether it is the home, the job, or the church. Submission is not negative as many conclude today. Every command of God is a privilege, not an albatross.

Jesus modeled this. Hebrews 5:8 tells us that even Jesus "learned obedience from the things which He suffered." Jesus always submitted to do the will of his father, even when facing the cross in Matthew 26:39, where he prayed, "My Father, if it is possible, let this cup pass from me; yet not as I will but as You will." Surely if Jesus willingly submitted himself to his father, we shouldn't see submission as onerous either.

This doesn't mean that a woman must subject herself to a physically abusive husband, or an alcoholic or addicted husband who threatens physical or emotional violence to her or her children. In these cases, the woman needs to extricate herself from the home to protect herself and her kids.

The primary task of husbands according to Ephesians 5:25 is to "love your wives as Christ loved the church and gave Himself up for her." He obeys this command by providing and protecting his family. Paul provides the complimentary instruction for a wife in v. 33 noting she "must see to it that she respects her husband" by supporting his work of providing and protecting.

Everything good in life flows naturally from an environment where the husband sacrificially loves his wife and she lovingly respects him. This is true for the husband and his wife as well as their children. When both parties understand and commit to this pattern, it's easier to move on in the dating relationship.

Submission does not infer inferiority. It is simply about function, not value. In a loving relationship where the husband sacrificially loves his wife, and the wife lovingly respects her husband, the relationship works like a hand in a glove. When couples try to establish a 50/50 relationship, both end up fighting for leadership at some point.

Properly applied, these principles work. And with the profile of the past two chapters firmly locked in place, we will see Solomon and Shulammite move on in their dating relationship.

SECTION TWO

TYING THE KNOT

*"Thanks to modern technologies, we can
have sex without babies, babies without
sex, and both without marriage. For many
marriage has become an irrelevancy."*

—— R. Albert Mohler

CHAPTER FOUR

THE DATING GAME
(Song of Solomon 2:8-17)

Most marriages are preceded by dating. That hasn't always been true. In Bible times, marriages were largely arranged by two fathers looking to advance the status of their family name by procuring a man of status for his daughter or a serviceable wife for his son. This is still practiced in many countries of the world today.

In Elizabethan times, ladies who had a position in the court of the king were wooed by knights and lords and other respected suitors through their charm, gifts, and skills. The fathers of the couple had the final say, and young men and women were never allowed to marry below or outside their social standing.

This was called "courting" because it was done in front of the whole community and was finalized with the blessing of family and friends. This practice was continued in America until the 20th century.

By the turn of the century a new form of prepping for marriage called dating came into vogue. In the book *From Front Porch to Back Seat: Courtship in Twentieth-Century America*, cultural historian Beth Baily noted that the word *date* originated as a slang word for booking a date with a prostitute.[41]

The advent of electricity and the automobile accompanied vast migration to the cities as the social interaction between unmarried men and women moved away from the family parlor. Men and women began arranging their own "dates" that included dinner, dancing, and other entertainment. As noted by Beth Baily above, too often dating moved from the front porch to the back seat.

After WWII the situation became murkier. Things changed drastically when 250,000 men never came home. The "man going off to war" syndrome caused panic among many women who thought they wouldn't be able to get a man. The average age for marriage declined as emotions clouded the decision to find the right guy and get married quickly.

To get your man, the practice of "going steady" for kids in high school and even junior high became prominent. This was sort of a "practice" marriage where class rings were exchanged and the couple made a vow to remain together forever – or until next Tuesday, whichever came first.

The hippie "free love" movement of the 60s brought the implosion of moral standards and authority. The sexual revolution rejected all biblical, cultural, and social norms of

---

[41] Beth Baily, *From Front Porch to Back Seat: Courtship in Twentieth-Century America* (Baltimore: The John Hopkins University Press, 1988), 22.

marriage as "make love, not war" became the standard. The feminist movement began the deconstruction of any barriers between men and women. They demanded sexual freedom just like men and received it with the advent of "the pill" and the 1973 Supreme Court decision *Roe v. Wade*, the case that legalized abortion. From that time on an unmarried woman could abort the unwelcome "evidence" of her sexual freedom and continue her promiscuity without repercussions.

The climate today can only be described as chaotic. The models mentioned above have all but disappeared. Some might "date" but it's hardly universal. Jean Twenge, professor of psychology at San Diego State University who studies generational differences, describes our modern context this way:

> Today's teens are also less likely to date. The initial stage of courtship, which Gen Xers called "liking" (as in "Ooh, he likes you!"), kids now call "talking"—an ironic choice for a generation that prefers texting to actual conversation. After two teens have "talked" for a while, they might start dating. But only about 56 percent of high-school seniors in 2015 went out on dates; for Boomers and Gen Xers, the number was about 85 percent.[42]

In addition to the increasing absence of dating, the "hookup" culture and "friends with benefits" have established sex as the most common norm in relationships with marriage seldom considered. Live-in arrangements, serial monogamy,

---

[42] Jean Twenge, "Have Smartphones Destroyed a Generation?" www.theatlantic.com, September 2017, accessed on June 6, 2020.

one-night stands, and even ignoring your own sexuality are all possible scenarios in the new genderless society that is forming.

These arrangements are a vicious attack on the very core of God's provision for mankind in Genesis 1-3. He created two sexes – man and woman. Likewise, God's approval of the sexual union of Adam and Eve in the first marriage has been shredded by all kinds of sexual deviancy and cheap substitutes.

This hasn't done anything to improve on God's provision. Instead, historical theologian Al Mohler notes, "Thanks to modern technologies, we can have sex without babies, babies without sex, and both without marriage. For many marriage has become an irrelevancy."[43] Our world regards marriage as antiquated as the 50s TV show, *Ozzie and Harriet,* and any kind of sexual restraint as damaging to our sexual libido.

But let's not throw in the towel just yet. Talking about dating and courtship may be as antiquated as the crank start Model T, but we must remember that sex and marriage are God's ideas. That means there must be a way to bring men and women together to enjoy God's provision of sexual union in marriage. This brings us to our discussion on dating.

DATING

Dating is not prescribed in the Bible. But we can see various couples brought together in marriage and learn from them. Solomon and Shulammite are one of those couples. So,

---

[43] R. Albert Mohler, *The Gathering Storm, Secularism, Culture, and the Church* (Nashville, Tennessee, Nelson Books, 2020), 58.

what can we learn from them about preparing for marriage? Obviously, they were not aware of the concepts of dating or courtship, so how did they do it?

I'm going to use the term *dating* and *courtship* loosely in the following discussion. I'm not trying to define or validate a certain style of relationship or provide a template or mandate. I will use the terms only because most people understand them, and we see elements of both in the way Solomon and Shulammite define their relationship before marriage.

Dating implies a sense of anticipation. Most people don't date several people at one time if they want to continue to live. That's because dating begins to imply exclusivity. Casual dating, without the goal of marriage in play, is potentially harmful because there is little interest in getting to know the other person or in learning how to deal with differences and conflict. These are not the skills needed for marriage.

Anticipation

But dating must begin somewhere. We already know that Solomon and Shulammite met as a result of Solomon being with his shepherds in the grazing country around the Sea of Galilee. One day he noticed a young shepherdess and began a conversation. The comments we have seen so far reflect the commitment they both had to behave respectfully even as they experienced deep feelings toward one another.

But now things rachet up a bit. Some say this section is a dream, but I don't see anything that would lead me to believe that. It seems as though time has passed between their first meeting and this new encounter. Solomon had gone back to the palace in Jerusalem and then returned to the country in the spring to attend to the shearing of his sheep.

Shulammite's reflections on this time are seen in Song of Solomon 2:8, "Listen! My beloved! Behold, he is coming, climbing on the mountains, leaping on the hills!" It seems as if she knew he would be coming. It's possible that he told her he would be returning to Jerusalem but would come back to see her in the spring. Well, its springtime and it is obvious that Solomon's thoughts have turned to love.

Jerusalem is a little over 60 miles from Galilee so Solomon may indeed have had to do some climbing in the Galilean hill country to get there. She is thrilled to see him, proclaiming in v. 9, "My beloved is like a gazelle or a young stag." He is as fast as a young male deer. Deer don't run, they bounce. He is so eager that he will do anything to get there quickly. I picture him sort of like a new puppy who wags his tail and jumps all over his master when he sees him.

And then he arrives. "Behold, he is standing behind our wall, He is looking through the windows, He is peering through the lattice." This sounds like some kind of voyeur but remember that he may have never been to her home. He is anxious but there is no address on the house. She probably told him something like, "My home is in the second valley past the stand of cedars on the hill."

The "wall" was the courtyard of her house. As he approached, he was "looking through the windows" for any sign of her. This is more than "I just happened to be in the neighborhood so I thought I would drop in." He told her he would return in the spring. Neither of them had been able to get the other person out of their mind all winter long. And now here they were, face to face in her home. Everything else is background noise.

Man is the initiator

We can make two observations here. The first is that Solomon is the initiator. He told her he would return and here he is. He traveled over 120 miles round trip to see her again. If his interest had waned, he might have forgotten all about the girl that he met in the fields several months ago. But he didn't. He made plans to return and he did.

This isn't a mandate for dating but it's a good idea. If the girl approaches the guy first it sends the wrong message. Paul's states in 1 Corinthians 11:3, "I want you to understand that Christ is the head of every man, and the man is the head of a woman, and God is the head of Christ." When the guy takes the lead, he is honoring that advice.

The other reason for this is that the woman has more to lose. If a woman approaches a guy first it can appear that she is interested in something that she isn't interested in at all. If a woman ends up in a sexual relationship, she bears the main responsibility if she ends up pregnant.

This model has become so perverted in our world. The modern feminist movement has made men unsure of what their role is to be. They've been told that men and women are equal in every way and that men are "toxic" and poten-tial abusers. So, it's natural for many young men to be unsure about making the first move.

However, it's still best for the guy to initiate the first date. I need to point out that a guy just might be shy or quiet. If a girl is interested in him, she may need to have a mutual friend drop the hint to have him call her. But guys need to man up and make the first call. If she turns you down, don't dwell on it. God has someone better for you.

They date in public

It's also interesting to note here that their rendezvous is completely public. He comes to her house. It's likely he met the angry brothers and her mom. And they did not retreat to some kind of private, secluded spot where no one could see them. He asked her to go for a walk outside where they could take the time to talk and get to know each other.

It sounds funny, but privacy is the enemy of growth in a young relationship. Conversation that takes place in the middle of sexual tension speaks the wrong language. The expectation today is that mom and dad are "in the way" of a blossoming romance. When the boyfriend comes over, parents are often expected to retreat to their room and stay there.

But snuggling on the couch watching a movie isn't building a relationship. It's preventing the very thing the couple needs most. Years ago, I read a piece called "Rules to Date My Daughter." I don't know who wrote it, but the rules made sense. Rule six is appropriate here:

> The following places are not appropriate for a date with my daughter: Places where there are beds, sofas, or anything softer than a wooden stool. Places where there are no parents, policemen, or nuns within eyesight. Places where there is darkness.

Places where there is dancing, holding hands, or happiness. Places where the ambient temperature is warm enough to induce my daughter to wear shorts, tank tops, midriff T-shirts, or anything other than overalls, a sweater, and a goose down parka – zipped up to her throat. Movies with a strong romantic or sexual theme are to be avoided; movies which feature chain saws are okay. Hockey games are okay. Old folks' homes are better.

You get the idea. And if you don't, you will if you ever have a daughter. Privacy will increase as the relationship grows, but it is never to be pursued to the exclusion of spending time around family and friends.

What do you do on a date?

There is also confusion about what you do on a date. It's somewhere between hanging out and jumping in the sack, but the lines are undefined.

Solomon ups the ante a bit in v. 10, "Arise, my darling, my beautiful one, and come along." The words "arise" and "come along" are both imperatives. He finishes the section in v. 13b with the same words. This is not a template or a mandate. But we can see that Solomon has taken the initiative and has some specific plans for the date.

Sandwiched in the middle of the imperatives of vv. 10 and 13 is the substance of his invitation. He says, "'For behold, the winter is past, the rain is over and gone. The flowers have already appeared in the land; the time has arrived for pruning the vines, and the voice of the turtledove has been heard in our land. The fig tree has ripened its figs, and the vines in blossom have given forth their fragrance. Arise, my darling, my beautiful one, and come along!' "

The first thing that strikes us are the many allusions to nature. But it's helpful to remember that Solomon is both a naturalist and a poet. 1 Kings 4:32-33 tells us that, in addition to being the author of three thousand proverbs and more than a thousand songs, "He spoke of trees, from the cedar that is in Lebanon even to the hyssop that grows on the wall; he spoke also of animals and birds and creeping things and fish." This confirms the author is Solomon and it shows that he is not just a "city boy." He knew and loved the country just like she did.

So, what did he invite Shulammite to do? We see six things here that all seemingly refer to spring. But there is more to the eye than that. He's not just inviting her for a walk in the park. The following phrases suggest an attitude as well as things to do. He invites her to:

1. <u>A new beginning</u> – "winter is past, the rain is over and gone" – Meeting someone new is exhilarating. But be cautious here. You can fall in love with anyone so don't let your heart get in front of your head. For a Christian this means no "evangelistic dating." That is, if you are planning on marrying a Christian then don't settle for anything else in your dating life. If you grow to love a non-Christian and they have to pretend they are a Christian before you get married, you will be in for a lifetime of disappointment.

2. <u>Stop and smell the roses</u> – "The flowers have already appeared in the land" – Our lives are often too busy to "stop and smell the roses." As a result, we miss the true beauty of life. Your dates don't have to cost a lot. Stop by Subway and enjoy a sandwich in the park. Go fishing with some friends. Play Frisbee golf in the park. Anything that gets you outside is usually cheap and enjoyable. Avoid inside events like watching movies or "just hanging out," unless it's with a group or family.

3. <u>Celebrate</u> – "The time has arrived for pruning the vines" – The ESV and KJV Bibles both translate this as "singing" because there is one letter difference between the words for "singing" and the word for "pruning." The context seems best to consider this as "singing" since pruning usually occurred in the fall and "singing" better fits the joy of spring. Celebrate by listening to a worship playlist on *Spotify* and see if your date knows any of the songs. Find out what they listen to and you'll find out what they celebrate.

4. <u>The right timing</u> – "The voice of the turtledoves has been heard in our land." This dove is different from the dove in v. 15. This dove is a migratory bird that returns to Israel in the spring. This is Solomon's invitation for Shulammite to join him because "the time is right" to pursue their love. I'm not trying to make too strong a tie here, but I think this indicates doing things that are in line with the particular length of your relationship.

Solomon was ready to get married, but maybe you're not. In the early part of dating life, do things with family and groups of friends. As you get more serious as a couple, continue to stress dates that keep you around groups of people, like ball games, church events, historical sites, museums, car shows, fairs, plays, and concerts. You will also see your relationship develop as you participate together in service projects, short term missions, and worship opportunities if you attend the same church.

5. <u>Be blessed</u> – "The fig tree has ripened its figs." The fig is one of the most important crops in Israel, along with the olive and grape. It ripens three times per year but the first crop in June is the sweetest. As figs were a blessing to enjoy, so Solomon invites Shulammite to enjoy the sweetness of their love.

    This seems to picture a more mature relationship, one that is focusing on sharing a future together. Your dating will be different then. It might include visiting potential grad schools, job fairs, trade shows, dinner with older married couples to pick their brains, and reading and studying the Bible together. The ripened figs of the fig tree reflect the sweetness of your relationship as you grow together.

Years ago, I performed the wedding for a couple who modeled this. Both sets of parents were active in our church and I knew them well. The parents told me privately that their kids were a "couple" but weren't telling anyone about it because they wanted to finish college before they got married.

The next summer we shared a houseboat on Lake Shasta in northern California with several families, including both of their families. You would have never known these two were a couple. There was no holding hands, no "pretzel people" displays, and no running off together. They acted with complete integrity and respect for each other. And all the younger kids on the trip (including mine) were watching them.

After I performed their wedding a couple of years later, I asked them about their behavior on that trip. They told me that they were not ready to get married at that time, so, even though they knew that's where they were heading, they didn't want to act in a way that would get ahead of the timing God had for them. That's maturity.

COURTSHIP

Couples like that have moved from dating to courtship. There is not a sharp division in Song of Solomon 3:13 and 14 but there are two more observations that seem to move the relationship of Solomon and Shulammite a little deeper. While I'm not using "dating" and "courtship" in a technical sense, these two observations fit better under the "courtship" umbrella we discussed at the first part of the chapter.

Pastor Tommy Nelson points out a telling distinction between dating and courtship when he says, "Dating is observation. Courtship is involvement. Dating is a time allotment; it is an end in itself. Courtship involves some mutual responsibility, more vulnerability, and a greater need for trust. Dating is marketing. Courtship is negotiating a potential sale to its close...Dating is casual and courtship is serious."[44]

Growing together

Solomon changes the tone between vv. 13 and 14 and moves the discussion to a deeper level. "O my dove, in the clefts of the rock, in the secret place of the steep pathway, let me see your form, let me hear your voice; for your voice is sweet, and your form is lovely." At first glance, this sounds like a lecherous old man. But that's not true.

A dove is quiet and shy. The female is coy and retiring, possibly intimidated. The "clefts of the rock" refers to the home of the dove lodged in the cleft of a hill. The "secret place of the steep pathway" indicates a tough climb for anyone who wanted to gain access to her nest. Even though Shulammite has not appeared shy and retiring to this point, Solomon still seems to be saying, "My love, you are out of reach to me, like a dove high up in the cliffs."

His next request shows that he knows there is still more to learn about her. His request is to "let me see your form." This is more than visual sight. The metaphorical sense of "see" means "to regard, perceive, feel, understand, learn, or enjoy."[45] He wants to see beneath the surface. He wants to deeply understand her.

---

[44] Tommy Nelson, *The Book of Romance: What Solomon Says About Love, Sex, and Intimacy* (Nashville, Tennessee: Thomas Nelson, Inc., 1998), 48-49.

[45] Robert D. Culver, "2095 הָאָר," ed. R. Laird Harris, Gleason L. Archer Jr., and Bruce K. Waltke, *Theological Wordbook of the Old Testament* (Chicago: Moody Press, 1999), 823.

The object of his desire to see is "her form." This is not a reference to her body. The word *mareh* means "appearance or countenance." And it's plural which points to the "extension and the totality of its parts." Old Testament commentators Keil and Delitzsch note the plural points to the "fulness of beauty and its overpowering impression."[46]

That's quite a descriptive desire. This is a man who is not satisfied with mere externals. He regarded her as physically beautiful, but that wasn't enough for him. He wanted to know everything about her – her emotions, her desires and dreams, her tastes and temperament, her fears and expectations. He wanted to know it all.

This does not mean that he was snoopy or trying to play amateur psychologist. It's the same thing the Apostle Peter talks about in 1 Peter 3:7 when he instructs husbands to " live with your wives in an understanding way, as with someone weaker, since she is a woman; and show her honor as a fellow heir of the grace of life, so that your prayers will not be hindered."

The word for "understanding" is *ginosko,* from which we get our word *knowledge.* It means to "experience, learn, get to know: what has been experienced becomes known to the one who has experienced it."[47] This is distinguished from *oida,* a different word in Greek which means "fulness of

---

[46] Carl Friedrich Keil and Franz Delitzsch, *Commentary on the Old Testament,* vol. 6, (Peabody, MA: Hendrickson, 1996), 536.

[47] E. D. Schmitz, "Γινώσκω," ed. Lothar Coenen, Erich Beyreuther, and Hans Bietenhard, *New International Dictionary of New Testament Theology,* vol. 2, (Grand Rapids, MI: Zondervan Publishing House, 1986), 392.

knowledge,"[48] or knowledge that is more intuitive. This indicates that understanding your wife is not intuitive. You have to gain that knowledge by the experience of living with her.

Why spend all this time on a bunch of archaic words? Because it is important to understand what both Peter and Solomon are saying. A wise man is one who takes the time to at least attempt to understand the woman he loves. Men sometimes feel out of their league here, but it's not necessary.

You can start the process of understanding your future wife (or husband) by learning to ask questions. "What do you want to be when the world grows up?" "What are you most afraid of?" "What did you learn about marriage from your parents?" "What makes you mad?" "What do you want to accomplish in the next ten years?" "Who are your heroes?" "What are you reading?"

The possibilities are endless. The only way that you will gain true knowledge is to ask questions. You may feel that the girl you are trying to get to know is like a dove high up in the cleft of the hills. But each question you ask, each note you log away in your brain, each attempt you make at clarification, takes a step to deeper understanding.

That doesn't mean she's playing games. Peter said that a woman is *"weaker"* but that means physically only. Her true status and value to you is as a "fellow heir of the grace of life." If she is to be a partner with you in this life experience, don't lock her out by stubbornly failing to even attempt to understand her.

---

[48] W.E. Vine and F.F. Bruce, *Vine's Complete Expository Dictionary of Old and New Testament Words* (Old Tappan, NJ: Fleming H. Revell, 1981), 298.

Peter provides a sobering reason for a husband to understand his wife in 1 Peter 3:7b. You do it "so that your prayers will not be hindered." Imagine that – an effective prayer life is directly tied to understanding this one you say you love.

Catching foxes

Solomon offers further insight for couples to consider in Song of Solomon 2:15, "Catch the foxes for us, the little foxes that are ruining the vineyards, while our vineyards are in blossom." Hebrew poetry provides a graphic picture for our consideration.

Foxes burrow into the ground in vineyards. They are known for digging around the roots of plants in the vineyard and eating their blossoms and tender shoots. They disturb the roots so plants can't grow. There is some debate about who is speaking here since he was speaking in the previous verse and she is speaking in the following verse.

But it really doesn't matter since the text refers to "us." The concern was that they needed to be on guard for whatever little foxes might attack their vineyard. It seems best to take this as a reference to their relationship.

Everyone faces certain things that will destroy a relationship if left unchallenged. We aren't told what foxes the young couple here was thinking of, but there are a number of contemporary foxes dating couples face today that come to mind.

Spiritual foxes

The first category might be called spiritual foxes. These are foxes that would cause you to question your faith or God's provision for you. A young person today might face this fox in what some call "evangelistic dating." That is, they don't believe that God will provide them a partner who loves Christ like they do so they let their emotions gain control and marry someone who is not a believer.

The Bible is clear about this. In the Old Testament God warned the nation of Israel against marrying those from other nations because they would turn them away from God. As we've seen before, this is exactly what eventually happened to Solomon. In 1 Kings 11:4 we read that "when Solomon was old, his wives turned his heart away after other gods; and his heart was not wholly devoted to the Lord his God."

You must recognize this fox before you marry someone who is not a believer. If you have to coax them through a coerced profession of faith now, don't be surprised when they renounce it later. If they won't go to church with you now, they won't go after you are married. If they won't pray out loud with you now, they won't pray with you later. When you can't worship or pray with your spouse, this leaves a hole that can't be filled even when you love them, and they love you.

Sexual foxes

Another fox every couple face is the sexual fox. This might be sex before you are married or sexual temptation after you are married. If you are sexually involved and you are not married yet, then you need to break up until a trusted pastor or friend can hold you accountable to remain celibate until you are married. "Cutting back" doesn't work. This might seem overly harsh, but sexual discipline now will be a sign of how you will handle sexual temptation with someone else after you are married.

If you have been sexually active in the past, then confess this to your fiancée and make a commitment to live a pure life until you are married. Sexual temptations in our society are enormous. But confession brings freedom from shame and guilt when it is brought to light and confessed. You don't have to let the past determine your future. That's what forgiveness of the cross is all about.

Emotional foxes

This might sound like a strange fox to look for, but the emotional fox is wily and devastating. I'm not talking about the normal swing of appropriate emotions. I'm talking about emotional immaturity.

A person who fails to keep a constant watch over their heart will find themselves enslaved to emotions that lead to all kinds of destructive behaviors. If the person you are dating is controlling, insecure, self-centered, dishonest, childish, domineering, clingy, jealous, possessive, impulsive, angry, moody, manipulative, easily offended, lazy, disrespectful, or impressed with signs of wealth, then take note. These issues will only intensify after you are married. Get some help in dealing with these foxes now. If you marry this person you are in for a long life of walking on eggshells and emotional pain.

There are many other kinds of foxes. Your situation is unique. But look for things like perfectionism, meddling and controlling parents, financial irresponsibility, fear of commitment, obsession with a hobby, or pornography and sexual perversions.

Foxes aren't fatal. But the more you see something that bothers you, the more it's possibly a fox that would undermine your love if you don't confront it. When you confront your partner, think through what you want to say and how to say it. If you need to get help, request help from a friend, a pastor, or a mature family member.

Think of what your marriage will be like if you do not confront these foxes. Please don't think that getting married will eradicate the problems. It won't.

No one is perfect. But two people striving to grow together through the time they are dating will be better prepared for the next step – marriage.

"...Love is not blind; that is the last thing that love is. Love is bound; and the more it is bound, the less it is blind."

— G. K. Chesterton

CHAPTER FIVE

ON EAGLES' WINGS
Song of Solomon 3:1-5

One of the greatest fears we have as humans is to be fully known. And yet that is one of our greatest desires. We desire to have someone stare us in the eyes and see all the hidden crevices and ravines and still love us. That's why marriage can be so intimidating. We long to be known and yet we're afraid we will be.

Surgeon Richard Selzer writes about a young couple who faced this dilemma, recounting his observations of a young husband seeing his wife after a delicate surgery.

> I stand by the bed where a young woman lies, her face postoperative, her mouth twisted in palsy, clownish. A tiny twig of the facial nerve, the one to the muscles of her mouth, has been severed. The surgeon had followed with religious fervor the curve of her flesh; I promise you that. Nevertheless,

to remove the tumor in her cheek, I had cut the little nerve.

Her young husband is in the room. He stands on the opposite side of the bed, and together they seem to dwell in the evening lamplight, isolated from me, private. Who are they, I ask myself, he and this wrymouth I have made, who gaze at and touch each other so generously, greedily? The young woman speaks.

"Will my mouth always be like this?" she asks.

"Yes," I say, "it will. It is because the nerve was cut."

She nods and is silent. But the young man smiles. "I like it," he says. "It is kind of cute."

All at once I know who he is. I understand, and I lower my gaze. One is not bold in an encounter with a god. Unmindful, he bends to kiss her crooked mouth, and I am so close I can see how he twists his own lips to accommodate to hers, to show her that their kiss still works.[49]

Getting married provides the best possibility to be known by another person that is humanly possible. But all of us have

---

[49] Richard Selzer, *Mortal Lessons: Notes on the Art of Surgery* (New York: Simon and Schuster, 1976), 46.

the fear that if we are fully known we will be rejected. The couple above reminds us that marital love conquers this fear.

But what happens if you are afraid to get married in the first place? What do you do if you fear that your fiancée sees something in you that makes him pull away? What happens if he sees something in you that makes him want to call the whole thing off and you end up losing him?

These are all dramatic questions that are felt by a number of people before they get married. Song of Solomon 3:1-5 immediately precedes the account of Solomon and Shulammite's wedding. It provides a realistic glimpse into the pre-marital jitters Shulammite was having.

Fear

The storyline takes an unexpected turn at the beginning of Song of Solomon 3. The road to a glorious wedding is interrupted by doubt. We often joke about "being left at the altar," or even being "The Runaway Bride" that the movie portrayed. But it's no laughing matter if you're truly experiencing second thoughts about getting married.

This new section actually begins in the last half of Song of Solomon 2:16. This might seem strange but remember that verse numbers were not added until the 16th century AD. So, at times a new thought might pick up in between verses or even in between the lines of a verse.

It would be nice to see that "My beloved is mine, and I am his" in v. 16 was followed by something like, "and they all lived happily ever after." But we all know that's not how it goes in real life, and that's certainly not how it goes for Solomon and his bride to be.

This is one of the things that makes this book such an authentic portrayal of marriage. It isn't just gloss and giddiness. Perhaps like most marriages, the reality of "pre-marital jitters" pops up in the last half of vv. 16-17, "He pastures his flock among the lilies. Until the cool of the day when the shadows flee away, turn, my beloved, and be like a gazelle or a young stag on the mountains of Bether."

At first it might seem like there isn't much going on. But a closer look reveals a cloud of doubt crossing her mind. Could this be one of the "foxes" in the previous chapter that she is concerned about?

She seems to be remembering their first meeting when she saw him as one tending his flock of sheep, not the king. She pictures the end of the day. Work is done and he beds the sheep down for the night. And then what?

The last sentence of v. 17 is curious. Why does she say, "Turn?" It's an imperative, a command. Why would she say this unless he had not turned toward her when she expected it? Could it be that she was reminiscing about the time in Song of Solomon 2:8 when he came bouncing over the hills like a gazelle eager to see her? Could it be that she was expecting the same eagerness to continue, but it hadn't?

We gain some insight in that last line of v. 17b with the reference to "the mountains of Bether." The ESV says, "cleft mountains" and the NIV translates it as "rugged hills." But the problem is that there was no mountain or hill in Israel at that time called Bether. So she is not referring to a real mountain. But is she looking at her situation as a mountain? An obstacle?

The word for *Bether* means "part, piece." It is only used three other times in the Old Testament. It always speaks "of halves of animals cut in two in making covenants."[50] So here it obviously refers to some kind of division. She seems to be saying, "I fear a large mountain of division could come between us."

We are left to wonder why she would implore him to "turn" and why she would see a potential "mountain of division" between them? Could it be that, after telling her he wanted to know her countenance deeply, he had to return to his duties? Maybe he had promised to come back that night but he got busy and couldn't.

Fear and questions are a part of every relationship. If you don't face your questions now, they will grow into fear and fear will develop into panic. Asking a question may reveal that there is no problem. But it might also indicate something more serious. It's important to face issues like constant fighting, possessiveness and unfounded jealousy, financial secrets, lack of spiritual commitment, and sexual pressure. Ignoring these types of issues could lead to huge problems after you are married.

Loss

The chapter break before Chapter 3 is unfortunate because it seems best to see Song of Solomon 2:16b – 3:6 as

---

[50] Francis Brown, Samuel Rolles Driver, and Charles Augustus Briggs, *The Enhanced Brown-Driver-Briggs Hebrew and English Lexicon* (Oxford: Clarendon Press, 1977), 144.

a unit. This section is right before the wedding in Song of Solomon 3:6-11 and reveals the questions and fears that were running through Shulammite's mind immediately before she got married.

Her second fear is expressed in a dream. While it's important to realize that Scripture indicates we are not to take direction from dreams, yet from time to time we can see they serve a purpose. Dreams can express unverbalized worries and concerns. That's what seems to be what is happening here.

She recounts the dream in Song of Solomon 3:1, "On my bed night after night I sought him whom my soul loves; I sought him but did not find him." This is not a sexual reference. It's a dream. It's at night. She's in bed, and this occurs "night after night." This indicates a nagging fear that something had come between them and she would lose him, perhaps to the demands of is kingdom. It could also indicate her fear that a country girl like her really didn't belong.

This feeling is solidified in v. 1. She sought him; she went into the city to look for him. There is no doubt about her love for him, "I must seek him whom my soul loves, I sought him," but panic set in when "I did not find him."

In her dream she also encountered the watchmen, indicating her desire to have someone help in her search. Feelings of loss and rejection must have overwhelmed her as she realized that he was gone.

I'm not trying to interpret a dream here, but we can surmise that this must have left Shulammite wondering if he would leave her in real life. Maybe she wasn't good enough for him. What if he decided he liked the fair skinned girls in the palace rather than her tanned look? What if he thought she wasn't sophisticated enough? Her mind was reeling with anxiety and fear.

LACK OF APPROVAL

It's also possible Shulammite experienced the fear of a lack of approval from her mom. Her father is not mentioned anywhere in the whole book, so it seems as if the only family she had in the picture was her mom and her brothers.

Thankfully this issue was resolved in v. 4, "Scarcely had I left them when I found him whom my soul loves; I held on to him and would not let him go until I had brought him to my mother's house, and into the room of her who conceived me." We aren't told where he was or how she found him, but he was back. That can happen in a dream.

The Hebrew grammar of this verse indicates that the main idea is in the middle clause – "I held on to him and would not let him go." The grammar also indicates excitement when she realized she had found him.

The interpretation of the end of v. 4 is problematic. She said, "I brought him to my mother's house." This is seen as a typical expression for an unmarried woman. She wouldn't say, "I took him home" because it was not her home and that would dishonor her mother. But being in her mother's house seems to indicate she thought of this as a secure place.

But the next phrase presents the problem. What does she mean by "and into the room of the one who conceived me"? Some feel this is simply the completion of the picture of the home. Others find a sexual invitation here. Neither seems correct.

It's best to view this simply as a conversation with her mother. Her dream occurred at night and she went out to search for him. Much like moms everywhere, she knew her mom would be waiting up for her. Presumably she woke her mother because it would not have been unusual for her to talk things like this over with her mom.

When she returned home with boyfriend in tow, they went to her mother's bedroom as a daughter might do in times of distress and told her relieved mother everything was okay. Bringing mom and boyfriend together in the dream indicated that mom approved, and all was well.

The symbolism of this should not be overlooked. Too often couples view themselves as an entity apart from the larger family. But God did not intend marriage to be "us against the world." In the optimal view of marriage, the parents of the couple add a son or daughter to their family and love them like their own. Their approval is a key component of the desire to be married.

IMPATIENCE

Patience is a key component in preparing for marriage. The decision to get married should not be made impulsively. This means that the wise person understands the importance of waiting for the right person. We saw that in the last two chapters. But it also means getting married in the right way, with no reservations as we saw above.

But patience also means getting married at the right time. This is what Shulammite is alluding to in v. 5, "I adjure you, O daughters of Jerusalem, by the gazelles or by the hinds of the field, that you will not arouse or awaken my love until she pleases." We have seen these exact words used before in Song of Solomon 2:7 when she asks her friends to help her keep her sexual temptations in place.

But here she means something else. We don't know if this is a part of her dream or not, but we do know that it's a reflection of her deep commitment to patience and preparing for marriage in the right way and the right time.

It would not be unusual to see a young woman like Shulammite preening at her good fortune in snagging the king. A woman of less character would be racing to the altar before the king changed his mind.

But we see none of that from Shulammite. She is asking her friends to hold her accountable and make sure that she is not rushing into this wedding without the proper checks in place.

Much like a pilot goes through a prescribed checklist before take-off, someone moving towards marriage needs to perform at least a mental checklist to ensure that the marriage will get airborne. At the very least that checklist should include:

1. The spiritual component. Is this person a believer? Do we share the same spiritual and relational goals? What is our mission in life?
2. The social component. Do our parents approve of this marriage? If not, why not? Do we both fit in the social

circles of the other person? Do our friends think this is a good match or have they verbalized concerns?

3. The timing component. Have we finished our basic education? Is there any good reason to wait to get married?

4. The financial component. Are we financially able to sustain our new home with no financial help from parents or anyone else?

Only when these criteria are met can a couple proceed with confidence in getting married and adding the physical commitment to their relationship. A couple who has sex in the back seat and are "deeply in love" but have no jobs aren't committed to each other and are not ready to get married.

This is not to say that every question must be answered, and every goal reached before you are ready to walk the aisle. Before I got married my mental checklist included owning my own home, having a thousand dollars in the bank, and being at least 23 years old. Well, I made it to 23, but the other goals were not reached.

But the basic questions had been asked and answered in an appropriate way. Despite the fact that Anne was a new Christian and had not been raised in the church, everyone in our circle of family and friends saw that she was a wonderful choice for me. Both sets of parents were enthused about our marriage. I had just graduated from college and was ready to start seminary. We both had jobs that could pay the bills, including graduate school.

Yet with all this in place, I almost got ahead of myself on the timing. Shortly after we were engaged Anne left for

Chicago to enter training as a flight attendant for United Airlines, a dream of hers from the time she was a child. But it turned into a time of great turmoil for both of us. We talked often on the phone which usually ended with her crying and saying she loved me and wanted to come home, despite the wishes of her parents who wanted her to stay.

I wanted to "put my foot down" and tell her Dad that I was running the show now and Anne was coming home to get married. But a friend wisely pointed out that I should not alienate her parents when they would be a part of my life for years to come.

Anne and I prayed about it and decided that we wanted her parents' blessing before she came home. Her Dad wasn't crazy about his youngest daughter living in New York so he said that she could come home if she was based in New York upon graduation. You guessed it! She was based in New York. God answered our prayer and answered our dilemma in a way that honored her parents and brought us together at the right time.

The wedding is not the apex of a love story. It's only the beginning. But if both parties don't approach the wedding with eyes wide open to any questions they might have about their potential partner, they are only postponing the day of reckoning. It causes much more heartache to end a problem than to prevent one.

In the book, *Marriage, Divorce, and Remarriage*, author Jim Newheiser lists ten questions that couples might ask during the dating process to determine if they are in agreement with moving ahead with the relationship. These questions are:

1. Are you both in love with the gospel, and is it impacting your lives?
2. Do you respect each other's character?
3. Do you have compatible life goals?
4. How do you function together in group settings?
5. Have you been able to work through the past?
6. Are you able to be honest with each other about sins and faults?
7. Can you love and accept each other as you are?
8. Why do you want to marry each other?
9. What are your expectations of marriage?
10. How well do you know each other and yourself?[51]

Discussions on issues like these will either dissipate questions or concerns one may have about their impending wedding, or they will confirm that the relationship should be terminated. As difficult as this may sound, it would be much better than discovering these things after the wedding.

In one of the first marriages I officiated as a young pastor, the young man called and asked if he could meet me alone before the next pre-marital counseling session. He poured out his previously unspoken fears that his fiancée was incredibly self-centered, insecure, and immature. We worked through a plan to talk to her about his questions at our next session. When he gently but firmly expressed his concerns at our next session she went to the bathroom and threw up. His fears were well founded, and they broke up. But he was delivered from a painful marriage.

---

[51] Jim Newheiser, *Marriage, Divorce, and Remarriage* (Phillipsburg, New Jersey: P&R Publishing, 2017), 65-68.

At times like that you need to know about God's sustaining presence. Isaiah 40:31 reminds us that "those who wait for the Lord will gain new strength; they will mount up with wings like eagles, they will run and not get tired, they will walk and not become weary." The "wings of eagles" refers to the strong wings of a mama eagle coming underneath to rescue her falling young eaglet after they have been pushed out of the nest in their first flying lesson.

Leaving the comfortable nest and jumping into marriage might seem like that to some. But if the boxes mentioned above are checked, and you have the affirmation of family and friends, then you can jump, trusting that God will bear you up on eagle's wings as you enter this new phase of life together.

Solomon and Shulammite are there. They have patiently done things right. They are ready to get married. It will be a wedding fit for a king.

"Rather, in a wedding you stand up before God, your family, and all the main institutions of society, and you promise to be loving, faithful, and true to the other person in the future, regardless of undulating internal feelings or external circumstances."

— Tim Keller

CHAPTER SIX

I DO! I DO!
(Song of Solomon 3:6-11)

Patricia McGerr had a story to tell. She told it in *Woman's Day* magazine in 1965. It was called, "Johnny Lingo's Eight-Cow Wife." When McGerr visited the South Pacific island of Kiniwata on an assignment she was told that she needed to visit a smaller island called Narubundi and find a man named Johnny Lingo. He's an expert "negotiator" she was told with a mocking laugh.

"Why are you laughing?" she asked. She was told that five months previous Johnny came to Kiniwata to buy a wife. The common price for a wife at the time was one or two cows. If a woman was thought to be exceptional the price might go as high as three or four cows.

Johnny wanted a girl named Sarita. Small and skinny, she walked with hunched shoulders and head lowered as if she was trying to hide. Her cheeks had no color. Her eyes never opened beyond a slit. Her hair was a tangled mess. She seemed to be afraid of her own shadow, even afraid of her own voice. She never laughed, never played with other girls. She had no chance of getting a husband.

But Johnny wanted her! Sarita's family told her father Sam Karoo to hold out for two cows, knowing that one would be a bargain. Johnny came into the tent. "Father of Sarita, I offer eight cows for your daughter!" Her father quickly agreed. Johnny delivered the eight cows and took his bride home to Narubundi. Everyone laughed and Johnny had not been seen since.

McGerr wanted to meet Johnny so she traveled to Narubundi. Upon finding Johnny she told him that the people in Kiniwata mocked him, saying he was a "sharp trader," and couldn't figure out why he had paid eight cows for his bride.

Just then a girl walked in with a bowl of flowers. McGerr remarked, "She was the most beautiful girl I had ever seen." She had some flowers pinned to her lustrous black hair. Her cheeks were glowing. She was tall and erect, and her eyes sparkled. She had the grace of a queen. She smiled sweetly at Johnny as she turned around and left.

McGerr asked Johnny how his wife could ever put up with such a beautiful woman in the house. "You admire her?" Johnny asked.

"Why, she's glorious," McGerr replied. "Who is she?"

Johnny proudly responded, "She's my wife! This is Sarita. But perhaps you wish to say she does not look the way they say she looked in Kiniwata."

McGerr was stunned. "She doesn't. I heard she was homely. They all make fun of you because you let yourself be cheated by Sam Karoo."

Johnny smiled and said, "You think he cheated me? You think eight cows were too many? She can see her father and her friends again. Do you think anyone will make fun of us then? Much has happened to change her. Much in particular happened the day she went away."

"You mean she married you?"

"That, yes. But most of all, I mean the arrangements for the marriage."

"Arrangements?"

"Do you ever think what it does to a woman when she knows that the price her husband has paid is the lowest price for which she can be bought? And then later, when all the women talk, as women do, they boast of what their husbands paid for them. One says four cows, another maybe six. How does she feel – the woman who was sold for one or two? This could not happen to my Sarita."

"Then you paid that unprecedented number of cows just to make your wife happy?"

"Happy? I wanted Sarita to be happy, yes, but I wanted more than that. You say she's different from the way they remember her in Kiniwata. This is true. Many things can change a woman ...But the thing that matters most is what she thinks about herself. In Kiniwata, Sarita believed she was worth nothing. Now she knows that she is worth more than any other woman on the islands ...I wanted an eight-cow wife."[52]

---

[52] Patricia McGerr, "Johnny Lingo's Eight-Cow Wife," *Woman's Day*, November, 1965.

THE PURPOSE OF MARRIAGE

There's a lot we can learn from this story, isn't there? The respect and dignity that is bestowed on women in a godly marriage is not seen in any other context. Rather than limiting women to patriarchal slavery, as some today claim, marriage frees a woman to participate with her husband in the awesome privilege of reflecting the gospel and perpetuating the human race.

Marriage is not a sociological construct that benefits men and enslaves women. Very simply, it exists because there are men and there are women, and for thousands of years the mutual attraction between men and women has led them to get married and set up house. No one forced them to. But in all civilized cultures, this has been the pattern.

Authors Sean McDowell and John Stonestreet have written about four goals accomplished in marriage. They conclude the purpose of marriage is:

1. To regulate sexuality—both in terms of procreation, but also to protect it from opportunism and the abuse of people, primarily women.
2. To socialize and domesticate the male nature—marriage settles a husband down and focuses him on caring for his wife, the mother of his children, and their common children.
3. To protect women from opportunistic men and empower them relationally—relationships where commitment is expected favors women. Relationships where commitment is not expected favors men.

4. To ensure that a child gets from both parents the attention, care and provision he or she requires until young adulthood is reached.[53]

These are the byproducts of a godly marriage. We don't see them explicitly in the Song of Solomon, but Solomon's wedding provides an ancient example that has been followed by millions of couples. The clues we glean from his example establishes a pattern for achieving the best life has to offer. Sociologists Linda Waite and Maggie Gallagher explain:

> Married people enjoy better mental and physical health, and generate greater wealth, more career satisfaction and less boredom and loneliness. What's more, 'married people are more satisfied with their sex lives. . .What the research shows is that married men and married women have better physical health than single people like them, that they live substantially longer lives.'[54]

A wedding is more than a date on the social calendar. It is a statement to society that two people are agreeing to form another building block in preserving this world. The glue that holds these blocks together is their own blood, sweat, and tears. No one else can do it for them. If their marriage

---

[53] Sean McDowell and John Stonestreet, *Same-Sex Marriage: A Thoughtful Approach to God's Design for Marriage* (Grand Rapids, MI: Baker Books, 2014), 32.

[54] Linda J. Waite and Maggie Gallagher, *The Case for Marriage: Why Married People are Happier, Healthier and Better Off Financially* (New York, New York: Doubleday, 2000), 51.

works well, it will secure their spot on the wall that holds off the marauders that would destroy our society.

SOLOMON'S WEDDING

Everyone loves a wedding. And we are invited to Solomon's wedding in Song of Solomon 3:6 which begins the third section of the book. This section describes the wedding of Solomon and Shulammite in colorful language that depicts Solomon's devotion to his new wife. This previously secluded farm girl was given the "eight cow wife" treatment by Solomon.

It's a public celebration

The last half of Chapter 3 jumps right into Solomon's wedding. For the first time in the book, neither Solomon or Shulammite are doing the talking. It's probable that this account is given by the daughters of Jerusalem, since they were the last group Shulammite spoke to in the previous chapter, and we know they were there since they helped build Solomon's stately sedan chair seen in vv. 9-10.

The wedding party

The wedding party makes their entrance in v. 6, where the rhetorical question is asked, "What is this coming up from the wilderness?" The literal translation is "Who is she?" Insiders and family would have known about Shulammite, but the general public would not have known this outsider whom the young king had chosen to be his bride.

Shulammite's hometown of Shunem was over sixty miles from Jerusalem so this would have entailed quite a procession that came "up from the wilderness" from Jericho to Jerusalem, a journey of four to five days.

According to v. 6 it was a grand procession that billowed out dust "like columns of smoke, perfumed with myrrh and frankincense, with all scented powders of the merchant." But it wasn't just a dusty parade. The smell of expensive perfumes from Arabia filled the air as various attendants, banners, musicians, and family passed by. Solomon put on quite a show to honor his new bride.

Solomon is also part of the parade. Royal protocol probably dictated that the king should not go out to fetch anyone. They should come to him. But there he is, creating quite a scene as his specially constructed mode of transportation passes by.

The "traveling couch of Solomon" is mentioned in v. 7. This was a bed, or royal cart of some sort enclosed with curtains on all four sides resting on posts carried by four men or horses, given the length of the trip. Today it would be a looooong limo or some kind of throw-back horse drawn carriage.

In vv. 7b-8 we see that Solomon was surrounded by sixty men, "the mighty men of Israel. All were wielders of the sword, expert in war, each man has his sword at his side, guarding against the terrors of the night." These men were part of the sixty-man contingent of "mighty men" who served his father David.

They were valiant men who never lost a battle. They were the cream of the crop, equivalent to our military generals, our SEAL teams, or our Secret Service. They comprised one-tenth of Solomon's royal bodyguard and they were all armed to the teeth as they rode beside him.

Solomon sat in his "sedan chair" in v. 9 as part of this over-the-top procession to honor his bride. In the next verse we find this was a portable sitting bed surrounded with curtains that Solomon had designed with " its posts of silver, its back of gold and its seat of purple fabric, with its interior lovingly fitted out by the daughters of Jerusalem."

This shows us that these women were not members of a harem. They were attendants to the court of Solomon who were talented in their own right and were tasked with decorating his sedan chair in a manner worthy of the event.

Someone might ask, "Why all this ostentatious display? Isn't a fancy wedding just an ego-driven display of a lot of pretentious do-dads that don't make any difference?" The answer is, maybe, if that's the purpose of the ones doing it. If a wedding is just an excuse for putting on the dog or impressing the neighbors, then the ostentatious display is meaningless. It does nothing to enhance the value or effect of the wedding.

I've officiated at wedding ceremonies where they barely had cake and coffee and yet they were just as meaningful as the ones that featured beautiful gowns, tuxedoes, and a fully catered reception. The value of a marriage has absolutely nothing to do with how much you spend on the wedding.

The value to society

On the other hand, the social value of weddings can't be overlooked. The wedding of Solomon and Shulammite was the event of a lifetime for Israel. Much like the public weddings of Prince Charles and Diana at St. Paul's Cathedral in London, or, more recently Prince William and Kate at Westminster Abbey in London, the attention of the whole country was fixed on this wedding. A royal wedding like this deserves all the pomp and circumstance that accompanies it because it's a source of national identity and pride.

There are three take-aways we can gain from the inclusion of Solomon's wedding in the Song of Solomon. *First,* the physical trappings of a wedding aren't the most important thing about a wedding. The Song of Solomon only spends six out of one hundred seventeen verses in the whole book on the wedding itself. So, the physical description was minimal, and whatever ceremony they observed wasn't even mentioned at all.

That tells me that Solomon, under the inspiration of the Holy Spirit, felt that all the hoopla surrounding the wedding itself was not as important as the other parts of the book.

Most couples give far more attention to the wedding dress, the flowers, the hair, the gowns, the music, the setting, the tuxes, the limo, the reception, the lighting, the photography, the cake, the first dance, etc., etc., etc., *ad nauseum,* than they do on pre-marital counseling or how they are going to live their lives after the wedding. I'm not saying there is anything innately wrong with any of that. But, if it is the apex of everything the couple is focused on, then something is really out of balance.

Second, the most important factor about a wedding is what comes before and after, not the ceremony itself. This is exactly opposite of public perception regarding weddings today. People spend thousands of dollars on their Pinterest wedding to ensure that every single detail is perfect. But most people, including many Christians, don't give a single thought to any kind of pre-marital counseling.

We have always demanded a minimum of five or six pre-marital sessions with an older, married couple, for anyone getting married in our church. Since there is no charge for this ministry, it's the least expensive item in their wedding budget, but absolutely the most valuable thing they can do in planning for their marriage. They are required to read a couple of books, do a marital inventory, and walk through a number of issues that will impact their marriage. Inevitably they become great friends with the couple counseling them.

Third, weddings have societal value because they legitimize the marriage in the eyes of society. That's why Solomon included the account of his wedding in the Song of Solomon. A wedding is not a meaningless public display of pride. It's more than a private commitment between two people or a means to pass along the family name.

A wedding holds two people accountable for their love. We've all seen the picture of the words *John loves Mary* carved on a tree with a heart around it. Cute! A wedding asks John to prove it. We ask him to stand up in front of God and all of his family and friends and pledge in front of everyone that he is going to love his bride for the rest of his life. And she does the same.

Then we hold them to it. When they sign their names on their wedding license and it's mailed to the County Recorder, it serves as a public record that these two people made a pledge to build a relational and financial wall around their family and take responsibility for the welfare of each other and any children that join their family.

What's wrong with that? If they don't live up to their promises, everyone will know that at least one of them is either a hypocrite or a liar, and the rest of their family and society at large will have to partially pick up the bill for taking care of them. That's why society has a vested interest in the success of marriage.

Without a wedding he (or she) can walk away with no repercussions. No harm – no foul. We began seeing this in the 60's when couples started living together without getting married. Sex became casual as it was removed from the context of commitment. All social indicators show that "shacking up" doesn't work because there is no commitment to the future.

Women pay the greatest price for this charade. Without marriage, women are forced to compete with men in the marketplace. They live without someone to protect them from forceful men, and place whatever children they may have in harm's way. Children who grow up without two parents are more susceptible to emotional instability, more likely to live in poverty, less likely to succeed in education, and less likely themselves to find a partner.

Author Mike Mason in *The Mystery of* Marriage comments,

It is no wonder that people love weddings. A wedding is one of the very few occasions when the formation of a true, lasting, and real bond between two human beings may be witnessed. In no other sphere (be it business, politics, or even friendship) is the forming of a voluntary bond of partnership so real or decisive, so permanent, nor so clear and simple. Marriage is the simplest (and also, despite its bad track record in current statistics, still the most successful and lasting) form of mankind's dream of an ideal community in this world. A good marriage is the closest thing on earth to the realization of a practical, enduring, and loving coexistence between people. It is a sign, a spiritual and social and political example, of depths of love and patience and forgiveness that are unknown in other areas of life. Every time a wedding takes place, the highest hopes and ideals of the whole community are rekindled. A wedding is the keynote address to the convention of human brotherhood.[55]

Those who view weddings as unnecessary and superfluous fail to grasp the necessity of holding society together by means of flourishing marriages. That's not easy and there are certainly marriages that fail. But that's not a reason to abandon the best hope society has of success.

When a wedding establishes a marriage that works, everyone benefits. Those who argue that marriage is a

---

[55] Mike Mason, *The Mystery of Marriage: As Iron Sharpens Iron* (Portland, Oregon: Multnomah Press, 1985), 75, 76.

patriarchal form of oppression or that it has outlived its use-fulness fail to look at the public benefits of marriage.

Seminary professor and author Wayne Grudem, in his book, *Politics*, lists the public benefits of marriage:

1. Marriage provides a better environment for having babies than any other relationship or institution.
2. Married couples raise and nurture children far better than any other human relationship or institution.
3. Marriage provides a guarantee of lifelong companion-ship and care far better than any other human rela-tionship or institution.
4. Marriage leads to a higher economic standard and diminished likelihood of ending up in poverty for men and women.
5. Marriage provides women with protection against domestic violence and abandonment far better than any other human relationship or institution.
6. Marriage encourages men to socially beneficial pur-suits far better than any other human relationship or institution.
7. Men and women in general have an innate instinct that values sexual faithfulness in intimate relationships, and marriage provides a societal encouragement of such faithfulness far better than any other relationship or institution.
8. Marriage provides greater protection against sexually transmitted diseases than any other relationship or institution.

9. The biological design of men's and women's bodies argues that sexual intimacy is designed to be enjoyed between only one man and one woman.[56]

The sociological benefits of marriage are undeniable. Mothers, fathers, children, grandparents, aunts, uncles, cousins, neighbors, employers, policemen, teachers, judges, pastors, churches, schools, and all society benefits when two young people set up housekeeping together and pledge to their world that they are going to pass the baton on to the next generation.

The degree to which marriages fail is the degree to which society fails. If marriages succeed, society flourishes. If marriages fail, society fractures as well.

It's a family celebration

Marriage also benefits families. Someone said that when the father of the bride hands off his daughter in marriage to his prospective son-in-law, it's like handing a Stradivarius violin to an ape. As a former ape and a father-in-law, I know both the thrill of one side of that equation and the fear of the other. Thankfully, I have two sons-in-law who have never caused me any regret for entrusting my daughters to their care.

Marriage is definitely a family celebration. A man and a woman are not only forming a new family. They are uniting the traditions, backgrounds, and the hopes and dreams of their two families. That's why the decision to marry is critical.

---

[56] Wayne A. Grudem, *Politics—According to the Bible: A Comprehensive Resource for Understanding Modern Political Issues in Light of Scripture* (Grand Rapids, Michigan: Zondervan, 2010), 223-225.

We see the involvement of Solomon's family in v. 11. "Go forth, O daughters of Zion, and gaze on King Solomon with the crown with which his mother has crowned him on the day of his wedding..." The crown Solomon wore was not the royal crown. The royal crown was placed on the head of the king by the high priest. This crown was made by his mother which means it could have been a crown of jewels or something as simple as a crown of garlands worn to express joy and gladness.

This is an interesting observation considering that Solomon's mother was Bathsheba, the woman who was caught up in an adulterous affair with Solomon's father David. When she became pregnant, David attempted to cover up the affair by orchestrating the murder of her husband. Unfortunately, the baby died, but following a time of grief, Bathsheba became pregnant again, giving birth to Solomon.

Given that background, the sign of approval from his mother is significant. It's possible that she understood what it was to be the "other woman" in an affair and wanted to make sure that her son's marriage was legitimate.

It's also possible that Bathsheba was giving her overt approval because Solomon was marrying an unknown farm girl from a remote part of the kingdom. She didn't want there to be any question about Shulammite's qualifications and her blessing. Both Solomon and Shulammite must have been very grateful for the visible sign of approval from Bathsheba.

We can make another deduction. Despite the fact that Solomon sinned by his political marriages and even allowed pagan worship later in his life, we also know that he loved the Lord and sought His wisdom. Moreover, 1 Kings 3:7-11 reflects his heart. "Now, O Lord my God, you have made Your servant king in place of my father David, yet I am but a little child; I do not know how to go out or come in ... give Your servant an understanding heart to judge your people to discern between good and evil. For who is able to judge this great people of Yours?"

How did he develop this love for the Lord? Much of this would have come from David, who, despite his own sin, was devoted to God. But it's also fair to assume that his spiritual instruction would have come from his mother, despite the fact that she had previously been married to a pagan Hittite.

But Bathsheba had lived under David's wisdom and counsel for over twenty years and she supported his wishes that Solomon be named as his successor. The mutual respect they shared and her loyalty to David was seen even on his deathbed in 1 Kings 1:15-17.

In addition, if King Lemuel ("to God") in Proverbs 31 is really a reference to Solomon, the author and compiler of the book of Proverbs as most rabbinical commentators agree, then the mother who gives such wise counsel to her son in Proverbs 31 is none other than Bathsheba. Her advice to her son in Proverbs 31:1-9 and her comments on a worthy woman in the remainder of the chapter, must certainly be regarded as godly advice for both Solomon and Shulammite.

Solomon had received a rich heritage of godly counsel from his father and mother during his formative years. With his father gone, his mother placed a crown on his head as a symbol of her blessing and thankfulness on his wedding day.

Parental instruction and blessing are so important in marriage. Unfortunately, in our modern context the vast majority of parents do little to prepare their children for marriage. They hope and pray that their kids figure it out and get lucky enough to meet someone who will be a good marital partner.

But there is so much more parents can do. They can be an example of love, commitment, forgiveness, sexual fidelity, integrity, and humility. Good marriages don't just happen. If parents are angry, judgmental, dishonest, hypocritical, immoral, or abusive, the chances are that their children will have no desire to duplicate that kind of marriage.

Parents can also teach their children. Solomon advocated this himself in Proverbs 22:6 where he wrote, "Train up a child in the way he should go, even when he is old he will not depart from it." How would he have known that unless it had been modeled from his parents?

Many parents have bought into the idea that they are not to "indoctrinate" their kids. But parents *must* teach their children about virtue, honesty, sexual integrity, hard work, and how to control their emotions.

Of course, for the Christian, the most important things to teach them are God's view of sin, the nature of man, the centrality of the person and work of Christ, and the work of sanctification. Don't depend on someone else to teach these truths. Parents are the most influential people in the life of a child. Don't abandon your position.

Kids also need to know what you think about marriage and the selection of a spouse. Giving them guidelines in advance and talking with them as they come of age will go a long way to maintaining sanity as they get ready to date and marry.

It's a personal celebration

The day of Solomon's wedding in v. 11 was "the day of his gladness of heart." And well it should be. Outside of salvation, our wedding day brings us more happiness and joy than any other day of our lives. So how do we get there?

Put God first

It begins with the commitment to honor God above all others in life. After all, the ultimate goal of life is not to get married. It's to please God. When we please God, we end up enjoying His provisions even more. Jesus offers this promise in Matthew 6:33, "But seek first His kingdom and His righteousness, and all these things will be added to you." You will never go wrong if you prioritize your life around the guidelines God provides in His Word.

Marry a believer

The second thing to focus on is to marry a believer. You must decide this way before you feel the emotional pull of a relationship. Paul gives us clear instruction in 2 Corinthians 6:14, "Do not be bound together with unbelievers; for what partnership have righteousness and lawlessness, or what fellowship has light with darkness?" A Christian and a non-Christian may have gone to the same school or belong to the same political party, but they will not have anything in common when considering the most important things in life.

When I met Anne, I was just starting to live a committed Christian life. I knew that Anne's family didn't go to church and she had not made any profession of faith. But she was so beautiful, and she had captured my heart. The longer we dated the more I knew that I was growing to love her. I always knew that I couldn't marry a non-believer, but I kept my mouth shut because I didn't want to lose her. The best I could do was ask her to go to church with me and she always did.

After dating her for over a year, I knew I was being dishonest with her. So, I took her to a football game and when we got back to her house I said, "I'm sorry, I love you, but I can't see you anymore." Nice guy! Real gutsy! She was heartbroken and so was I.

Several weeks later a mutual friend told me she wanted to talk to me. So, I did. She asked why I had broken up with her and I told her that I was a Christian and I couldn't marry someone who wasn't. In her quiet voice she asked, "Well, how do you know I'm not a Christian?"

She then told me that she had never put all the pieces together until she started coming to church with me. She had prayed one night in church on her own to receive Christ and I never knew about it. My heart jumped into my throat with joy. That began our life of walking together with Christ and we have never looked back.

So, I know the personal pain of dealing with this question. And yet so many Christians ignore this before they get married. A number of years ago, Pastor Ray Stedman shared a letter from a Christian about to marry a non-believer.

Dear God, I can hardly believe that this is my wedding day. I know I haven't been able to spend much time with You lately, with all the rush of getting ready for today, and I'm sorry. I guess, too, that I feel a little guilty when I try to pray about all this, since Larry still isn't a Christian. But oh, Father, I love him so much, what else can I do? I just couldn't give him up. Oh, you must save him, some way, somehow. You know how much I've prayed for him, and the way we've discussed the gospel together. I've tried not to appear too religious, I know, but that's because I didn't want to scare him off. Yet he isn't antagonistic, and I can't understand why he hasn't responded. Oh, if he were only a Christian. Dear Father, please bless our marriage. I don't want to disobey you, but I do love him, and I want to be his wife, so please be with us and don't spoil my wedding day.[57]

If that young lady is truly a believer, the day will come when she will want to stand beside her husband as they sing praises to God and sit under the teaching of the Word, but he will want to sleep in. She will want to pray about the situations they face, and he will let her pray – by herself. She will want to take their kids to Sunday School, and he will tell them they don't have to go if they don't want to. Oh, she will still love him. But her heart will ache to have a partner in her walk with the Lord – but she won't have one.

[57] Charles Mylander, *Running the Red Lights: Putting the Brakes on Sexual Temptation* (Ventura, CA, Regal Books, 1986), 168-169.

111

Maintain sexual purity

Sexual activity before marriage is perhaps the greatest negative influence on marriage. Nothing destroys the spiritual confidence of both men and women like sexual sin. Too often something done in the heat of the moment plagues someone for a lifetime. Of course, this is especially true for women because of the possibility of pregnancy, but the shame and guilt felt by men who have been trapped in sexual sin can be just as real.

Sexual lust focuses on self because it operates in the flesh and not the Spirit (Galatians 5:13, 17), it leads to frustration because you can't get what you want (James 4:2), it continually wants more (Ephesians 4:18-19), it enslaves self by becoming the focal point of life (Romans 6:16), it excludes Christ, which will lead Him to give you over to a depraved mind (Romans 1:28-29), it is done to gratify your desires (Ephesians 2:3), it entices with evil desires (James 1:14), it wars against the soul (1 Peter 2:11), and it avoids commitment and leads to tragedy (Proverbs 6:25-26).[58]

On the other hand love focuses on the other (Philippians 2:4), it leads to fulfillment (Ephesians 3:19-20), it brings a "harvest of righteousness and peace for those who have been trained by it (Hebrews 12:11), it demonstrates self-control (1 Corinthians 9:27), it lives by the Spirit which denies the lusts of the flesh (Galatians 5:16), it is a reflection of Jesus ((Romans 13:14), it seeks God to give you the "desires of your heart" (Psalm 37:4), it prevents sin (Galatians 5:14-15), it

---

[58] Daniel L. Akin, *Exalting Jesus in the Song of Songs* (Nashville, Tennessee, B&H Publishing Group, 2015), 109-112.

sanctifies your soul and keeps you blameless (1 Thessalonians 5:25), and it commits to serve one another (Galatians 5:13).[59]

God calls a young man who acts on his sexual impulses a fool. In Proverbs 7:7 Solomon says this man is "naïve...a young man lacking sense...and a fool." The word for fool means "thick-brained, or stupid." He is "morally deficient.[60]

But Solomon also describes an immoral woman in Proverbs 7:21-23, "With her many persuasions she entices him; With her flattering lips she seduces him. Suddenly he follows her as an ox goes to the slaughter, or as one in fetters to the discipline of a fool, until an arrow pierces through his liver; as a bird hastens to the snare, so he does not know that it will cost him his life." Solomon calls her a "harlot, adulteress, and a strange (loathsome, enemy) woman" in Proverbs 6:26 and 2:16.

Unfortunately, in our sexually permissive climate today, most young people have had sex before they get married, often with multiple partners. This often applies to Christians too.

The Christian must take full advantage of God's forgiveness if there has been sexual activity before marriage. Many Christians continue to be plagued by their past sexual sin when they don't have to be. King David reminds us in Psalm 103:12 that "as far as the east is from the west, so far has He removed our transgressions from us." In Romans 8:1 Paul emphatically states, "Therefore there is now no condemnation for those who are in Christ Jesus. For the law of the Spirit

---

[59] Ibid.

[60] Louis Goldberg, "44 לוא," ed. R. Laird Harris, Gleason L. Archer Jr., and Bruce K. Waltke, *Theological Wordbook of the Old Testament* (Chicago: Moody Press, 1999), 19.

of life in Christ Jesus has set you free from the law of sin and of death."

No one is perfect when they get married. But repentance, confession, and forgiveness provide a clean slate for those entering marriage as well as maintaining spiritual health in the years to come.

It's a spiritual celebration

The final picture of marriage is not overtly seen in the Song of Solomon, but it is the most important celebration of marriage in the whole Bible. I'm referring to the spiritual celebration of marriage that occurs when two believers marry.

As mentioned in the introduction to this book, the Song of Solomon is not an allegory picturing all the nuances of Christ's love for the church. But the theme of marriage seen in the Song of Solomon is indeed a precursor to the theology of marriage provided in the New Testament.

Weddings are wonderful events for anyone, but especially for Christians. They recognize marriage is the picture of God's love for man as seen in the work of Christ. The Bible begins with the first marriage in the Garden and ends with the Marriage Supper of the Lamb in Revelation 19. Why? Because marriage is a picture of the gospel.

The gospel reminds us that we seek for a greater romance than our marriage. We yearn for the love of our eternal bridegroom because we understand that our earthly spouse can't measure up to our expectation of perfect love and can do nothing to cover our sin.

A fancy wedding dress, beautiful flowers, wonderful music, and all the trappings of a storybook wedding won't turn a bride into an "eight cow wife." But the gospel can. The same goes for the husband. To think that God would elevate His bride – His church – to the status of being holy and blameless is beyond my ability to comprehend, but Paul tells us in Romans 6:8 that "while we were yet sinners, Christ died for us."

Nothing elevates our status and perception of who we are like the gospel. It transforms us from sinners into saints, from being angry and hostile to God, to being his beloved child.

Husbands and wives know the truth about each other in ways that can only make every honest person wish for something better. We love each other, but both partners in an honest marriage realize they have a long way to go. We accept the dirty socks, burned biscuits, coming home late, dishes stacked in the sink, grease tracks from the garage to the refrigerator, talking endlessly on the phone to mom, and forgetting birthdays, because we realize that we're not there yet. But praise God, we will be!

The Apostle John gives a poignant description of this in the last book of the Bible. In Revelation 19:7 he writes, "Let us rejoice and be glad and give the glory to Him, for the marriage of the Lamb has come and His bride has made herself ready."

This verse references a Jewish wedding which consisted of three phases. The first phase was the betrothal, usually negotiated by the parents when the couple was quite young. The presentation followed when the agreed upon time arrived and the bride was presented at a family festival that could last for up to a week. Finally, the vows were exchanged at the conclusion of this time.

The bride of Christ, betrothed before the foundation of the earth (Ephesians 1:4; 2 Thessalonians 2:13), will be presented to the groom in all her beauty and glory at the return of Christ (John 14:1-3; 1 Thessalonians 4:13-18). This adornment of the bride for the groom will be carried into the thousand year millennium (Revelation 21:2) when Christ will "wipe away every tear from their eyes; and there will no longer be *any* death; there will no longer be *any* mourning, or crying, or pain; the first things have passed away" (Revelation 21:4).

But we might ask, how has the bride "made herself ready?" The next verse tells us. "It was given to her to clothe herself in fine linen, bright *and* clean; for the fine linen is the righteous acts of the saints." The word for *bright* is the Greek word *lampo,* from which we get our word *lamp.* It means "beaming, bright, shining, radiant, gleaming, beautiful."[61] In the New Testament the word always pictures the brilliance of the righteousness of God.

This righteousness given to the bride of Christ is the righteousness of God applied to the Christian as a consequence of salvation. 2 Corinthians 5:21 states, "He made Him who knew no sin *to be* sin on our behalf, so that *we might become the righteousness of God in Him*" (emphasis mine). This makes the Christian *positionally* perfect at the moment of salvation in a way that changes our lives. We don't lean on our own righteousness, we fully depend on the righteousness of Christ!

---

[61] C. H.-Hahn, "Light, Shine, Lamp," ed. Lothar Coenen, Erich Beyreuther, and Hans Bietenhard, *New International Dictionary of New Testament Theology* (Grand Rapids, MI: Zondervan Publishing House, 1986), 484.

This is reflected in the "righteous acts of the saints" as we emulate His righteousness in our own actions towards each other. We will never live perfect lives on this earth. But when the trumpet of God sounds at His return, Christians will "be changed" and "put on immortality" when "death is swallowed up in victory" (1 Corinthians 15:52-54). Jesus will "present to Himself the church in all her glory, having no spot or wrinkle or any such thing; but that she would be holy and blameless" (Ephesians 5:27).

I will never forget the moment I saw my beautiful bride appear at the rear of the church for the first time in her wedding dress. As I looked down the long aisle her radiance and beauty was all I could see as she walked down the aisle on the arm of her father to become my wife. Our lives have certainly not been perfect from that time on. But, praise God, our sins and disappointments and failures have been covered by the righteousness of Christ.

What a phenomenal promise that our identity on earth isn't all He sees in us. And some day we will be like Him and we will see Him as He is in heaven because He is sanctifying us right now and preparing us for the ultimate Marriage Supper of the Lamb in heaven. So, congratulations Mr. and Mrs. Christian! When you say, "I do!" your marriage becomes a picture of that ultimate reality.

"The factor most strongly related to sexual satisfaction among married couples was not age or gender or work status but traditional attitudes toward sexual morality."

—— Linda J. Waite and Maggie Gallagher

CHAPTER SEVEN

WHEN A MAN LOVES A WOMAN

(Song of Solomon 4:1-16)

Ancient Corinth is a beautiful city to visit. Located on the Greek Peloponnesus in southern Greece, you can still see the remains of much of the city of biblical times. The remains of the Temple of Aphrodite remind the visitor of the Greek goddess of love, beauty, and procreation. However, she lived in constant infidelity. As a result, she bore many children, two of whom were *Phobos* and *Eros*. *Phobos* represented the fear of sex, and *Eros* represented the insatiable desire for sex.

Both of these influences are still with us. *Phobos*, the fear of sex, was seen early on in the teachings of the Roman Catholic Church. The fourth century Church father, Augustine, lived a promiscuous life before he picked up the Bible and became a Christian. His past promiscuous sexual escapades resulted in an overreaction against sex.

He formulated the Roman Catholic doctrine of concupiscence (sexual lust), which identified the opposition between sensual appetite and reason. He taught that concupiscence referred to the transmission of original sin through sexual intercourse.[62] This led to the perverted Catholic elevation of Virgin Mary, the condemning of sex even in marriage, and the heinous practice of celibate priests.

On the other hand, sex in our culture is rampant *eros*. Russian-born Pitirim Sorokin, the first professor and chairman of the Sociology Department at Harvard wrote *The American Sex Revolution* in 1956. His words were prescient sixty years ago.

> The sex drive is now declared to be the most vital main spring of human behavior. In the name of science, its fullest satisfaction is urged as a necessary condition of man's health and happiness. Sex inhibitions are viewed as the main source of frustrations, mental and physical illness and criminality. Sexual chastity is ridiculed as a prudish superstition. Nuptial loyalty as an antiquated hypocrisy. Sexual profligacy and prowess are proudly glamorized...The traditional "child of God" created in God's image is turned into a sexual apparatus powered by sex instinct, preoccupied with sex matters, aspiring for, and dreaming and thinking mainly of,

---

[62] Derek and Rosemary Thomas, *A Biblical Guide to Love, Sex, and Marriage* (Carlisle, PA: EP Books USA, 2007), 61.

sex relations. Sexualization of human beings has become so preoccupied with sex that it now oozes from all pores of American life.[63]

And it hasn't gotten any better since then. Our culture has the collective morality of rabbits. A time-traveler from the 1950s to our culture today would think that we are operating with half a brain if they could see the number of STDs, the rise of out-of-wedlock pregnancies, shattered relationships, same-sex marriage, and the transgender movement.

The rising distortions about sex have been astounding. Sociologists Mark Regnerus and Jeremy Uecker in *Premarital Sex in America* chronicles "Ten myths about sex in emerging adulthood." I've listed them below with my comments in parentheses:

1. Long-term relationships are a thing of the past. (But everyone wants them. No one gets married with the idea of being ditched later by their partner.)
2. Sex is necessary to maintain a struggling relationship. (Not true. It won't repair communication, lack of respect, fake intimacy, or feeling dirty and cheap.)
3. The sexual double standard between men and women is wrong and should be resisted. (This doesn't remove the risk of pregnancy for women. It also ignores the fact that women are seldom the initiators of sex for a variety of reasons.)

---

[63] Pitirim Sorokin, *The American Sexual Revolution* (Boston: Porter Sargent Publisher, 1956), 58.

WHEN A MAN LOVES A WOMAN

4. Boys are sexual beings and cannot be expected to follow sexual norms. ("Boys will be boys" sets a low standard for social propriety, sexual abuse, and rape. And most men indeed do follow sexual norms of society and remain faithful to their wives.)

5. You are entirely in charge of your own sexuality; others' decisions don't matter. (It matters to parents, your future spouse, your children, sexual partners, and most in society who still frown on promiscuous sex.)

6. Porn will not affect your relationships. (Porn presents a completely distorted view of what most women look like, that women "want it," and that sex is "only" physical. It is addictive and robs you of your time, confidence, and fulfilling relationships. It destroys relationships because no woman can live up to the fantasy, and soon the fantasy is not satisfying either.)

7. Others are having more sex than you. (Not true for married people. And "so what?" Sex is not the pinnacle of a fulfilling life.)

8. Sex doesn't need to mean much – it's just a physical drive. (This regards sex purely as animalistic. This ignores the need for boundaries on needs and appetites. I like Krispy Kreme doughnuts, but I can't eat them every time I want them!)

9. Marriage can wait for later. (This ignores the fact that marital chances decrease with age.)

10. Living together is a positive step towards marriage.[64] (This is never true. Linda J. Waite and Maggie

---

[64] Mark Regnerus and Jeremy Uecker, *Premarital Sex in America: How Young Americans Meet, Mate, and Think about Marrying* (New York: Oxford University Press, 2011), 242-249.

Gallagher in *The Case for Marriage: Why Married People Are Happier, Healthier, and Better Off Financially* note that "on average, cohabiting couples are less sexually faithful, lead less settled lives, are less likely to have children, are more likely to be violent, make less money, and are less happy—and less committed—than married couples."[65])

If the above accurately represents society's current attitude toward sex, it differs dramatically from that intended by God who, after all, invented sex! Chapter 4 of the Song of Solomon contains an account of the wedding night of Solomon and his bride Shulammite. But before you start reading ahead looking for the steamy parts you need to know that there is nothing tawdry or scintillating here. This is not an exercise in theological voyeurism.

Unfortunately, many interpreters have taken that view, finding a sexual reference behind every tree. If their interpretations are true, then Solomon and Shulammite were over-sexed teenagers who couldn't keep their hands off each other. But this doesn't uphold a virtuous example of marriage and would not be worthy of inclusion in the Bible.

And the temptation to "be relevant" has trapped many pastors in the clutches of sensationalism needed to sell books. One pastor used such graphic descriptions that I can't quote them. Another prominent megachurch pastor launched a series on sex from the roof of his church while in bed with

---

[65] Linda J. Waite and Maggie Gallagher, *The Case for Marriage: Why Married People Are Happier, Healthier, and Better Off Financially* (New York, NY: Broadway Books, 2000), 201.

his wife. Perhaps he should float back to earth and take his space suit off!

IT'S PERSONAL

So, how should we handle this passage on sex? We are certainly not to fear it nor eroticize it. We are to look at it honestly and thankfully. If God chose to have Solomon write this and put it in the Bible, then it is for our good.

One of the first rules of biblical interpretation is observation. It's a good practice to simply read through a passage you're studying and write down your first observations. This is especially true of difficult passages.

One of the first things you notice as you read Song of Solomon 4 is that "you" or "your" is used twenty-six times in this chapter. In addition, "my" is used twelve times, and "my bride" is used five times. This is very personal!

The chapter opens with Solomon's expressive description of his wife. He wasn't trying to win her because they were already married at this point. But he is definitely trying to summarize his feelings of love for her. This is possibly meant to be sung since grooms often sang to their brides during the wedding procession and it is written in such an organized style.

But it's also probable that this is the language of foreplay. There is an old saying that says men give romance to get sex and women give sex to get romance. There is a degree of truth to that – if the man is smart enough to go slow.

There are seven (the number representing perfection in the Bible) allusions to the beauty of his bride Solomon enumerates as they face each other after the wedding, ready to make love. It's obvious that he thinks of her as perfect.

He begins in Song of Solomon 4:1, "How beautiful you are, my darling, how beautiful you are!" Similar words end the section in v. 7, "You are altogether beautiful, my darling, and there is no blemish in you." He is commenting on her beauty as he begins to comment on her physical features in anticipation of enjoying her sexual pleasures.

The first allusion refers to her eyes in v. 1, "Your eyes are like doves behind your veil." Women commonly wore head-dresses at their wedding, but not veils. Her eyes were the first things Solomon noticed, comparing them to turtle doves.

Solomon also notes in v. 1, "Your hair is like a flock of goats that have descended from Mount Gilead." The mountains of Gilead were known for rich pastureland and abundant herds of black goats. This is a reference to Shulammite's long lustrous black hair flowing down onto her shoulders. A Jewish woman never wore her hair down except when alone with her husband, so we can almost imagine her taking her hair down as he watches.

The third observation in v. 2 seems a little odd to us, but Solomon's poetic eye noticed "your teeth are like newly shorn ewes which have come up from their washing," that is, they are white and perfect. Furthermore, "all of which bear twins," indicating she had a matched set, top and bottom. Lastly, "not one of them have lost their young," so she hasn't lost one of them! This probably alluded to her beautiful smile.

Fourth, in v. 3 he comments, "Your lips are like a scarlet thread." As in our day, cosmetics were common. This was evidently a reference to her red lipstick. He also noticed, "your mouth is lovely" indicating he loved the curve of her lips.

Solomon continues his checklist of beauty, noticing "your temples are like a slice of a pomegranate behind your veil." This referred to her cheeks, not the temple. Most likely he noticed she was blushing the color of pomegranate behind the veil.

The sixth item also sounds strange to us. In v. 3, he also noted, "Your neck is like the tower of David, built with rows of stones on which are hung a thousand shields, all the round shields of the mighty men." Men don't try this at home! As she stood in front of him her neck reminded him of the stately towers at the corner of his palace that were stately and tall. It's possible the "rows of stones" referred to a necklace that he reached to undo.

The seventh allusion in v. 5 has sexual overtones but is natural and wholesome for a husband to observe. "Your two breasts are like two fawns, twins of a gazelle which feed among the lilies." Gazelles are shy and skittish when approached. The allusion of two young fawns lying in a meadow of lilies pictures her shyness at revealing her breasts.

The cumulative effect of all of these pictures is to show us that these are the personal reflections of a young man on his wedding night. Commenting on her beauty is not a cheap trick to get her into bed. It is the thoughtful discourse of a man who wants his wife to know exactly how he feels about her and who knows how to prepare her emotionally for making love.

It's Private

The next observation is that sex is intended to be private. This is possibly the most egregious depreciation of sex in our culture today. There is no such thing as "propriety" when you can view every form of sexual deviancy in living color on your iPhone. Nothing is sacred because nothing is private.

The language of vv. 1-5 has all been in the second person "you." But now it switches to the first person, "I," in v. 6 where Solomon said, "Until the cool of the day when the shadows flee away, I will go my way to the mountain of myrrh and to the hill of frankincense."

The first problem is identifying the one who is speaking. Solomon makes the most sense because the flow indicates that he is moving from his description of her beauty to his specific plans for the night. He describes his vision in v. 6, saying, "Until the cool of the day when the shadows flee away…" He seems to be saying this party is going to last all night long! After all, this is his wedding night!

He also describes his intentions, "I will go my way…" which depicts his sense of urgency and desire. And where is he going? He is going "to the mountain of myrrh and to the hill of frankincense." This seems to picture the constant sweet aroma that filled the night air as they enjoyed their first night of marriage.

But this indeed is a private affair, meant for a party of two. In v. 8 he shows that he is aware of her potential fears of all these new experiences. He extends his invitation, "Come with me from Lebanon, my bride, may you come with me from Lebanon. Journey down from the summit of Amana, from the summit of Senir and Hermon, from the dens of lions, from the mountains of leopards." Both of them no doubt would have been familiar with the landmarks Solomon mentioned.

But he also does something curious with them. He lists three native mountains, Amana, Senir, and Hermon that contained dangers from lions and leopards. Why would he mention that? It seems that in his poetic way Solomon was expressing the journey that Shulammite had made in following him from her home to Jerusalem. He is saying, "Come, trust me, I will protect you from the lions and leopards."

Solomon continues his allusion to the privacy of this trust. In v. 12 he comments, "A garden locked is my sister, my bride, a rock garden (spring) locked, a spring sealed up." There are three pictures here. A garden (vineyard) behind locked gates, a rock garden, or spring with blocked access, and a spring which has a seal over the entry, protecting water for the rightful owner. A wall would be put around a garden to protect it from animals and strangers. A fresh spring would be covered with clay which would harden, protecting it from strangers. These all refer to her so it's clear this is a picture of virginity.

Solomon's terminology is very intimate. A garden was the primary picture of a woman in the Song of Solomon. Here in v. 12 we see the garden, rock garden, and spring are all locked or sealed. These are all seen as protecting the virginity of his bride before marriage. A young woman is to be protected from strangers and predators who would violate her by taking what doesn't belong to them.

This not only protects the emotional well-being of the woman, but it is a barrier against bringing a child into the world outside of marriage. The husband who enters her garden takes on the protection of her honor and emotional well-being and commits to a lifetime of raising their child together if she becomes pregnant.

Solomon also uses an intimate term to describe Shulammite. He calls her "my sister, my bride" four times in this passage. In doing so he uses the terminology of the day that saw a bride as a family member as close as a biological sister. Even though a husband and wife don't share DNA, they form the most intimate relationship that is humanly possible.

The protection of the virginity of a young woman is not seen as pejorative. If you listened to many of the purveyors of perverted sex in our culture today, you might think that virginity is like a tumor that needs to be removed as quickly as possible. "Losing it" is almost seen as a humorous rite of passage for sexual sophisticates today.

Though we've lost our sense of protecting virginity today, some have taken that much too far in the past. Jerome, the fourth century Catholic scholar who translated *The Vulgate*, said that marriage was good because it produced virgins. He also asserted that married saints have always remained virgins.[66] That is certainly not God's view.

Surprisingly, the Puritans emerged in the sixteenth century to contradict the heretical Catholic views on sex and marriage (more on this in Chapter 11). It may surprise you that they had a wonderfully balanced view of sex.

---

[66] Leland Ryken, *Worldly Saints: The Puritans as They Really Were* (Grand Rapids, Michigan: Zondervan Publishing House, 1990), 40.

Leland Ryken spoke of their view of sex: "The Puritan doctrine of sex was a watershed on the cultural history of the West. The Puritans devalued celibacy, glorified companionate marriage, affirmed married sex as both necessary and pure, established the ideal of wedded romantic love, and exalted the role of the wife."[67]

An anonymous Puritan described the union of two people in marriage was so they "may joyfully give due benevolence one to the other; as two musical instruments rightly fitted do make a most pleasant and sweet harmony in a well-tuned consort [concert]."[68]

It's Pleasurable

There is no escaping the erotic nature of Solomon's love poem as he and his bride move to consummate their marriage. The passion expressed here is neither prudish nor licentious. It's pure joy because of the attitude and commitment of the couple.

In this marital union there is no need for a sex manual to explain technique. When a husband and wife come together in mutual honor and respect, making love is as right as rain. Solomon expresses his passion in v. 9 by telling his bride "you have made my heart beat faster with a single glance of your eyes, with a single strand of your necklace." Literally this

---

[67] Ibid., 53-54.

[68] Ibid., 44.

means to "ravish, excite, or arouse my heart," or "you have aroused my sexual passion."[69]

In a continuing litany of his attraction to her beauty, he exults in vv. 10-11, "How beautiful is your love, my sister, my bride! How much better is your love than wine, and the fragrance of your oils than all kinds of spices! Your lips, my bride, drip honey; Honey and milk are under your tongue, and the fragrance of your garments is like the fragrance of Lebanon." The fragrance was from her "night dress" or negligee which was possibly kept in a cedar hope chest that brought the smells of the cedars of Lebanon with her.[70]

Solomon continues in vv. 13-14, "your shoots are an orchard of pomegranates with choice fruits, henna with nard plants, nard and saffron, calamus and cinnamon, with all the trees of frankincense, myrrh and aloes, along with all the finest spices." The combination of all the aromatic spices mentioned is symbolic of the sexual fruit of Shulammite's exclusive garden offering to her husband.

The word for "shoots" means "sprout" and obviously refers to the fruit coming from Shulammite's garden. Likewise, "orchard," means "enclosed garden" and has the connotation of "paradise."[71] What an apt picture. Solomon wouldn't be the last one to describe the sexual enjoyment of his wife as paradise.

---

[69] G. Lloyd Carr, *The Song of Solomon*, Tyndale Old Testament Commentaries, vol. 19, (1984; repr., Downers Grove, IL: InterVarsity Press, 2009), 131.

[70] Robert Davidson, *Ecclesiastes and the Song of Solomon*, The Daily Bible Study Series (Philadelphia: The Westminster Press, 1986), 131.

[71] R. Laird Harris, "1808 פַּרְדֵּס," ed. R. Laird Harris, Gleason L. Archer Jr., and Bruce K. Waltke, *Theological Wordbook of the Old Testament* (Chicago: Moody Press, 1999), 733.

Solomon continues the barrage of praise in v. 15 by telling Shulammite, "you are a garden spring, a well of fresh water, and streams flowing from Lebanon." Notice that there is no reference to her garden being locked or sealed here. He sees her as the source of the refreshment from the fresh water of running springs. All are pictures of refreshing sexual pleasure.

By this time Solomon's senses are on overload. His engine is running and he's ready to go. And Shulammite is too. In v. 16 she replies, "May my beloved come into his garden and eat its choice fruits!" She is as ready as he is to share the delights of the marriage bed.

This was essentially sexual foreplay. A man doesn't have to recite poetry and rehearse the various features of his attraction to his wife, but he does need to remember that the man climbs the mountain much faster than his wife.

The guy who says, "Let's just forget about all this fancy talking and get down to business" is focusing only on his own needs and ignoring the way God made his wife. That's why loving comments, advance planning, and providing a romantic setting are important considerations for every husband to observe.

This is also a good place to mention another issue. It's sad to say but some studies show that as many as a third of American women have endured some type of sexual abuse before marriage. A wise man and woman talk this through before they get married. Love and respect and gentleness go a long way to helping someone who has experienced sexual abuse talk about before marriage and develop new attitudes toward sex.

If your wife was used for the sexual gratification of an abusive family member or friend before she got married, she will need an understanding husband to help her gain a better understanding of what God intended sex to be. If you don't take the time to do this, she may regard sex as a burden or even continued abuse. And that will eventually make you feel angry and cheated when you don't know what she went through. Take the time to gently ask some questions and help her work through these difficult issues.

IT'S PROPER

Shulammite has expressed her desire to remain a virgin until the proper time in Song of Solomon 2:7 and 3:5. Now it's time. We come to Song of Solomon 4:16 which deserves a comment about the placement of this verse before we look at what it says.

There are exactly 111 lines of Hebrew text (60 verses in English) from Song of Solomon 1:1 to Song of Solomon 4:15. And there are exactly 111 lines of Hebrew text (55 verses in English) from Song of Solomon 4:16 to the end of the book in Song of Solomon 8:14.

What does that little tidbit of information indicate? Obviously, Song of Solomon 4:16 is the exact middle verse of the book. This isn't an accident. Hebrew poetry often makes a statement by how it is arranged. This is like God has placed a giant neon sign above this verse to indicate that the central theme of the book is the joy of marital sex.

Shulammite's invitation is clear in v. 16, "Awake, O north wind, and come, wind of the south; make my garden breathe out fragrance, let its spices be wafted abroad. May my beloved come into his garden and eat its choice fruits!" If her body is her garden, then this is a clear invitation to her husband to enjoy the physical pleasure of sex with her.

Shulammite is adamant in her desire. She uses three imperatives in her invitation to Solomon. The first word is "awake." It's the opposite of "do not arouse or awaken my love" she used earlier in Song of Solomon 2:7 and 3:5. The second is "Make my garden breathe out fragrance" which stresses, "let the winds blow the smell of my fragrance to my lover." The last imperative is "May my beloved come into his garden." This is her open invitation and her voluntary sexual surrender.

Chapter 5 is another example of an unfortunate chapter break because the first verse of the chapter is an obvious continuation of her invitation. He speaks, "I have come into my garden, my sister, my bride; I have gathered my myrrh along with my balsam. I have eaten my honeycomb and my honey; I have drunk my wine and my milk."

Notice the nine usages of "my," indicating possession. This sounds harsh, even misogynistic. But that is a wrong assumption.

The New Testament teaches *mutual* possession in the sexual relationship. We have seen this before when we looked at 1 Corinthians 7:2-5. The husband's body belongs to his wife and the wife's body belongs to her husband.

We also notice that all the verbs in Song of Solomon 5:1 are present tense, indicating progressive action. The last phrase, "Eat friends; Drink and imbibe deeply, O lovers," seems best to be understood as the well-wishing of family and friends as the lovers go off to consummate their marriage.

There is nothing unseemly or tawdry about this. Those who view an open discussion of sex in that way miss the honorable way this is presented. It is not voyeuristic or titillating. It is a simple statement of the natural, unfettered joy of two people who have prepared well for marriage and now enjoy the fruits that God created their bodies to give them.

Think about what would happen if somehow all sexual encounters outside of marriage vanished. The heartache and shame caused by these acts would disappear, all because the simple, profound, and proper act of marriage allows the best things in life to flourish for the husband and wife as well as their children.

Puritan poet John Milton broke with the heretical Catholic views on sex to depict the beauty of the private sexual relationship between a husband and wife.

> Hail wedded love, mysterious law, true source
> Of human offspring, sole propriety
> In Paradise of all things common else.
> By thee adulterous lust was driven from men
> Among the bestial herds to range, by thee
> Founded in reason, loyal, just and pure,
> Relations dear, and all the charities
> Of father, son, and brother first were known.
> Far be it, that I should write thee sin or blame,
> Or think thee unbefitting holiest place,
> Perpetual fountain of domestic sweets,

Whose bed is undefiled and chaste pronounced.[72]

God has provided sex for the joy of two people in marriage in a way that can't be matched by any other relationship. The exhilaration that a husband and wife find in the privacy of their bedroom is matched only by the rest and peace in knowing that all is well in God's perfect provision.

[72] John Milton, *Paradise Lost* (New York, New York: Penguin Books, 2000), 93.

SECTION THREE

TROUBLE IN PARADISE

"I know, I told my audience, why over 50% of Christian marriages end in divorce: because Christians act as though marriage redeems sin. Marriage does not redeem sin. Only Jesus himself can do that."

—— Rosaria Champagne
Butterfield

CHAPTER EIGHT

MAKING A MESS
(Song of Solomon 5:2-8)

I graduated from college and Anne and I were married two months later, the same month I entered seminary. I was on my best behavior as a new husband and a pastor in training, whatever that means.

One night in our first month of marriage, Anne asked me to unload the dishwasher after dinner so I gladly obliged. The dishwasher was at the end of an L shaped part of the counter with cabinets right above it. I made the first couple of trips up and down without incident, but the third trip from the dishwasher all the way up to the cupboard exposed my pretty little wife to an ugly scene.

As I straightened up from the dishwasher, the cabinet door swung open and attacked me, hitting me on the head.

OWWW! That hurt! Instantly, I did the first thing that came to my mind. I counter punched! I hit that door! With my fist! Hard!

Now, I had never done anything like that before and I have not done anything like that since. But I did it that time. Oh, how I did it. I hit it so hard that I left the imprint of my knuckles in the perfectly formed hole that I put through the veneer on the inside of the cheap apartment style cabinet door.

Wonderful. My wife did the only thing she could think of. She laughed. She laughed loud and she laughed long. She laughed until she cried. And me? As I was washing the blood off my knuckles at the sink, I realized I was at a crossroads in my marriage. Would I put the fear of God in her for daring to ask me to unload that stupid dishwasher when I didn't know how, or would I join her on the floor laughing?

Thankfully, I chose the latter. It was, indeed, funny. In fact, I just asked her about it now as I was writing this, and she laughed again. So did I.

This was a little incident. We all endure moments like this. But it could have turned into something bigger if I had given vent to my temper and embarrassment. I could have made her fear me by exposing her to my childish anger.

This is the same kind of childish incident that Solomon and Shulammite encountered in their young marriage in Chapter 5 of the Song of Solomon. It was a small incident, but it set the tone for the rest of the entire book.

The tone of the book changes dramatically in Song of Solomon 5:2. The warm glow of the wedding night has faded, and the couple experience their first conflict. This lends a dramatic sense of realism to the whole book because every married couple knows that it isn't long before marriage feels a little like living with your sister. The vows sound good at the wedding, but after about six days, not so much.

It's also significant that the remaining four chapters of the book are devoted to this conflict and how it is resolved. That's four chapters to get them to the altar, and four to learn how to keep the vows they made in a fallen world to a fallen person.

Even if you're a king married to a beautiful bride, the fairy tales are wrong. No one lives happily ever after unless you live in Disneyland. As we walk through their conflict, every married couple will recognize the following issues that every married couple encounter.

ADVERSITY

It appears that Shulammite has a dream to begin this new section in Song of Solomon 5:2. But listen to her words carefully, "I was asleep but my heart was awake. A voice! My beloved was knocking: 'Open to me, my sister, my darling, my dove, my perfect one! For my head is drenched with dew, my locks with the damp of the night.'"

This is not a dream. She had been asleep, and she woke up to the voice of her husband. And so married life begins. The wedding is a memory. The honeymoon is over. She's asleep and her husband comes home late. She's already in bed – by herself. This is not a good look for newlyweds.

He's not there at bedtime which means he missed dinner and with no cell phones she had no idea where he was. She's tossing and turning trying to decide if she's worried or mad.

That really doesn't matter because her expectations have not been met.

As she tries to close her eyes again in the dark, she hears him at the door but it's locked. He can't get in. But he doesn't merely knock and say, "Hey, it's me. Let me in." No, he's got something else in mind. Imagine the tone of his voice in v. 2, "Open to me, my sister, my darling, my dove, my perfect one."

Freeze the camera right there. What do you see? He's either incredibly naïve or extremely calloused. He's home late yet he's expecting another wedding night? He's a guy. He doesn't get it. He had no idea that his wife might be worried or mad – or he's putting on an incredible act. Either way, the perfect Pinterest wedding is history.

APATHY

Listen to Shulammite's mood in v. 3, "I have taken off my dress, how can I put it on again? I have washed my feet; how can I dirty them again?" What happened to "May he kiss me with the kisses of his mouth! For your love is better than wine?" This is a flimsy excuse wrapped in an apathetic tone thick with irony. They are not on the same page.

He had not come home when she expected him. She waited up for him but then washed her feet, took off her robe, and went to bed. She faded in and out of sleep, listening to every sound of the night, not knowing if something had happened to him, or he was just that stupid.

Realistically, she *could* have run to open the door without putting her robe on and getting her feet dirty. But she was unwilling to do so, even for Solomon. I detect a whiny, high-pitched voice as she expressed her flimsy excuse.

This doesn't speak well for either of them. At the very least he is naïve. He knew it was late because he said his hair was wet with the dew of the night. We have a clue to his mysterious location later in Song of Solomon 6:11-12 when he said, "I went down to the orchard of nut trees to see the blossoms of the valley, to see whether the vine had budded or the pomegranates had bloomed. Before I was aware, my soul set me over the chariots of my noble people."

He was inspecting his orchards and on the way home he stopped by the stables to check on his horses and chariots. It sounded like a lame excuse, but it was true. He was working late and simply lost track of the time.

Now he was pounding on the door after midnight looking for love in the wrong place. He was completely oblivious to how his wife would feel when he was later than expected. *And* he has no concept of what she might be thinking as he waltzes up to his room with romance on his mind, only to find she has her first marital "headache." Ever been there guys?

I'm betting that he learned it's not too smart to come home late at night smelling like a stable hand and expect your wife to instantly respond to your sexual whims. Hopefully he learned that a woman needs time to catch up to the sexual inclinations of her husband.

That's not to let her off the hook. Surely, she must have realized that kings are busy people. Solomon had vast holdings and projects. If she thought she could keep track of him every moment of every day, then she too was naïve. She could have waited up for him and explained her concern and asked if they could come to some kind of understanding regarding his schedule.

Instead, she goes to bed rehearsing her lines. "Where have you been? You always do this. You are so inconsiderate. And then you think you can just come home and jump into bed. Well, it doesn't work like that buddy!" She could already taste the venom as she spit the words out as she grilled him. And it would taste good! She was mad and she was going to punish him with flimsy excuses about not being able to get out of bed because she didn't want to get her feet dirty.

ALIENATION

We need to be clear that this section is not primarily about sex. This is about two young people who don't have the emotional maturity to think about the other person in the marriage. Life has thrown them a curve and they don't know how to handle it.

Let's have the camera pan back out again to Solomon standing in the dark hallway outside his room. He has had a fruitful day checking out his orchards and his horses. He loves his wife dearly and has been thinking about what awaits him when he gets home. And when the door is locked, he compliments her with some of those beautiful, poetic words he's famous for.

But she turns him down. Flat! Talk about, "You've lost that lovin' feeling!" She won't even bother to get out of bed and cross the room a few feet to open the door for him. As he listens to her whine a new emotion washes over him. He's never felt this toward his wife before. He is confused, hurt, angry, and stunned all at the same time.

All he can think to do is run out into the night trying to figure out what just happened. This is the equivalent of jumping in your car and laying rubber to the end of the street. Way to go Romeo! Is there an adult in the house?

Now I'm not saying that any man should have his sexual impulses met at the drop of the hat. But I am saying that when a man is turned down with such a flimsy excuse, it does something to him. This is not insurmountable, but without the proper tools and context, he doesn't know how to handle it, so he runs away like a hurt child.

Solomon feels alienated, cut off from the wife he loves. But he doesn't realize that Shulammite's been feeling the same alienation for the past several hours. The tragedy is that they both feel the same thing and it could be solved with a little understanding from both of them.

But hope springs eternal. In Song of Solomon 5:4 we find the words that she must have recounted later to Solomon to tell him how she felt at the moment, "My beloved extended his hand through the opening, and my feelings were aroused for him." Maybe it was the sound of his voice or maybe she came to her senses as she walked across the floor. The words are a little difficult to understand but they seem to indicate there was some kind of opening in the door where it was possible to slip your hand through to try to reach the latch and unlock the door. But she had locked it.

How quickly feelings change. Seconds ago, she was angry and hurt but now she feels deep love for him. She continues in v. 5, "I arose to open to my beloved; and my hands dripped with myrrh, and my fingers with liquid myrrh, on the handles of the bolt."

It's hard to tell what this means, but it probably refers to the practice of dipping your fingers into a bottle of myrrh to use as perfume. Myrrh will flow out of a tree when the bark is pierced. Perhaps Solomon had done this right before touching the door. I guess if you can't catch a quick shower before you romance your wife, you could splash on a little foo-foo juice and announce, "Hey baby, I'm home. Come to Papa." Or not.

His hands must have left some of the myrrh on the door handle as he tried to open it. She felt it as she opened it. Too late. In v. 6 she continues, "I opened to my beloved, but my beloved had turned away and had gone!" The tragedy of moments like this is we can be so close yet so far away. They missed each other by mere seconds but the seeds of alienation had been sown.

The sad thing is that in reality this is not a very big problem. It started with a very reasonable desire. Shulammite wanted and expected her husband to get home on time. Even in homes where both spouses work this could still pop up. The issue is that the wife wanted to be with her husband. That's all. That's not too much to ask, is it?

Men might miss this. As a rule, they are out of the home more and possibly more inclined to get caught up in work or have some kind of distraction on the way home and ignore the courtesy of getting home at a certain time or calling to let her know he will be late.

The other side of this, of course, is that the woman might not be doing much to make sure that her husband doesn't find an excuse for not coming home. Martin Luther said, "Let the wife make the husband glad to come home and let him make her sorry to see him leave."[73]

Both men and women need to look at their side of this equation and see how they stack up. If a woman is always grinding on her husband about her "honey-do" list, or if she and the house constantly look like a tornado touched down and left dirty dishes are left all over the kitchen, with laundry, toys, magazines, pizza and cheerios scattered all over the floor and the kids running around like escaped convicts, he might find it less than appealing to come home. Ladies, if you struggle with housekeeping, you may need to get some help on ways to make your home an attractive place for all to enjoy.

And if the husband is always angry, foul-mouthed, unkind, demeaning, and abusive in words and deeds, then it would be understandable if she were to feel like, "Why don't you just leave and come back two months from next Thursday or whenever you can get your attitude cleaned up, whichever comes later." Guys, if your wife is not glad to see you and your kids run and hide when you get home, you've got a problem.

None of these problems existed for Solomon and Shulammite. They both wanted to be together. But they let the childishness of hurt feelings come between them. The desire to be together, simply to enjoy the company of one another should never be ignored. All Shulammite wanted was for Solomon to come home. And Solomon wanted the same thing. Incredible. How did they miss that?

---

[73] Erwin W. Lutzer, *Rescuing the Gospel: The Story and Significance of the Reformation* (Grand Rapids, MI: Baker Books, 2016), 133.

Anger

The short answer is that they both let their initial feelings get the best of them. They both felt alienation first, but then it grew to anger. Her alienation took several hours to turn to anger, but he made this move very quickly. The sound of her voice means he knew she was in there. And the locked door must have been bewildering and confusing at first. But when the reality of her refusal to get out of bed set in, he immediately was angry – and he was gone!

The Hebrew word for "gone" in v. 6 is dramatic. It doesn't mean just "leave." It means "to pass over, alienate, take away, or transgress."[74] Solomon emphatically and completely turned away from his wife because he was mad! The tone of her voice had told him to cool his jets and left him standing like a beggar at his own bedroom door.

It's easy to see how he must have felt. "You're kidding me! She doesn't want to come to the door just because she'll have to wash her feet again. Doesn't she know who I am?! I'm the king. How dare she treat me this way. I'll show her. I'm outta here."

The reality of marriage is that the person we love the most in the whole world can get under our skin. That's because they aren't perfect, and neither are we. Author Mike Mason describes this phenomenon well:

> The person we love is inevitably a cross, as well as being a helper in the carrying of our own cross.

---

[74] "1556 רָבַע," ed. R. Laird Harris, Gleason L. Archer Jr., and Bruce K. Waltke, *Theological Wordbook of the Old Testament* (Chicago: Moody Press, 1999), 640.

Why must this be so? Simply because it is impossible to love anyone without seeing intimately into the tragedy of their lives, and everything that we see becomes a weight of grief in us. To love is not to view someone as being the most wonderful person in the world or to think of them as a saint. On the contrary, it may mean to see them as we must come to see ourselves, even as the 'chief of sinners.' It is to see all their weakness, their falseness and shoddiness, to have all their very worst habits exposed—and then to be enabled, by the pure grace of God, not only to accept them, but to accept them in a deeper way than was ever before possible. Love works for two people, in other words, the way faith works for one. For faith always begins with a frank recognition of one's own sinfulness (called repentance), which paradoxically opens up the way for deeper self-acceptance through forgiveness. Similarly, before love can really begin to be love, it must face and forgive the very worst in the person loved.[75]

AGONY

This feels like a bad movie. We want to yell, "Hey you two! Wait a minute. Don't turn away from each other. Just wait a few more seconds and you can resolve this. It's not that big of a deal!"

---

[75] Mike Mason, *The Mystery of Marriage: As Iron Sharpens Iron* (Portland, Oregon: Multnomah Press, 1985), 163.

Shulammite realized this first, but she enjoyed her personal pity party a few seconds too long. Her change of heart in v. 6 was too late, "My heart went out to him as he spoke. I searched for him but I did not find him; I called him but he did not answer me." Now it was too late to solve the problem on the spot. Each step Solomon took as he was leaving increased the chasm between them.

It's more agonizing to mend a broken heart than prevent one. Rather than take a few steps to open the door, she had to put her robe and sandals on and run out into the night. In v. 7 we see, "The watchmen who make the rounds in the city found me, they struck me and wounded me; the guardsmen of the walls took away my shawl from me."

These security guards were different than the ones in her dream in Chapter 3. These were the real deal. And they were not kind. It sounds as if they probably thought she was a prostitute plying her trade in the streets around the palace, so they treated her roughly, not realizing she was Solomon's wife. Devastated, she returned to the palace and woke up some of her girlfriends in v. 8, "I adjure you, O daughters of Jerusalem, if you find my beloved, as to what you will tell him: for I am lovesick."

Where do we go from here? It's always easier to make a mess than make amends. But that's what we will look at in the next chapter. Thankfully, Solomon was honest enough to include their own childish mistakes in his love song, but he was also willing to include the road they walked to making amends. Let's walk it with them.

"Can it be that it was all so simple then, or has time rewritten every line? If we had the chance to do it all again, tell me, would we? Could we?"

— Alan Bergman, Marilyn Bergman,
Marvin Hamlisch

CHAPTER NINE

MAKING UP IS HARD TO DO
(Song of Solomon 5:9-6:13)

Anyone can make a mess of their marriage. It's not hard to do. Wounding someone is easier than stopping the bleeding and beginning the healing process. But making up is hard to do. That's probably why the last chapter was half as long as this one.

Outside of death, few things are more difficult to watch than the disintegration of a marriage. Ron Lavin describes what happens when conflicts go unresolved. They inevitably pile up into a mountain of indifference.

Their wedding picture mocked them from table, these two minds who no longer touched each other. They lived with such a heavy barricade between them that neither battering ram or words nor artilleries of touch could break down. Somewhere between the oldest child's first tooth and the youngest daughter's graduation, they had lost each other. Throughout the years, each slowly unraveled that tangled ball of string called self, and as they tugged at stubborn knots, each hid his searching from the other. Sometimes she cried at night and begged the whispering darkness to tell her who she was. He lay beside her, unaware of her winter, for she warmed herself in self-pity. She took a course in modern art, trying to find herself in colors splashed on a canvas, and complained to other women about men who were insensitive. He climbed into a tomb called the office, wrapped in his mind a shroud of paper figures and buried himself in customers. Slowly the wall between them rose, cemented by a mortar of indifference. One day, reaching out to touch each other, they found a barrier they could not penetrate, and recoiling from the coldness of the stone, each retreated from the stranger on the other side. For when love dies, it is not a moment of angry battle. It lies, panting and exhausted, expiring at the bottom of a carefully built wall it could not penetrate."[76]

---

[76] Harold E. Helms, *God's Final Answer: A Series of Studies on the Book of Hebrews* (Maitland, FL: Xulon Press, 2004), 42-43.

GET SOME HELP

The decisions you make at the first sign of trouble in your marriage are critical. Without thinking, most tend to impulsively respond in kind – "Oh yeah, well so's your mother." Or they may run to a sympathetic friend to get backing for their position. This often includes parents or other family members. Another option is to do nothing at all, hoping it will all blow over.

None of these are good decisions. When there is an obvious problem like Mr. and Mrs. Solomon faced in the last chapter, something needs to be done. Let's look at Shulammite's response and see what we can learn from her.

Shulammite is back in the palace after failing to find her husband. She is deeply concerned and reaches out to her friends in Song of Solomon 5:8, "I adjure you, O daughters of Jerusalem, if you find my beloved, as to what you will tell him: For I am lovesick."

This is understandable since they were her close friends. This is one of the seven times she consulted them in the book, so this is not unusual. Shulammite probably stirred up a commotion as she went out looking for Solomon and when the guards confronted her it caused quite a stir in the palace.

Talk it through together

But seeking the counsel of friends right away may not be the best idea. We have no indication that Solomon had done this before or that there was anything particularly egregious in Solomon's departure. The wisest course of action would have been to step back and wait for him to come home. Then they could sit down and talk about her expectations and work it out. Establishing good communication patterns is especially important for young married couples.

Nevertheless, she consults her friends, who were also Solomon's friends. They knew him before she even came into the picture. So, their response in v. 9 is curious. "What kind of beloved is your beloved, O most beautiful among women? What kind of beloved is your beloved, that thus you adjure us?"

These are harsh words coming from her friends. They are knocking Solomon and mocking Shulammite. Twice they ask, "What kind of beloved is your beloved?" They are saying, "What kind of guy is this who would run off in the middle of the night like that?" They also mock Shulammite, intimating "Why are you so upset country girl? What makes Solomon any different than any other man? This is just the way men are."

Stop!

Before we proceed, let me say that this is where the climber meets the hill. This is the precise point where marital vows are tested. Women are inclined to run to mama and guys usually clam up or blow up when they encounter a problem like this. Unfortunately, few people stop long enough to examine their response to problems and dig deep into God's Word to see what he might have to say about marital conflict.

That's because most people, possibly even most Christians, have adopted what sociologist Christian Smith calls "moralist therapeutic deism" as their default position on theology. They believe that God is a nice guy but don't really believe he has anything to say about things like marital conflict.

Read and apply the Bible!

But God created mankind, invented marriage, and understands conflict, so he has a lot to say about issues like this. Here are some biblical instructions for working through conflict. They aren't spiritual aspirin – you know – "take two and call me in the morning." They aren't magic. But when applied, they can reverse the trend of sin and blame.

PLEASE! If you are married, read these slowly and thoughtfully. If you are experiencing conflicts in your marriage you may want to write down your responses to them. The first five are from Ephesians 4:

1. Speak the truth in love – v. 25 – "Therefore, laying aside falsehood, speak truth each one of you with his neighbor, for we are members of one another." Verse 15 adds, "speak the truth in love." PAUSE before you begin a heated discussion. Modulate your tone and volume. Don't sugarcoat it, but don't seek to wound. Avoid, "You never ..." and "You always ..." Try, "My perception is ...," and "When you do this, I feel ..."

2. Don't avoid conflict – v. 26-27 – "Be angry, and yet do not sin; do not let the sun go down on your anger, and do not give the devil an opportunity." Deal with any anger or bitterness *every day before you go to bed*. If

you don't, it tends to get buried and become a festering issue that will be brought up the next time you get mad.

3. Use words that build up, not tear down – v. 29 – "Let no unwholesome word proceed from your mouth, but only such a word as is good for edification according to the need of the moment, so that it will give grace to those who hear." Don't curse or call each other names. Clearly communicate what you are feeling and what you might do to avoid future conflicts. Choose to change your conversation to that which will build up, not tear down.

4. Recognize your sinful reactions ASAP! – v. 31 – "Let all bitterness and wrath and anger and clamor and slander be put away from you, along with all malice." Bitterness occurs when issues go unresolved. Passive anger and explosive outbursts are expressions of anger at God since He could have changed the situation but didn't. Clamor and slander are loud exaggerations intended to tear the other person down so you can look down on them. Malice is the intent to cause harm, not bring resolution. You can't control the other person, but you can confess your own sinful response.

5. Check your heart – v. 32 – "Be kind to one another, tender-hearted, forgiving each other, just as God in Christ also has forgiven you." Ask God to soften your heart. Remember that you love them. Forgive liberally and often. This means you don't hold a grudge or keep score.

6. Listen before you speak – James 1:19-20 – "But everyone must be quick to hear, slow to speak and

slow to anger; for the anger of man does not achieve the righteousness of God." It's been said, "It's better to keep your mouth shut and have everyone think you're stupid, than to open it and remove all doubt." This is especially true if you are a talker. DON'T JUMP TO CONCLUSIONS! ASK CLARIFYING QUESTIONS!. DON'T INTERRUPT!

7. Don't seek to get even – 1 Thessalonians 5:15 – "See that no one repays another with evil for evil, but always seek after that which is good for one another and for all people." Don't keep score. Don't retaliate. Look for the good in the conflict.

8. Consistently focus on the good in the other person – Philippians 4:8 – "Finally, brethren, whatever is true, whatever is honorable, whatever is right, whatever is pure, whatever is lovely, whatever is of good repute, if there is any excellence and if anything worthy of praise, dwell on these things." Look for the bad and you will find it. Look for the good and you will find that too. Learn to look past the part in the other person that causes conflict to see them as a whole person, not just the part that causes conflict.

9. Be willing to be wronged – 1 Peter 2:20 – "For what credit is there if, when you sin and are harshly treated, you endure it with patience? But if when you do what is right and suffer for it you patiently endure it; this finds favor with God." Demanding justice will not bring reconciliation. "Leave room for the wrath of God ...'Vengeance is Mine, I will repay,' says the Lord"

(Romans 12:19). Trust God to work. He can bring conviction and change when you can't.

10. Pray – Philippians 4:6 – "Be anxious for nothing, but in everything by prayer and supplication with thanksgiving let your requests be made known to God." <u>This single act will do more to resolve marital conflict than anything else you can do! Face each other, hold hands, then pray out loud specifically for what the *other person asks you* to pray for, not what you think they need</u>. Don't weaponize prayer by directing it to the other person. Ask for prayer for your needs and pray for the needs they have expressed.

Seek biblical counseling

If the two of you can't resolve a conflict after trying these things, then you may need to seek counsel from someone else. Every marriage goes through what you are facing, so don't be afraid to do this. Your marriage is worth seeking godly help.

Here are some guidelines on seeking help:

1. In general – Don't ever talk to anyone about a problem in your marriage unless you both agree to do so! This means family, friends, neighbors, and people at church or work.

2. Parents – Don't talk to your parents unless both of you are present and you agree they can be trusted. You don't want your problems discussed by your parents-in-law and neither does your spouse. If parents

are both committed Christians, and you both agree, they could be a great source of help.

3. Friends – Don't talk to your friends unless both of you are present. If you talk to them by yourself, most of them will take your side and tell you what you want to hear. If you both trust a friend or a couple who are committed Christians, then they could prove to be helpful if you both talk to them.

4. Opposite sex – Don't seek counsel from, or talk about your problems with anyone of the opposite sex without your spouse present. Ever! Don't listen to other's marital problems either. This is a good way to begin an affair.

5. Church groups – Don't mention your "situation" in prayer at your small group in church unless both of you agree to do so in advance. "Silent" prayer requests are meaningless and do nothing but create curiosity and gossip. A solid group of friends can be a wonderful asset if both people are willing to open up to a limited group who can be trusted to keep your situation strictly confidential. Marital problems should never be shared in larger groups unless church discipline is involved.

6. Continuing sin – If either spouse is involved in continuing, unrepentant sin, then the process of church discipline (Matthew 18:15-17) may be appropriate according to the guidelines of your church. If your church doesn't practice church discipline it is appropriate to tell your sinning spouse that you are going to ask a pastor or elder from the church to intervene.

If you still can't resolve your issues, then you need to follow God's pattern for counseling in your local church. Caring for the spiritual needs of believers is the job of pastors and elders in a local church. Hebrews 13:17 indicates that Christians are to "Obey your leaders and submit to them, for they keep watch over your souls as those who will give an account. Let them do this with joy and not with grief, for this would be unprofitable for you." This biblical task is not entrusted to non-believers outside the church because they cannot possibly address the issues of sin, repentance, confession, grace, forgiveness, and salvation.

The first choice for counseling should not be a "professional" outside the church who will charge for their services. God's pattern is explained in Galatians 6:1, "Brethren, even if anyone is caught in any trespass, you who are spiritual, restore such a one in a spirit of gentleness; each one looking to yourself, so that you too will not be tempted."

In 1 Thessalonians 5:14 Paul urges believers to "admonish the unruly, encourage the fainthearted, help the weak, be patient with everyone." This might be a pastor, an elder, or a mature person in the church who knows the Bible well, who has a solid marriage, and can help you resolve your conflicts.

If you can't find someone who can provide biblical counseling, contact biblicalcounseling.com. They can provide you with helpful resources for biblical counseling anywhere in the country.

Divorce is the last option in resolving conflict and can only be pursued in two situations. The first is if sexual immorality is present (Matthew 5:32), and the second is if a non-believing spouse leaves a believing spouse and files for a divorce (1

Corinthians 7:15). This doesn't mean divorce is mandated. But sexual immorality and abandonment by an unbeliever break the "one flesh" nature of marriage and can cause such a wound that the innocent party is allowed to divorce under these circumstances.

In rare situations, separation (without filing for divorce) might be advisable if severe drug or alcohol problems, physical abuse, or financial irresponsibility are present. This should always be done with the purpose of reconciliation.

HER PART

Let's return to Solomon and Shulammite to see how they handled this problem. They both did some very wise things, so we will first look at what she did to resolve the situation, and then we will see what he did.

We must remember that marriage is the union of two sinners, not two angels. Solomon sinned against his wife by his inconsiderate lack of communication. Then Shulammite sinned by her anger and her petulance in locking him out. It doesn't matter who sinned first.

If the answer to conflict is to assume you are right and your spouse is wrong, you're headed for deep trouble. If you look to friends and family for help, most of them will say, "Trust your heart." This is completely wrong even if it's written into every movie you've ever seen! Proverbs 28:26 tells us, "He who trusts in his own heart is a fool, but he who walks wisely will be delivered." Your heart is an idol factory built to protect the one inside. If you trust your heart, you will be led into error, not truth.

She defends her husband

Shulammite seemingly knew that and answers her "counselors" in a wonderfully surprising way – by defending her husband. Despite what the daughters of Jerusalem said about Solomon, Shulammite wasn't buying it.

She understood that her response was sinful and wrong. In response to her friends questioning him, Shulammite's response was to say, "No, that's not what my husband is at all. Let me tell you about him."

She began by telling them about his physical features. This sounds out of place at first. This almost sounds like a girl who has just met a guy and is saying, "Wow! What a hunk!" But this is more than just physical attraction. This is a wounded wife putting aside her hurt feelings to remember just how much she loves her husband.

Conflict resolution can't occur if you're focusing on getting even. If you see the act of sin committed against you as the whole person, you will never regain the footing you had before the offense. Shulammite is reviewing her feelings about the whole person, not just the offense Solomon committed against her.

His physical features

She begins by commenting on his general appearance in Song of Solomon 5:10, "My beloved is dazzling (general impression) and ruddy (normal reddish complexion of a young man), outstanding among ten thousand." That is, he stands out in a crowd. I can just hear some women saying,

"Well, duh! Give me the smartest and richest man on earth and I'll be a good wife too!"

That misses the point. She is not commenting on his position as the king. She is reminding herself that people notice him. Every man is not a king, but every man likes to think that his wife looks up to him and respects him. Women who fail to respect their husbands fail him at his point of greatest vulnerability (Ephesians 5:32).

She also comments about his looks. But notice that he isn't even around. This is not meant to stroke his ego. She is simply reflecting on the physical features that she loves in him:

1. v. 11 – "His head is like gold, pure gold; his locks are like clusters of dates and black as a raven." His bronzed face and curly black hair suggest he is ruggedly handsome.
2. v. 12 – "His eyes are like doves beside streams of water, bathed in milk, and reposed in their setting." She copies his poetic flair because he said the same thing about her eyes in Song of Solomon 4:1. His translucent pupils are calm and penetrating.
3. v. 13 – "His cheeks are like a bed of balsam, banks of sweet-scented herbs." This probably refers to the common practice of perfuming the beard. "His lips are lilies dripping with liquid myrrh." She likes the sweet smell of kissing him.
4. v. 14 – "His hands are rods of gold set with beryl; His abdomen is carved ivory inlaid with sapphires." He wears fine jewelry and his abs are cut! I heard former NFL quarterback Peyton Manning once say on TV

that the only guys with a cut six pack are 18-year olds and professional athletes. So, don't worry guys. This applies to very few of us.

5. v. 15 – "His legs are pillars of alabaster set on pedestals of pure gold; His appearance is like Lebanon, choice as the cedars." His legs are like columns of white marble, strong and sturdy, like the beautiful carved pillars of an ornate building. His whole appearance is like the massive cedars of Lebanon depicting strength. His general appearance was tall and strong.

Personal features

But she's attracted by more than his physical features. In v. 16 she comments, "His mouth is full of sweetness and he is wholly desirable. This is my beloved and this is my friend, O daughters of Jerusalem." Notice what she says about his personality.

The "mouth" most often refers to speech. The word for "sweetness" is used in connection with honey, meaning it was smooth and completely agreeable. He was not loud or abusive. He was thoughtful, reasonable, and measured. The man who is known as a loudmouth or crude doesn't impress anyone, including his wife.

He is also "wholly desirable," that is, "he is all I ever wanted in a husband." A "desirable" man is not the Dos Equis "most interesting man in the world" kind of guy. If that were true, then the man who's a "player" with the ladies would be desirable. That's not what she means. Solomon was a man of integrity; honest, respected, virtuous, competent, strong, loving, and committed to her. That's what made him desirable.

She expresses partnership

Shulammite also says, "This is my beloved." The emphasis is on possession. She uses this phrase twenty-four times in the book, leading us to believe she meant it! She was proudly saying, "This is my guy!" She treasured him. He belonged to her and she belonged to him.

Partnership is one of the key elements of a healthy marriage. The New Testament writers created a manifesto of God's desire for men and women partnering in marriage, even though this idea was completely unheard of throughout the Roman Empire at that time. Romans regarded marriage as a necessity to bear children but sexual encounters outside of marriage and multiple divorces were accepted norms.

Christian marriage ran counter to the cultural norms for the first three hundred years of the Christian era, despite the persecution they endured under the Roman Empire. Eventually the biblical model of Christian marriage was largely forgotten for a thousand years due to the erroneous teaching of the Roman Catholic Church.

This changed with the Reformation in the sixteenth century. During the conflict with the Catholic Church, Martin Luther recovered the primacy of Scripture as the standard for theology and life, as opposed to the Catholic standard of subordinating Scripture to the authority of church tradition and church councils.

In renewing the emphasis on Scripture as the primary authority, Luther changed the institution of marriage. He did this innocently at first by helping to smuggle priests and nuns out of convents to free them from the constraints of the Catholic Church and help them find husbands and wives. He smuggled one group of nuns out of a convent inside barrels used to transport herring!

One of the nuns was a young woman named Katie von Bora. His eventual marriage to Katie changed Luther's theology on marriage from theoretical to practical. Since he couldn't find a suitable husband for her, she finally asked, "What about you?" When he saw that his marriage would "please his father, rile the pope, cause the angels to laugh and the devils to weep,"[77] he consented, and they were married. She was 26. He was 42.

Despite the shallow (and almost laughable) reasons Luther gave for marrying, he and Katie grew to love each other deeply and had six children. In a letter to her in 1533 Luther wrote, "Katie, you have a god-fearing man who loves you." He further declared, "You are an empress ...If I should lose my Katie, I would not take another wife though I were offered a queen."[78]

Luther learned first-hand the benefits of God's gift of marriage. If he had not married Katie he would have missed out on the joy of marriage and failed to be an example to

---

[77] Gene Edward Veith Jr., David Vaughn, gen. ed., *A Place to Stand: The Word of God in the Life of Martin Luther* (Nashville, Tennessee: Cumberland House, 2005), 98.

[78] Michelle Durusha, "A Sixteenth Century Scandal," https://credomag.com/article/a-sixteenth-century-scandal, May 7, 2018, accessed on June 2, 2020.

the thousands of disenchanted Catholics who had such a distorted view of marriage at that time.

She maintains their friendship

Shulammite also called Solomon "my friend." Some people think that friends are people who like the same kinds of things. That may be true, but there is much more to friendship. Solomon fleshes out the meaning of the word by noting, "a friend loves at all times," even in adversity (Proverbs 17:17), "a friends sticks closer than a brother" (Proverbs 18:24), and "faithful are the wounds of a friend (Proverbs 27:6).

Anne and I aren't friends because we like to wallpaper together (we don't), because we love to play volleyball together (we don't), or because we both love cars (we don't). We are friends because we have built a life *committed to the same things.* We are passionately committed to the Lord, to His Church, to giving our lives to serve Him in His Church, to see our kids grow to love these same things, and to turning our house into a home that reveals our deepest values in every way.

Friendship is more than sharing the same last name. Friendship is what we build into each other's lives with the raw materials of life. When we build with friendship the big bad wolf of adversity might show up and huff and puff trying to blow your house down, but the only result will be hyperventilation. The poet explains friendship this way:

> I love you not only for what you are
> But for who I am when I am with you.
> I love you, not only for what

You have made of yourself
But for what you are making of me.
I love you for the part of me that you bring out;
I love you, for putting your hand
Into my heaped-up heart
And passing over all the foolish, weak things that
you can't help dimly seeing there,
And for drawing out into the light
All the beautiful belongings
That no one else had looked quite far enough to find.
I love you because you
Are helping me to make of the lumber of my life,
Not a tavern but a temple;
Out of works of my every day
Not a reproach but a song.
I love you because you have done more than any
creed could have done to make me good,
And more than any fate could have done to
make me happy.
You have done it without a touch, without a word,
without a sign.
You have done it by being yourself. Perhaps that is
what being a friend means, after all.[79]

She is determined to succeed

Shulammite also shows her determination as she continues her search for Solomon. She is not blaming him or

---

[79] Roy Croft, "Why Do I Love You?" in Albert Lewis Alexander, *Poems that Touch the Heart: America's Most Popular Collection of Inspirational Verse* (New York, New York: Doubleday, 1962), 3-5.

giving up on him. She doesn't accept the critiques of even her closest friends. Instead, she reveals that she will continue to love him and that she knows him well.

She knows him

As she defends Solomon to her friends, she seems to have had an epiphany in Song of Solomon 6:2 when she said, "My beloved has gone down to his garden, to the beds of balsam, to pasture his flock in the gardens and gather lilies." When she stopped long enough to think about it, she realized, "I know where he has gone." Like any man when he is annoyed or hurt or simply wants to get away, Solomon has gone to his man cave. He's gone to the place where he is most comfortable.

This describes more than her knowledge; it describes her attitude. She could have said, "He's such a baby. Let him go down to his little garden and pout. I'm not going after him." But she didn't. She's already indicated she wanted to reconcile, and now it's apparent she was fighting for her marriage.

Ladies, do you know where your husband would go if you had a strong misunderstanding? Would he go to the den? The garage? To work? Would he go to a friend's or neighbor's house? More importantly, would you go seek him out?

She recommits to him

But she doesn't leave it there. She doesn't know what he is thinking, and it doesn't even matter if he is mad, or pouting, or whatever. Song of Solomon 6:3 re-states the same phrase used in Song of Solomon 2:16 but reverses the order. There she said, "My beloved is mine, and I *am his*." Here she says, "I am my beloved's and my beloved *is mine*" (emphasis mine). Is this coincidence or does she switch the order on purpose?

I think it's on purpose. This indicates that *she knew* that Solomon felt exactly the same way she did even though the conflict had not been resolved. Don't miss that. When there is disagreement or conflict, it's easy to forget that with the first hurt feeling or harsh word. One of the greatest keys to resolving conflict is to think the best about the other person rather than succumb to the natural tendency to think the worst – to cast blame, to see them only in light of their recent failure.

There is no faltering here with Shulammite. In essence she was saying, "It's not "me vs. him", it's just "us." If you want to win the argument, forget reconciliation. If you want to wait for him (or her) to say, "I'm sorry," you won't resolve conflict. If you vow to meet him halfway, you'll never get there!

I once heard that old time movie star Ginger Rogers could do every dance step Fred Astaire could do – but *backwards*. Marriage is a dance. Partners are committed to each other. One leads, the other follows, but they step in unison as they gaze into each other's eyes. Of course, they step on each other's toes occasionally, but they keep dancing. They don't allow anyone to cut in as they grow in commitment to each other.

At times you won't even *like* your spouse. But that's not the question. The question is, do you *love* them? Christians should understand this. The biblical idea of love is much deeper than merely liking each other.

In John 15:17 Jesus said, "This I command you, that you love one another." It's hard to visualize this as a commandment to feel something. Instead, the word agape is distinguished by action, not feeling.

This is the way God loved us in Romans 5:8, "But God demonstrates His own love toward us, in that while we were yet sinners, Christ died for us." He didn't merely feel emotional about us. He took the necessary action to save us, even when we were still wallowing in our sin. This is redeeming love, and every marriage must have it in spades. It looks out for the interests of another above its own interests.

This is the love of husband for his wife and vice versa. It is not centered in fanning the flame of our emotions. It's not about discovering a new romantic rendezvous. It's not about trying harder or turning over a new leaf. It's about *doing* something. Let's see what Solomon does.

HIS PART

He leads with love

The scene changes drastically in the Song of Solomon 6:4. We are not told why or how but all of a sudden Solomon is back, and he immediately begins his explanation. His initial response is profound. Simply put, he leads with love, not by defending himself.

His decision to front the argument with his true feelings about his wife is astounding. Solomon must have realized by now that, as 50's TV star Ricky Ricardo used to say to his wife Lucy, "I've got some splainin' to do." But *before* he got to any debate about who did what to whom, he wanted to tell her how much he loved her.

Wow! Often in counseling a couple will trade accusations for hours before it finally seems like they are spent. When I finally ask if they really love each other, they are usually quiet and then tears begin to flow before they quietly answer, "Yes." That may be a little simplified but not much. The point is, why not *start* there?

That's what Solomon does. He turns on the poetic charm in v. 4, "You are as beautiful as Tirzah, my darling, as lovely as Jerusalem." Tirzah was a beautiful city in northern Samaria. It was filled with beautiful gardens and orchards fed with an abundant supply of water. Tirzah was close to her home, so she knew of its beauty.

Jerusalem, of course, was the capital of Israel. In Lamentations 2:15 the city is called "the perfection of beauty, the joy of all the earth." Solomon is comparing his wife to the two most prestigious cities he can imagine. It might be like saying, "You remind me of the beauty of Rome or Paris at night."

But he also uses the analogy of war in v. 4, saying she was "as awesome as an army with banners." We've seen that a banner was a military sign of identity and conquest. Soldiers gathered around their banner as they marched into a conquered city. Solomon is saying, "I've been captured by your beauty. Take me, I'm yours."

Remember, Solomon has no idea why she locked him out or why she wouldn't get up and come over and unlock the door for him. But to him, it doesn't matter! MEN AND WOMEN – GET THAT – IT DOESN'T MATTER! Solomon is saying something like, "Honey, I don't know why you're mad, but let me tell you that I love you and you're still the most beautiful person I can imagine."

Why would he say that? Because he didn't care about his rights. Today we are told to stick up for our rights, but that's the opposite of the instruction of scripture.

The Apostle Paul gives us valuable insight on seeking our rights in 1 Corinthians 9:4-6, "Do we not have a right to eat and drink? Do we not have a right to take along a believing wife, even as the rest of the apostles and the brothers of the Lord and Cephas? Or do only Barnabas and I not have a right to refrain from working?"

He is asserting his rights as an apostle. But having a right and using it are two different things. Later on, in 1 Corinthians 9:12 Paul clarifies, "If others share the right over you, do we not more? Nevertheless, *we did not use this right,* but we endure all things so that we will cause no hindrance to the gospel of Christ" (emphasis mine). Paul asserts his rights but recognizes that by doing so he might hinder the gospel, so he willingly gave up his right to assert his rights!

The application to marital conflict is easy to see. I may have certain rights, but most of the time it's wiser to forego those rights for the sake of easing the conflict. That's what Solomon is doing here. He is certainly not coming in hot with a bunch of questions and accusations. That would defeat any attempt at reconciliation by placing his wife on the defensive and he doesn't want that.

Guys, it takes guts to give up your rights. Peter showed the way to do that in 1 Peter 2:20, "For what credit is there if, when you sin and are harshly treated, you endure it with patience? But if when you do what is right and suffer for it you patiently endure it, this finds favor with God."

Do you want to get credit for being right, or do you want resolution? One finds favor with God and the other one doesn't.

He admits confusion

Leading with love doesn't mean the discussion is over. Solomon is still confused. In v. 5 he pleads, "Turn your eyes away from me, for they have confused me." He still doesn't know what hit him. He's looking at her looking at him and they are both speechless at this point. She may have an idea of where he was but all he remembers is the locked door and her refusal to get out of bed to unlock it.

She's quiet at this point so it's quite possible that she is also confused. Loving each other doesn't mean that you will never be confused about the actions of the one you love. It just means that more questions need to be asked and answered when the emotions have quieted down.

He humbles himself

In light of her silence you've got to give Solomon credit for trying. With no other information from her he just keeps ploughing ahead with more compliments. In fact, he doubles down by repeating the words that he said to her on their wedding night.

He again comments in vv. 6-7, "Your teeth are like a flock of ewes which have come up from their washing, all of which bear twins, and not one among them has lost her young." So, he starts with the fact she still has all of her teeth and then moves on to her cheeks by stating, "Your temples are like a slice of a pomegranate behind your veil." These are comments about her smile and the blush of her cheeks.

But he quickly adds more substantive comments. In v. 8 he adds, "There are sixty queens and eighty concubines, and maidens without number." He is comparing her to other women "without number." In other words, she is more valuable to him than any other woman he can imagine. Maybe it just took him a bit to circle the plane trying to figure out where to land, but he gets there.

He continues with these words of commitment in vv. 9-10, noting, "my dove, my perfect one, is unique: She is her mother's only daughter; She is the pure child of the one who bore her. The maidens saw her and called her blessed, the queens and the concubines also, and they praised her, saying, 'Who is this that grows like the dawn, as beautiful as the full moon, as pure as the sun, as awesome as an army with banners?'"

As they say in the South, that's tall cotton. She is perfect and one of a kind. She is her mother's favorite child. Her friends and women in court hold her in high esteem, and she is only getting more beautiful with time. She has the presence of an army entering a conquered town with their victory banners unfurled and flying high.

There are very few actual beauty queens around. But your wife wants to know that you think of her as *your* beauty queen. She wants to know that she is the only one for you. She wants to know that she still possesses your heart. You don't have to be a poet, but guys, you need to consistently find the words to express your feelings to your wife in a way that sounds authentic to who you are.

Why don't men say these things? It's not because we don't have a working knowledge of the English language. It's because we are proud. We don't like feeling weak. Like Fonzie, we don't like to admit, "I was wr ...wr ...wrong!"

Neil Diamond and Barbra Streisand sang, "You don't bring me flowers anymore." What happens to a woman's heart when she realizes those days are over? A guy at a men's conference I spoke at once told me, "If I brought my wife flowers, she would say, 'What have you done now?'" I replied that's probably because it had been too long since he'd done it.

Marriages don't end in one big bang. They are murdered over time by a thousand tiny cuts before they finally bleed to death.

But don't lose heart when your marriage hits a rough patch like this. Be encouraged that it's entirely possible for couples to turn a troubled marriage around. Linda Waite and Maggie Gallagher, in their book *The Case for Marriage* report that:

1. 86% of unhappily married people who stick it out find that, five years later, their marriages are happier. Most say they've become very happy.
2. 60% who said their marriage was unhappy but stayed married rated their marriage "very happy" or "quite happy" when re-interviewed a decade later.
3. The very worst marriages showed the most dramatic turnarounds: 77% of the stable married people who rated their marriage as very unhappy (1 on a scale

of 1-7) said that the same marriage was either "very happy" or "quite happy" five years later.

4. Permanent marital unhappiness is surprisingly rare among the couples who stick it out.
5. Just 15% of those who initially said they were very unhappily married (and who stayed married) ranked their marriage as not unhappy at all five years later.[80]

Most people assume that when trouble creeps in the marriage is doomed. But that's just not true. Disagreements are inevitable, even in a good marriage. But there are tools for working through these disagreements if you use them.

A WORD FROM THE APOSTLE JOHN

The apostle John provides three tools for doing this. In Revelation 2:4-5 John records Jesus' words to the church of Ephesus, "'But I have this against you, that you have left your first love." This also applies to marriage. Jesus' advice is threefold:

1. The first thing – "'Therefore remember from where you have fallen." Sit down together and talk about your favorite dates and the events and places you most enjoyed when you first got married.
2. The second thing is "repent." In reality, I can't do anything about the sin of my wife and vice versa. All I can do is examine my own heart for sin and repent.

[80] Linda J. Waite and Maggie Gallagher, *The Case for Marriage: Why Married People Are Happier, Healthier, and Better Off Financially* (New York, NY: Broadway Books, 2000), 148-149.

3. The third thing is, "do the deeds you did at first." Do some of the things you did when you first fell in love. Revisit the place where you spent your honeymoon. And treat each other the way you did back then.

Making up is hard to do. Repairing the wounds of marital conflict isn't easy. But it's worth it. When a wound heals, that place is stronger than it was before the injury. The same with a marriage. Healing the wounds is what makes a stronger marriage.

"The reason some people have never been able to forgive is that if they forgave, the last rug would be pulled out from under them and they would have no one to blame."

— David Seamonds

CHAPTER TEN

GET OVER IT!
(Song of Solomon 6:10-13)

Corrie ten Boom was a Dutch survivor of the Ravensbruck concentration camp in WWII. Her family was imprisoned for hiding Jews and resistance members in hidden chambers in their home in Amsterdam. She lost her father and older sister in the camp while she was imprisoned. Fifteen days after the death of her sister Betsie, Corrie was released due to a clerical error and she returned home to Amsterdam. A week after her release all the women in her age group were sent to the gas chambers.

The horrors of these camps are something few can comprehend. Anyone who has visited one of them can attest to the physical revulsion one feels when confronted with the atrocities of the Nazi Regime.

Corrie and her family were committed Christians who believed in the absolute sovereignty of God. As she lay dying,

Betsie told Corrie that she must not be bitter and angry. She told her that she must live to tell people that "There is no pit so deep that He [God] is not deeper still."[81] This became Corrie's message when she was released. God used her in a mighty way to proclaim His love even in the middle of hellish circumstances.

Years later Corrie was confronted with a situation she hadn't anticipated. After years of an extensive speaking ministry that took her around the world speaking of God's love, her beliefs were put to the test in a dramatic way. She tells it this way:

> It was at a church service in Munich that I saw him, the former S.S. man who had stood guard at the shower room door in the processing center at Ravensbruck. He was the first of our actual jailers that I had seen since that time. And suddenly it was all there—the roomful of mocking men, the heaps of clothing, Betsie's pain-blanched face.
>
> He came up to me as the church was emptying, beaming and bowing. "How grateful I am for your message, Fraulein," he said. "To think that, as you say, He has washed my sins away!"
>
> His hand was thrust out to shake mine. And I, who had preached so often to the people in Bloemendaal the need to forgive, kept my hand at my side.

---

[81] Corrie ten Boom, *The Hiding Place: The Triumphant True Story of Corrie ten Boom* (1971; repr., Peabody, Massachusetts: Hendrickson Publishers, 2009), 240.

Even as the angry, vengeful thoughts boiled through me, I saw the sin of them. Jesus Christ had died for this man; was I going to ask for more? Lord Jesus, I prayed, forgive me and help me to forgive him.

I tried to smile, I struggled to raise my hand. I could not. I felt nothing, not the slightest spark of warmth or charity. And so again I breathed a silent prayer. Jesus, I cannot forgive him. Give me Your forgiveness.

As I took his hand the most incredible thing happened. From my shoulder along my arm and through my hand a current seemed to pass from me to him, while into my heart sprang a love for this stranger that almost overwhelmed me."[82]

Events like this remind us of the critical nature of biblical doctrine. But they also remind us that sometimes obeying these doctrines is tough.

This certainly applies to marriage. Any married person who is honest will admit that extending forgiveness, even when it isn't asked for or deserved, is part of the DNA of a Christ-honoring marriage. Forgiveness is necessary for matters large and small as we will see in the lives of Mr. and Mrs. Solomon.

---

[82] R. Kent Hughes, *Are Evangelicals Born Again?: The Character Traits of True Faith* (Wheaton, Illinois: Crossway Books, 1995), 68-69.

TAKE YOUR TIME

We've seen the genesis of the misunderstanding between Shulammite and Solomon, and we know that they both still love each other and want to reconcile. Now what?

There is no such thing as a pat answer for marital conflict because every couple is different and so is every situation. But there are several things that are common that must be done before genuine reconciliation can take place.

A couple of things show us this couple is on the road to recovery. This first thing is the passage of time. If Shulammite had immediately gone to the door to open it they may have had a reasonable discussion and solved their problem, but I doubt it. Shulammite had been stewing all evening and Solomon was completely oblivious to what his wife was feeling.

Time and distance can be your friend in situations like this that flare up quickly. Usually that's when harsh words and accusations are made. It takes a very mature couple to recognize the danger of an eruption like this and solve it on the spot. Most of us need some time and space to think things through.

Solomon and Shulammite didn't plan for that, but Solomon's departure gave both of them a little time to pause and reflect. We've seen that Shulammite's heart changed almost immediately, though it was too late to talk with her husband. It's also possible that Solomon may have needed a short time away to process how he was feeling and consider his response.

Whatever your tendency is, don't ever let the day end without trying to reconcile after an argument or misunderstanding. The Apostle Paul provides this profound principle in Ephesians 4:26, "don't let the sun go down on your anger." If you find yourself in the middle of an argument, there is nothing wrong with saying, "Give me a minute here. I need some time to think this through." Some people need minutes, others need hours. But the sun goes down every day. Whatever time you need, make sure that you come back and sit down to solve the problem before the day is over.

We've already seen that both of them expressed their love for the other person. Solomon hasn't heard her expression of love yet, but we know that's what she feels. If you can't put your pain and anger aside for a moment and know that you still deeply love your spouse, then you will probably not reach a reconciliation.

In those beautiful words that the Apostle Paul expressed in 1 Corinthians 13:5-7, love "does not act unbecomingly; it does not seek its own, is not provoked, does not take into account a wrong suffered, does not rejoice in unrighteousness, but rejoices with the truth; bears all things, believes all things, hopes all things, endures all things."

This may not be on the surface during the course of an argument, but you need to remind yourself that you don't have to dig too deep to find it. Love doesn't seek perfection or justice. Love seeks to absorb the pain from the other person and respond to them in the way that is best for them.

The points of disagreement are critical in every marriage. Initially it may come as a surprise to a young married couple, but in time they grow to understand that loving each other is not merely a nice Hallmark moment. Loving means living with your spouse as they really are – not as you thought they were when you got married.

Facing the worst in the person loved might even mean confronting serious, blatant sin. A guy once asked me if it was okay for a husband to watch porn with his wife?! The lecherous smile on his face told me he was more interested in porn than his wife. That person was not loving his wife at all and deserved to be confronted in the strongest way possible.

But the sins of Shulammite and Solomon also needed to be confronted. At the very least both of them were self-centered and reacted with childish petulance. In this kind of situation there is no one better to help someone confront their sin than the one who loves them most. Taking the time to reflect on what happened is the first step in figuring this out.

GET THE FACTS

Solomon and Shulammite finally had the time to cool down a bit and find out exactly what happened. After profusely complimenting his wife and assuring her of his love, Solomon explained in Song of Solomon 6:11, "I went down to the orchard of nut trees to see the blossoms of the valley, to see whether the vine had budded or the pomegranates had bloomed." It's not immediately clear what he is referring to. Is he explaining why he got home late or where he went after she shut him out?

It seems best to see this as his explanation of why he got home late. This ties in well with his fuller explanation in v. 12, "Before I was aware, my soul set me over the chariots of my noble people." This is a simple, logical explanation. He was

GET OVER IT!

overseeing some of his agricultural interests and lost track of the time.

That is a reasonable explanation. If she had given him a chance to explain that before she offered her weak excuse, this whole disagreement might have been avoided. She could have explained her desire for better communication which would have prompted him to apologize and be more considerate next time.

But that didn't happen. And now the overlay of shutting down his sexual advance and his resultant childish retreat have added other sin to the original layer. But at least they both now know the full facts of the situation.

Getting the facts is critical in resolving conflict. Innuendo, assumption, and jumping to conclusions doesn't help anyone. These are fact killers.

In our legal system a person has the right to due process in determining guilt or innocence. The same is true in marital conflict. Due process means the couple takes the time to find out exactly what happened before they pronounce judgment. It's always best to think the best of the other person rather than the worst until proven otherwise.

A good technique to use in getting at the facts is simply asking questions. Shulammite could have let him in and then asked, "Where have you been?" "Why didn't you let me know if you thought you might be late?" Judging from her quick change of heart, it's not too much to assume that, upon hearing his answers, she might have said, "I'm sorry Honey. I jumped to conclusions about your intentions. Will you forgive me?"

185

If Solomon had stayed at the door and not rushed away, she would have come to the door and opened it. He would have seen immediately that something was wrong and asked, "What's wrong?" When she told him, he would have apologized and said that he understood and that he would make every effort to get home on time or give her advance notice in the future, and the situation would have been over.

But none of that happened. They had both sinned in childish fashion. Solomon told her where he had been, yet the issue is not resolved. Solomon shows remarkable wisdom as he continues to move toward reconciliation.

LEAVE YOUR BAGGAGE BEHIND

Several years ago, a UAE plane crash landed in Dubai. The pilot landed too late and ran out of runway. The plane skidded to a halt, the chutes deployed, and 300 people began to exit. Onboard video showed people immediately reaching for the overhead compartments to get their luggage despite flight attendants being heard saying, "Please exit the plane immediately. Leave your luggage behind."

That's good instruction for conflict resolution in marriage – please leave your baggage behind. The temptation is to unload your baggage when conflict occurs. You've been packing it for years with old insults, grudges, creative name calling, bad advice, and plenty of tired, repeat performances.

But you must leave it behind if you want to move forward. "But he was so inconsiderate" – leave it! "But she locked me out!" – leave it! "But I deserve an apology!" – leave it! "I deserve her respect!" – leave it! "He should tell me he was wrong!" – leave it! "She had no right to do that!" – leave it! "If I don't stick up for myself now, he'll do it again!" – leave it! "She is just like her Mom!" – leave it! Leave all of these in the overhead compartment and never retrieve them.

Solomon is attempting to do that. In v. 13 he pleads, "Come back, come back, O Shulammite; Come back, come back, that we may gaze at you!"

Solomon is a desperate man, pleading with Shulammite to "Come back" four times! He has expressed his deeply held love for her in no uncertain terms and she has remained silent. The reference to *"we"* indicates this discussion has taken place in the presence of the daughters of Jerusalem. Solomon returned to find Shulammite in the company of her friends and expressed his love to her in their presence. Now he waits for her answer.

FORGIVE

This is where the heavy lifting begins. They are face to face. Solomon has expressed his love to Shulammite. She can see the desperation in his eyes. He has asked her four times to *"Come back."* These words communicate a lot. He's told her where he was, but she hasn't said anything about what she was thinking from behind the locked door of her bedroom. To him, it doesn't matter. In essence he is taking the blame for the situation and asking her to forgive him and come back.

Every couple has to learn this lesson. Reconciliation is not about claiming rights and demanding justice. If you want to assert your rights, you will never be fully satisfied. If you demand justice, you will never feel like you get it. Ultimately the only way to deal with the offense is to forgive.

Jesus taught this in Matthew 18:21-35. Peter came to Jesus and asked, "Lord, how often shall my brother sin against me and I forgive him? Up to seven times?" The word for "forgive" means "let go, cancel, remit, leave." It points to "the voluntary release of a person or thing over which one has legal or actual control"[83]

When Peter posed his hypothetical question, "Up to seven times?" he expected Jesus to pat him on the head and commend his magnanimous spirit. After all, seven is the number of perfection, indicating that Peter thought he had the perfect formula for forgiveness.

But Jesus had a different idea. In v. 22 He responded, "I do not say to you, up to seven times, but up to seventy times seven." He then told Peter a parable.

A king wanted to settle the accounts with his slaves. The large amount of money involved suggested the slaves were some kind of provincial governors who owed back taxes on the land.

The king found that one of these slaves owed him 10,000 talents. The talent was the largest denomination of money known at the time, so this pictured an amount that was 10,000 times that amount. This debt was impossible to repay.

The man's negligence and the principle of compounding interest had raised this amount to something that was impossible to repay. So, the king ordered the slave's wife and

---

[83] H. Vorländer, "Forgiveness," ed. Lothar Coenen, Erich Beyreuther, and Hans Bietenhard, *New International Dictionary of New Testament Theology*, vol. 1, (Grand Rapids, MI: Zondervan Publishing House, 1986), 697.

children be sold to pay the debt, not an unusual practice in biblical times.

But the man prostrated himself on the ground and begged for mercy, promising to repay the amount in time. Any logical person, including the king, would realize that he didn't have the ability to repay the amount he owed. So, the king did something totally unexpected. We're told in Matthew 18:27 the slave owner "felt compassion and released him and forgave him the debt." Wow! Happy ending! Not quite.

Immediately the forgiven servant went out and found a fellow slave who owed him a hundred denarii, about a hundred days' wages. When the man couldn't repay, he threw him into prison.

Word of this got back to the king. He called in the first slave who had been forgiven 10,000 talents and said, "What's the deal? I forgave you a huge amount that you never could have repaid and now you go out and throw a guy in jail because he can't repay you a measly three month's wages?"

Jesus concluded the parable by saying, "And his lord, moved with anger, handed him over to the torturers until he should repay all that was owed him. My heavenly Father will also do the same to you, if each of you does not forgive his brother from your heart." That is a dramatic climax and a powerful message about forgiveness.

So, you don't want to forgive your spouse? The clear teaching is that one who refuses to extend forgiveness even for the smallest offense, doesn't grasp the enormity of the forgiveness extended to him by his heavenly Father. And if you do not forgive, then "the torturers" await, meaning you will be cast into hell.

That's quite weighty, don't you think? This can have a major impact in marriage. In marriage we take on the debts of the one we love when they offend and hurt us, thereby owing us something. Refusal to forgive that debt means that we ignore the fact that our larger debt has been forgiven by our heavenly father.

If we drill down on this a bit, this means that each of us has piled up a list of sins that we could never repay. If you go to court for a traffic violation, the judge checks to see if you have any "priors," meaning prior offenses. If we could see our list of "priors" that God sees, it would shock and demoralize us. We could never repay the collective debt of our sin. So why do we refuse to forgive the small offenses committed against us by our spouse?

Perhaps it's because we have a wrong view of forgiveness. Forgiveness does not mean that the offense or sin committed against us is OK or that you agree with it. Forgiveness also does not mean you are obligated to continue to give someone the chance to offend you. If I loan you $10 every day for 10 days and you refuse to pay me back, I can forgive the debt. But I also don't have to continue lending you money.

An extreme example of this principle in marriage would be a husband who comes home drunk every night for a month and beats his wife and kids. Does she have to forgive? The answer is yes, but that doesn't mean she has to continue to subject herself and her kids to a dangerous situation to prove her willingness to forgive. In that case, she can still forgive him, but she needs to get out of the house with her kids.

Forgiveness means you let go what is owed to you. If someone owes you an apology – let it go! If you say, "I'll forgive you when you forgive me," – let it go! If you wait until they promise never to do it again – let it go! If you want them to admit that you were right, – let it go! If you hold on to the right to retaliate, – let it go! If you want to claim the moral superiority because their sin is worse than yours, – let it go!

Author Mike Mason comes to our rescue again:

> To the Christian, however, submission means much more: it means a willing and fearless involvement in another's sin. It does not mean complicity with sin, but it does imply a sharing of its cost, its wages. A Christian finds the strength to forgive another person, first of all in the fact of his own forgiveness, but second in the knowledge that he himself is being crushed by their sin. He must forgive, in short, or be destroyed himself.[84]

Some things can only be eradicated through forgiveness. You can't reclaim lost innocence. You will never get complete justice. You can't pull the words back out of the air once they are spoken and stuff them back into the bag. The only solution is to forgive.

A lack of forgiveness is corrosive. Like acid it will eat at your stomach because you still carry the anger of the wrong that was done to you. You might be partly at fault, but you must be fully forgiving. This is Jesus' way. And it's the only way to reconciliation.

---

[84] Mike Mason, *The Mystery of Marriage: As Iron Sharpens iron* (Portland, Oregon: Multnomah Press, 1985), 165.

Forget

Back to our young married couple. This is where it gets dicey. Solomon has complimented her and told her there is no one who compares with her. He gave her an explanation of why he didn't come home on time. He asked for forgiveness without expecting anything back from her. But she hasn't said anything to this point.

But that changes in the last two lines of Chapter 6 where there is a change in the speaker. As Solomon finishes his plea, all eyes are on her. In v. 13 she responds with a rhetorical question, "Why should you gaze at the Shulammite, as at the dance of the two companies?" The word for "companies" refers to companies of soldiers. Some say this is a sexually tinged plea from him to have her dance for him like she's entertaining the troops. But that's reading into the text and it is inconsistent with the context.

The best interpretation of this text is that Shulammite feels like she is on the spot in front of her friends who are still standing there, and she wants to talk to Solomon in private. She dismisses them with a little sarcasm, saying in effect, "Why are you staring at me like I'm some kind of lewd dancer for a bunch of soldiers?" In other words, "Get out of here. I want to talk with my husband alone."

Well done Shulammite! Friends should not be privy to these kinds of discussions. The process of reconciliation is between a husband and his wife. Relatives, friends, and other counselors don't belong in the discussion. Husbands and wives must learn to face each other and do the necessary repair work.

And now she has dismissed her friends. They are eye to eye after their first marital "fight." When Shulammite dismissed her friends, she signaled her intentions to Solomon. It was as if she was saying, "Now where were we when you knocked on the door?" She has forgotten all about what happened just a couple of hours before. It's over! Done!

This is the fruit of forgiveness. It allows you to start over. You don't have to score. You go back to where you were before the offense occurred. It restores the wounded relationship as if nothing had ever happened. Do you really want to get over it? Then you *must* forgive – and forget.

Shulammite chose to forgive because she wanted to return to the vibrant relationship she had enjoyed with her husband. They are now in a position to forget what had happened and complete their reconciliation. As happens often when true reconciliation occurs in a marriage, this drives the couple to the embrace of love.

SECTION FOUR

STAYING IN LOVE

"It is important to remember not only that the Bible for-bids sex outside marriage, but that it commends sex within marriage."

— Christopher Asch

CHAPTER ELEVEN

THE ACT OF MARRIAGE
(Song of Solomon 7:1-9)

Despite our current fascination with all things sexual, sex is one of the most distorted issues of our time. Sadly, one of these distortions sees sex as dirty and perverted. It was spawned by the Roman Catholic Church. There were all sorts of sexual perversions that permeated the Catholic Church throughout the Middle Ages.

Early church fathers Tertullian and Ambrose preferred the extinction of the human race to its propagation through the "sin" of sexual intercourse. Augustine, the great church father from the fourth century, said the sexual act was innocent in marriage but the passion that always accompanies it was sinful. A third century theologian named Origen took Matthew 19:10-12 (which clearly teaches the supremacy of marriage over celibacy) so literally that he had himself castrated before being ordained.[85]

Their perverted teaching regarding sexuality eventually resulted in the Catholic Church issuing edicts forbidding sex on Thursdays, the day of Christ's arrest, on Fridays, the day He was crucified, on Saturdays, in honor of the Blessed Virgin, and on Sundays in honor of departed saints. Are you counting? They also included bans on sex for 40-day fasts before Christmas, Easter, and Pentecost. In the end a married couple was left with only 44 days a year where they could lawfully enjoy their sexual relationship.[86]

This is what led the Catholic Church to allegorize the Song of Solomon to remove all sexual inferences. Eventually this led to the perverted teaching of the Virgin Mary and celibacy for priests in the Catholic Church.

This demented approach to sexuality carried over to the teaching of the Anglican Church when Henry VIII broke with the Catholic Church. In Victorian England, Queen Victoria, the head of the Anglican Church, said sex was "dreadful" and spoke of it as "the animal side of our nature." She advised women who had to have sex with husbands to "lie back and think of England."[87]

These are gross misinterpretations of the view of sex in the Bible. But we face different perversions today. Rather than demonizing sex as something to be hidden, we have practically made it the central point of our identity. When

---

[85] Leland Ryken, *Worldly Saints: The Puritans as They Really Were* (Grand Rapids, Michigan: 1986), 40.

[86] Philip Yancey, "Holy Sex," *Christianity Today* (October 2003), 48-49.

[87] Gary Inrig, *Whole Marriages in a Broken World; God's Design for a Healthy Marriage* (Grand Rapids, MI: Discovery House Books, 1996), 198.

the world takes the God-given gift of purity in a sexual relationship between a married man and woman and perverts it, it ends up in shame, guilt, abuse, and loss of dignity – mostly for women!

Today we regard sex as a right, not a privilege. We demand sexual gratification because "it's a basic need" just like food. So, we treat it like our fast food culture where we supersize everything and fill our plates with calories to indulge our every appetite. It seems as if our sex saturated society knows no bounds.

Unfortunately, this fascination with sex doesn't result in more and better sex. It results in the depersonalization of the act intended for the greatest degree of human intimacy, and degrades it with vile, cruel acts against thousands of innocent, naïve, or helpless individuals, all done in the name of sexual freedom.

Years ago, I performed a wedding ceremony for a young couple in our church. He was a godly young man who wanted to be pure in all his relationships. The young woman was a stunning beauty. She too professed Christ and our pre-marital counseling didn't turn up any red flags.

But within a month he came home to an empty closet and found that she was gone. She called me several weeks later. She told me a tale of sexual abuse that had dominated her life from the time she was ten years old into her teenage years. She was used as a sexual object in every form of perversion you could imagine.

When she finally got married, she felt incredible shame and didn't know how to react to the normal sexual advances of her husband. In fact, she was repulsed by sex. Stories like this have been repeated thousands of times in our sex saturated culture.

HONEYMOON SEX VS. MARITAL SEX

This chapter is about sexual love in marriage. In some ways it is more explicit than Song of Solomon 4:1-5:1 where the couple enjoyed what might be called "honeymoon" sex. So why go over the same ground again in this chapter? Is there a difference between "honeymoon" sex and "marital" sex?

The answer to that is yes. I'm going to use these terms in this chapter to describe the difference between what I wrote in Chapter 7 and this chapter. If you compare the content of Song of Solomon 4:1-5:1 with that of Song of Solomon 7:1-9, you will find some differences even though they are both talking about sex.

The difference between the two chapters is the setting of each. Chapter 4 occurs on their honeymoon night. Chapter 7 takes place after a major argument that dominates the rest of the book. It makes sense to view this as Solomon's desire to maintain a vibrant sex life even after an argument, *especially* after an argument. I will address this again at the end of this chapter but for now, think of how this section on "marital" sex might be different than the passage on "honeymoon" sex.

It's private

In this section we see Solomon and Shulammite in a virtuous and healthy sexual encounter. They are married. They have resolved their conflict through the grace of forgiveness. She has dismissed her friends and they now retreat to the privacy of their bedroom. They are now free to talk this through and pick up where they left off when Solomon appeared at the door several hours before saying, "Honey, I'm home."

That is the biggest difference between the sexual discussion in this chapter and the sexual description in Chapter 7. The argument they had could have set the tone for the defeat of their marriage. But they resolved it in an honest, mature way and are now ready to resume their marital relationship.

That's important. Sex doesn't solve a problem, but it is an important part of reconciliation. Call it "make-up" sex if you want, because it's vitally important for a couple to re-connect in the most intimate way after they have cleared the air and asked for forgiveness. Sex now communicates that nothing has changed. Sex says, "We are still committed to the same level of sexual intimacy we enjoyed before our argument."

It's more meaningful

This section in Song of Solomon 7:1-5 sounds like a repeat but it is actually more graphic in content than the account of their wedding night in Song of Solomon 4:1-5:1. Solomon exhibits a poet's ability to craft pictures that portray deeper truths than the physical. This is a desperately needed corrective to the dominant view of sex as purely a physical desire.

Solomon is not just describing his wife's body here. He is describing a unique set of characteristics that increases his love for her. He knows her better now that they have been through their first fight. His words are deeper and sweeter as he contemplated the object of his love.

Every woman has hips and breasts and lips and the other body parts Solomon mentions. But these don't make sex intimate. Men can function sexually with any woman. But he is domesticated in a good way and drawn to one woman through his increasing knowledge of her inner qualities that he has never known in any other woman. This is what Solomon reveals in this passage as opposed to the earlier account of their wedding night.

There is one other thing about the setting we should notice. In the previous account of her physical attractiveness in Song of Solomon 4:1-5:1, Solomon began his description of Shulammite's beauty from the top of her head and worked his way down, though he never described anything below her waist.

In Song of Solomon 7:1, Solomon begins his description of her body with her feet and works his way up to the top of her head. Is that significant? Yes, it is. Think back on Shulammite's words in Song of Solomon 5:3 when she gave her transparent excuse for not getting out of bed to unlock the door for him. She said, "I had bathed my feet, how could I soil them?"

Now he began his description of her with her feet. Could it be that he had bowed before her and was washing her feet? We're reminded of the need to wash feet after one had walked outside in the desert climate and we know Shulammite had gone outside to look for Solomon. What a setting to demonstrate the powerful nature of forgiveness as well as a compelling enticement to fall into each other's arms as they weep over their estrangement and renew their love through having sex.

In the following list from Song of Solomon 7:1-5, Solomon uses 10 metaphors to describe Shulammite's personal characteristics that increased his love for her:

1. Trustworthy – v. 1 – "How beautiful are your feet in sandals, O prince's daughter!" Wealthy homes and palaces in Bible times had tile floors covered with beautiful rugs. Slaves and women went barefoot but sandals were worn by those trusted to go outside and return. He saw her as a "prince's daughter" because she was royalty and he could trust her.

2. Sacred femininity – v. 1b – "The curves of your hips are like jewels, the work of the hands of an artist." This refers to her thighs, hips, and loins as a reference to her reproductive organs. The curve of her hips as the "work of the hands of an artist" refers to the unique shape of a woman that Solomon found sexually attractive. This is one of the marvels of God's masterful artistry that is not only attractive to a man, but physically necessary to allow a woman to conceive, carry, and birth a baby.

3. Happiness – v. 2 – "Your navel is like a round goblet which never lacks mixed wine" Wine was a sign of celebration and joy. Solomon was saying, "You make me happy!"

4. Fruitfulness – v. 2b – "Your belly is like a heap of wheat fenced about with lilies." This pictured wheat that

was thrashed and winnowed. Often rows of heaped wheat were fenced to prevent them from blowing away. Flowers were planted around them in celebration of the bounty of the harvest. Her belly also held the potential fruitfulness of housing a child.

5. Propriety – v. 3 – "Your two breasts are like two fawns, twins of a gazelle." Fawns are baby deer or in this case, gazelles. They are known for being swift and shy, alluding to her being shy about displaying her body, a sense of propriety.

6. Strength and purity – v. 4 – "Your neck is like a tower of ivory" Watchtowers were often erected on the walls of a city to demonstrate strength and vigilance. The color of ivory depicted purity. Solomon saw this quality when he first met her in Chapter 1.

7. Refreshment – v. 4b – "Your eyes like the pools in Heshbon by the gate of Bath-rabbim." Heshbon was a Levitical city, so priests would have lived there. The pools were deep pools used for storing water. Solomon saw a deep sense of holiness in her eyes. He saw refreshing forgiveness in her eyes – not accusation.

8. Security – v. 4c – "Your nose is like the tower of Lebanon, which faces toward Damascus." Men, don't say this to your wife unless you understand what you are talking about! This is not a reference to a big nose. Since there is no known tower of Lebanon, Solomon is referring to the mountains that overlooked Damascus which was the seat of power for the Assyrian Empire to the north of Israel. The Assyrians were a perennial enemy of Israel, so Solomon was particularly

interested in what went on north of his border. The nose is the dominant feature of the face, so Solomon is saying that one of the primary characteristics of his wife was her alertness and wisdom. He could trust her to be aware of dangers and attacks against him.

9. Exemplary – v. 5 – "Your head crowns you like Carmel." Mt. Carmel is on a range of mountains that dominates the western coast of Israel. It is visible to all. Solomon considered her as someone who is worthy of being seen and emulated by all.

10. Honorable – 5b – "And the flowing locks of your head are like purple threads; the king is captivated by your tresses." Solomon has previously commented on her raven black hair that she took down in his presence. But the emphasis here is on the color purple which was either a purple thread or the sheen of her dark black hair in the light. Purple was the color of royalty. He felt that his wife brought honor to his throne.

These character qualities are what distinguish this section from the "honeymoon sex" section in Song of Solomon 4:1-5:1. Solomon saw qualities in his wife that he had not seen before. No other man would have known these things about her. This is the thrill of a growing relationship. This makes the act of making love even more meaningful because of this unique knowledge that no one else sees.

Whenever men are asked to comment on the deeper character qualities of their wife, they usually say something like, "I just can't do that. I'm no Romeo." Well, guess what men? You may not be a Romeo, but you're married to Juliet. And her heart is longing for some *Juliet talk* before you get to your *Romeo part*.

Physical body parts are certainly necessary for sex and they are a major component of a man's sexual attraction to a woman. This physical, sexual attraction is part of God's gift to every married couple.

But every woman possesses the same body parts. However, every woman does not possess the same ten character qualities Solomon admired in his wife. Finding similar qualities in your wife and expressing them is more important to a vibrant sex life than a recitation of physical qualities. This is what turns sex into "making love."

Men, if you want to unlock your wife's heart, find something you admire about her character and tell her about it. You might want to comment on her constant smile and cheerfulness, or her willingness to live within your budget. You might tell her how much you appreciate her hard work and her desire to learn. It will go a long way in expressing your love if you tell her that you trust and respect her, and that you admire her devotion to the Lord and your family.

It's more pleasant

Solomon's poetic chops continue. As the chapter unfolds, we see the movement from foreplay to intercourse to rest afterward in an innocent and beautiful expression of marital sex.

In doing so it's important to note that sex is not presented as the natural culmination of reconciling after an argument. Sex is not the answer to marital discord. The hard process we outlined in the last three chapters is. Better sex won't solve misunderstandings or make for a better relationship. *You have to solve the problems first!*

But sex is certainly a pleasurable part of the marital experience. Solomon proceeds to describe the sexual encounter with his wife. In v. 6 he sums up all her charms by proclaiming, "How beautiful and how delightful you are, my love, with all your charms!" Solomon is caught up in the whole package. His wife was beautiful, she was devoted to him, he deeply respected her, and he wanted to make love to her.

Verse 7 introduces some graphic pictures of sex. He remarks, "Your stature is like a palm tree, and your breasts are like its clusters." Palm trees grow tall and slender. The fruit of the palm tree hangs in clusters at the top of the tree. The round, firm appearance of the cluster reminds Solomon of her breasts.

His intentions are clear in the next verse. "I said, 'I will climb the palm tree, I will take hold of its fruit stalks.' Oh, may your breasts be like clusters of the vine, and the fragrance of your breath like apples." This isn't hard to understand. His determination is seen in the verb "I said," meaning "I think I will," or "I want to," or simply "Yes!" When he says, "Oh, may your breasts . . .," he is using a form of exultation like "Oh, let me have your breasts . . ."[88] A contemporary Solomon might say, "Ohhhhh, yeah!"

He finishes his description in v. 8, saying, " And your mouth like the best wine!" Everything about her is fulfilling and satisfying. She doesn't even have bad breath! The taste of her kiss is like prize winning wine.

---

[88] Graham S. Ogden and Lynell Zogbo, *A Handbook on the Song of Songs*, UBS Handbook Series (New York: United Bible Societies, 1998), 205.

And Shulammite responds. In the last half of v. 9 she addresses "my beloved" which is used exclusively by Shulammite. She responds, "It goes down smoothly for my beloved, flowing gently through the lips of those who fall asleep." After all of his talking she may have been saying, "Shut up and kiss me!" She felt the same satisfying passion that he did. This is how God intended sex to be.

Sex is the icing on the cake, but it is not the cake. Sex is God's gracious design for the most pleasant physical encounter men and women can experience on earth. God's plan in Genesis 2:22 tells us that after He created woman out of the rib of the man, He "brought her to the man." God designed woman as a gift for man, not a playmate, but a "helpmate."

We've all heard the jokes about men needing help and it's true. But a man needs the softness, the gentleness, and the sensitivity of a woman to complete him. And guess what? Women need men too. In general, men are physically stronger, more task oriented, and use their strength and creativity to protect, design and build things that provide for their families and culture at large.

Genesis 2:23 contains Adam's exclamation of delight when he first saw Eve. He said, "This is now bone of my bones, and flesh of my flesh; she shall be called Woman, because she was taken out of Man." The literal translation of the first phrase is "this time." Adam was overjoyed because he had named Mr. and Mrs. Giraffe, Mr. and Mrs. Lion, and even Mr. and Mrs. Cockatoo, but he looked around and there was no "Mrs. Adam." Now there was! "Finally, a mate for me!"

Genesis 2:24 continues, "For this reason a man shall leave his father and his mother, and be joined to his wife; and they shall become one flesh." Adam didn't have a mother or a father, but He is God's pattern for the future generations of all mankind.

The word for "joined" means "cling, stick to, follow closely, keep close to, join to." It can also refer to welding two pieces of metal together (Isaiah 41:7) and carries the sense of "clinging to someone in affection and loyalty." We see the word in Jeremiah 13:11 where "the waistband clings to the waist of a man, so I made the whole household of Israel ...cling to Me."[89]

The picture of *one flesh* is a double picture of a man and a woman intertwined in sex almost as if they are trying to become one, and the creation of a baby that comes out of that union. Nothing comes as close to the image of two people becoming one flesh as sexual union. In marriage it brings joy to God as well as a husband and wife.

Solomon is saying that marital sex is more pleasant than honeymoon sex. His description is more expressive. Their sex here comes after an argument, so the feelings are more intense. There are tears of sorrow and repentance mixed in with the joy of ecstasy. Call it *make-up* sex if you want. Only lovers who have felt the arrows of sharp words can fully appreciate the soothing refreshment of forgiveness and restoration in marital sex.

That's not to say that *make-up* sex is the only reason that marital sex is more pleasurable. As couples grow older they

---

[89] Earl S. Kalland, "398 קָבַד," ed. R. Laird Harris, Gleason L. Archer Jr., and Bruce K. Waltke, *Theological Wordbook of the Old Testament* (Chicago: Moody Press, 1999), 177.

relax and don't feel the pressure of sexual performance as much. They also learn more of what brings pleasure to each other and grow in their desire to make sex pleasing for both people.

The constant wonder of God's gift to married partners is enough to thank God for the blessing of continued sexual encounters throughout the married life. Every young married couple should look forward to this continued wonder.

HINDRANCES TO MARITAL SEX

Sexual intimacy is so important that I want to offer some suggestions for holding onto this wonder. I'm speaking here of marital sex, not honeymoon sex. There is very little that will stand in the way of honeymoon sex. *But the joy of marital sex can be dulled and even killed by inadequate attention.* This isn't exhaustive but let me suggest some "joy killers" of romance in marriage:

1. Sin – Romance dies when wounds go unhealed. Sinful words, actions, resentments, and attitudes that go unconfessed go unforgiven. When this happens the two retreat to their corners and romance dies. Proverbs 18:19 says, "A brother (or sister) offended is harder to be won than a strong city, and contentions are like the bars of a citadel." *Learn to actively cultivate* confession, repentance, and forgiveness in your marriage. Your sex life will suffer if you don't.

2. A wandering eye – The tsunami of pornographic images creates a thirst for perfection which is

unattainable and unquenchable. Sex outside of marriage can't deliver what it promises because God didn't design it that way. Solomon came to know this from first-hand experience. He wrote about the pain of sexual sin in Proverbs 5:3-14, "For the lips of an adulteress drip honey and smoother than oil is her speech; But in the end she is bitter as wormwood, sharp as a two-edged sword. Her feet go down to death, her steps take hold of Sheol." To those who commit adultery he warns, "you will give your vigor to others," and "strangers will be filled with your strength," resulting in wasted years, physical consumption, and utter ruin.

3. <u>Laziness</u> – After the wedding, the mundane nature of life takes over too easily. This leads to romantic laziness and boredom in the bedroom. Men, remember that you are a *microwave* and your wife is a *crockpot.* If you forget this, you might be left with leftovers or cold pizza. There is nothing wrong with spontaneity, but romance takes time and effort. If you don't know what your wife thinks is romantic, ask her. Then do it!

4. <u>Kids</u> – Ya gotta love 'em but they do complicate your love life. A wife especially needs to remember that she was a wife before she was a mom. Couples need to have a lock on their bedroom door and regularly plan for time away from the kids. They are not your first priority. Your husband or wife is. If you don't prioritize like this, when your kids are gone you won't know each other. Believe it or not, this is also healthy for your kids too.

5. <u>Age</u> – The passing of time adds pounds and lines to everyone, and your gym time, facial cremes, diets, and supplements can't stop it. But that doesn't mean you have to lose the romance. Don't believe the lie that only people with perfect bodies can enjoy sex. That's not true! Many studies show that married people are more satisfied with their sex lives than singles, and that continues into their 50s, 60s, and beyond. Sex is not just physical, it's mental. Just ask the empty nesters you know. They're the ones smiling right now because they know what I mean.

6. *Rumors and lies* – Don't fall for the lies that married people are boring and out of touch with modern thinking, that everyone "falls out of love" in marriage and needs some extra-curricular activity to "spice up" their marriage, that better "technique" makes for better sex, that pornography is a healthy outlet for sex, or that marriage should be some kind of transcendent experience that brings ultimate fulfillment.

Let me close this chapter on a repetitive note to men. Guys, if you expect "honeymoon" sex only, you might get sex for a night, but not for the long term. A woman is more than a body, and sex is more than rubbing flesh together. Sex is the culmination of a thousand other things that bind a couple together. Solomon provided a wonderful example here. Learn from it and your sex life will be as satisfying for both of you and it will "stay," as we see in the next chapter.

"A good marriage is the closest thing on earth to the realization of a practical, enduring, and loving coexistence between people. It is a sign, a spiritual and social and political example, of depths of love and patience and forgiveness that are unknown in other areas of life."

—— Mike Mason

CHAPTER TWELVE

MAKING LOVE STAY

(Song of Solomon 7:10-13)

I don't know where this came from, but it illustrates the natural tendency toward letting love die in marriage. See if you can relate.

THE SEVEN AGES OF THE MARRIED COLD

1st year – "Sugar dumpling. I'm really worried about my baby girl! You've got a bad sniffle and there's no telling about these things with all the strep going around. I'm putting you in the hospital this afternoon for a general check-up and a good rest. I know the food is lousy there, so I'll be bringing you food from Tonsini's. I've already got it all arranged with the floor superintendent."

2nd year – "Listen darling. I don't like the sound of that cough! I've called Dr. Miller to rush over here. Now you go to bed like a good little girl for Papa."

3rd year – "Maybe you better lie down, honey. Nothing like a little rest when you feel bad. I'll bring you something. Is there any canned soup?"

4th year – "Now look dear, be sensible! After you've fed the kids, washed the dishes and finished vacuuming, you'd better lie down."

5th year – "Why don't you take a couple of aspirin?"

6th year – "If you'd just gargle or something instead of sitting around barking like a seal!"

7th year – "For Pete's sake, stop sneezing! You'll be giving me pneumonia!"

We laugh at the potential realism because it's true for many marriages. But it doesn't have to be. In good marriages, love changes and grows over the years. It doesn't become stagnant. But it takes work. The question is, how do you keep 1st year love from devolving into 7th year apathy? As songwriter Dan Fogelberg asked years ago, "How do you make love stay?"

Every couple who is serious about their marriage seeks an answer to this. Solomon and Shulammite exhibit some qualities that help answer that question.

Desire

Following the sexual encounter that capped their reconciliation in the previous verses, the young couple continues to talk about their relationship. In Song of Solomon 7:10

Shulammite speaks, repeating a phrase she has used twice before but building on the meaning this time.

In Song of Solomon 2:16 she said, "My beloved is mine, and I am his; he pastures his flock among the lilies," indicating her desire to be regarded differently than the prostitutes who followed shepherds around trying to sell their services or find a husband. In Song of Solomon 6:3 she adds a reciprocal phrase, "I am my beloved's and my beloved is mine, he who pastures his flock among the lilies," indicating their mutual commitment even in the middle of conflict.

Her usage of the term in Song of Solomon 7:10 indicates a maturation of her love, noting, "I am my beloved's, and his desire is for me." Is there any difference in her meaning? The answer is yes, given the context of their recent conflict. After their reconciliation she recognizes that her questions about his commitment to her were unfounded. She now acknowledges his "desire" for her shows his commitment to her.

It's also likely from the most recent context that "desire" also has a sexual connotation. His words and actions leading up to their sexual intimacy obviously show that his sexual desire for her was strong. And her response shows she loved it.

Maintaining sexual desire usually isn't much of a problem for a man, but unless the couple work at it, the woman can end up feeling used and uninterested. Dr. Willard Harley in his book entitled *His Needs, Her Needs* points out the differing priorities of men and women in his studies:

A man desires:
1. Sexual fulfillment
2. Recreational companionship

3. An attractive spouse
4. Domestic support
5. Admiration of his wife

A woman desires:
1. Affection
2. Conversation
3. Honesty and Openness
4. Financial Support
5. Family Commitment[90]

Of course, this list isn't ultimate truth, but it's interesting to note the lack of sexual fulfillment anywhere on the woman's list. That doesn't mean women aren't interested. It just means that the things listed are the ways she perceives love. A husband who fails to understand that will feel his wife pull away from him over the years, especially if he thinks that having more sex will solve the problem.

PLANNING

Song of Solomon 7:11 takes us into uncharted territory for many married couples. Shulammite is speaking and, actually gives four commands, "Come, my beloved, let us go out into the country," followed by "let us spend the night in the villages," followed by, "Let us rise early and go to the vineyards," and finally, "let us see whether the vine has budded

---

[90] Willard F. Harley Jr., *His Needs, Her Needs: Building an Affair Proof Marriage* (Grand Rapids, MI: Revell, 2001), 18.

216

and its blossoms have opened, and whether the pomegranates have bloomed."

What is this? A bossy lady making plans without telling him? I don't think we have to see it that way. Up until this time Solomon pursued her by telling her where to meet him, coming to her house to court her, introducing her to his family and friends in the palace, and planning the wedding.

But now she is finding her voice. Maybe she realized that she had put him off in their misunderstanding and she wanted to make up for it by showing him that she really did want to spend time with him. Whatever it was, she had some definitive ideas. This illustrates how important it is to listen to your wife's voice.

Years ago, Anne and I were having one of those "I don't know what's wrong, but I can see you're upset about something" conversations late at night lying in bed staring at the ceiling in the dark. Several things came up but the one I remember the most is my dear, sweet, quiet wife who wants to please me in every way she can, telling me, "You make all the decisions."

Mind you, she wasn't really complaining or rebelling in any way. What she meant was that I seldom consulted her on various issues in our life. When I probed a little, she said that I always picked what kind of car she had and where we go on vacation. I must admit that my first reaction was, "So?" But I recovered a bit of sanity to ask her what she meant. She ended up telling me that her preference would be to have a smaller car and she would like to go to the Oregon coast on vacation some time.

Wow! Is that all? Now, I'm 6'4" and I like big cars or trucks, so when I asked her what kind of car *she* wanted I was afraid she was going to say a Toyota or some other dinky car that I couldn't fit into. So, when she said she had always wanted a Mustang I readily agreed. That's a small car I could get enthused about. Was I glad I asked!

Our kids were older by that time. We didn't need a larger car anymore, so we ended up buying a used Mustang – a convertible! We were both happy. She still has a Mustang convertible and she even lets me drive it once in a while. And the next year we enjoyed a wonderful vacation traveling through Northern California up to the Oregon Coast.

My point is that I needed to listen to the voice of my wife. Planning is a corporate responsibility. Marriage is not a one-way street with the guy making all the decisions. Shulammite expressed her desires here and no doubt Solomon welcomed that. This has nothing to do with roles in the marriage. 1 Peter 3:7 says wives are to be honored as "fellow heirs of the grace of life." Part of a grace-filled marriage is working together on planning.

TIME

It's also instructive to notice what she suggested. In Song of Solomon 7:11b she said, "let us spend the night in the villages." She's saying, "Let's get out of town." They were in the palace in Jerusalem so it's possible that the disagreement they had was because he was spending too much time at work. It's possible she was thinking that time in the country where she grew up might be helpful.

She grew up outside tending vineyards. They met while he was tending his flock of sheep. They dated among the cedar and cypress trees. There is something refreshing about being outside. It clears the brain, slows things down a bit, and helps us get in touch with God's creation. That's a good proposal any time, but especially after a stressful time of tension or disagreement.

We also saw that she knew where he had probably gone when he fled into the night. In Song of Solomon 6:2 she said, "My beloved has gone down to his garden, to the beds of balsam, to pasture his flock in the gardens and gather lilies." And v. 11 tells us she was right. He had been in his "man cave," his comfort zone. He went down to his orchards and to the stables to check on his chariots and horses.

So, notice what she was doing. She was saying that she wanted to go spend time *doing something he wanted to do!* That doesn't necessarily mean that she enjoyed it. But she wanted to enter his world. She wanted to share it with him. She may have been thinking of this as a business trip away from home or merely as a vacation. It's clear that she wanted to spend some time with him alone.

I'm not trying to build a theology of vacations here. I'm just pointing out that Shulammite was expressing her desire to spend some time with her husband. This isn't a mandate of Scripture, but the principle of rest is present in the creation account as well as God's instructions on the Sabbath and the various festivals in the Old Testament.

This doesn't mean you have to spend a lot of time or money on this. My dad worked two jobs to support a family of eleven kids, so he didn't have much time for this kind of "getaway" with my mom. In fact, I doubt if they had a weekend with just the two of them in over thirty years. That doesn't mean they didn't love and cherish each other. It just meant they didn't have the time or money to splurge like that.

But if you can, this type of getaway is important for your marriage. Shulammite's request is the equivalent of "Let's get away to Maui or Cancun or the local Marriott or Motel 6." You don't have to spend a lot of money. The point is for you to be together.

Shut off your computer. Unplug your phone and take a walk. Plot a "staycation" where you drop the kids off at a friend's house, get a pizza and watch a game or Hallmark movie on TV. Come on guys, it won't kill you. If you can, splurge and go to the mountains, the beach, the desert or the big city – anyplace that you can afford, and you can be alone. Just do it!

MUTUALITY

Lest there be any doubt about Shulammite's enthusiasm for a sexual relationship with her husband, look at the last line of Song of Solomon 7:12, "There I will give you my love." She is as interested in a vibrant sex life as he is. While God has created man to take the initiative in sex, that doesn't mean that He designed the woman to be a disinterested spectator.

A wife an take the initiative in a number of ways. She can plan for the obvious. Shulammite isn't just suggesting a getaway. I don't think she's thinking only about walking around the old home place and catching up on things. She is thinking about being with her husband for the purpose of sexual enjoyment.

There is nothing wrong with a woman clearing the calendar, planning an early dinner and putting the kids down early and letting her husband know that she is available. I'm sure he won't mind! After all – what's more important – finishing your housework, falling asleep in front of the TV – or taking time to enjoy the gift God has given you in each other?

A woman might also get a book like *Sex, Romance, and the Glory of God* by C.J. Mahaney and ask her husband if he would like to read it with her. I predict he'll take the bait and read it with you. There is plenty of great advice in that book.

But Mahaney also gives a good example of bad advice in his book. He quotes a book written in 1894 called, *Instruction and Advice For the Young Bride on the Conduct and Procedure of the Intimate and Personal Relationships of the Marriage State for the Greater Spiritual Sanctity of this Blessed Sacrament and the Glory of God*, by a woman named Ruth Smythers, who was the wife of Pastor L.D. Smythers. She explains there may be a positive side of the wedding but:

> On the negative side, there is the wedding night, during which the bride must "pay the piper," so to speak, by facing for the first time the terrible ordeal of sex.
>
> At this point, dear reader, let me concede one shocking truth. Some young women actually anticipate the wedding night ordeal with curiosity and pleasure. Beware such an attitude! A selfish

and sensual husband can easily take advantage of such a bride. One cardinal rule of marriage should never be forgotten: GIVE LITTLE, GIVE SELDOM, AND ABOVE ALL, GIVE GRUDGINGLY! Otherwise, what could have become a proper marriage could become an orgy of sexual lust.[91]

I'm not sure what that lady had in her background, but I pity poor Mr. Smythers and all the young women who took that advice. May her tribe not increase! 'Nuff said.

ROMANCE

The last ingredient in keeping the flame alive is romance. I'm not talking about Hallmark cards or boxes of chocolate or flowers. If those things do it for you, fine. I think Shulammite had something different in mind in v. 13 when she continued, "The mandrakes have given forth fragrance; and over our doors are all choice fruits, both new and old, which I have saved up for you, my beloved."

Mandrakes were some kind of "love apple" thought to be sexually stimulating. Whether they were or not, Shulammite invited it. Romance isn't just the act of sex. It's everything that goes along with it. Each person should explore what things are sexually stimulating for them and let their spouse know what it is. If you don't know, ask them. As long as it isn't physically repulsive to either one or motivated by some

---

[91] C.J. Mahaney, *Sex, Romance, and the Glory of God: What Every Christian Husband Needs to Know (Wheaton,* Illinois: Crossway Books, 2004), 107.

kind of kinky sex trick learned from a porn-site, the couple is free to explore it.

Shulammite continues in v. 13, "over all our doors are all choice fruits." The same picture was used on their wedding night in Song of Solomon 4:16. Remember that she invited him to "come into his garden and eat its choice fruits!" That verse is the exact middle of the book, indicating the central theme Solomon wanted to communicate.

She wasn't shy. She also indicated in v. 13 that all their choice fruits were "both new and old." There's nothing that can throw a wet blanket on your sex life like boredom. If sex degenerates into ritualistic habits, one or the other will soon lose interest. Different times, places, and environments – some new and some old – help to keep the spice in your sex life. Again, this is only true if both people are open for it and it doesn't destroy the trust between them.

These were all things "which I have saved up for you, my beloved." Solomon was the recipient of a willing wife's desire to be sexually pleasing to him. He was always "my beloved," to her and she was always "beautiful and pleasant" to him.

Remember men – you must touch her heart and soul before you touch her body. I believe that's why Shulammite expressed herself so freely here. His foreplay was planned and exquisite in detail. He paid her the highest compliments and communicated incredible value and trust before he approached her sexually.

Robert Capon summarized the marriage bed this way:

> The bed is the heart of the home, the arena of love,
> the seedbed of life, and the one constant point of

meeting. It is the place where, night by night, forgiveness and fair speech return that the sun may
not go down on our wrath; where the perfunctory
kiss and the entirely ceremonial pat on the backside
become unction and grace. It is the oldest, friend-
liest thing in anybody's marriage, the first used and
the last left, and no one can praise it enough."[92]

It seems difficult for most people to think of romance as
something they have to work at. After all, in the movies it just
happens. But, like anything else that is worthwhile in life, if
someone doesn't think about it in advance, it's not going to
happen. Feelings that aren't expressed in actions are often
neglected and forgotten.

Why not do a little survey of your romantic inclinations
with your spouse. Find out where each would like to go for a
getaway. Ask about what things on Harley's list at the beginning of the chapter are important to your mate. The goal is
not to get what you want, it's to find out what your husband or
wife wants. That will go a long way in making your love stay.

---

[92] Robert Farrar Capon, quoted in Debra Evans, *The Mystery of Womanhood*
(Wheaton, Ill.: Crossway Books, 1987), 265.

"Married people enjoy better mental and physical health, and generate greater wealth, more career satisfaction and less boredom and loneliness. What's more, married people are more satisfied with their sex lives...and they live substantially longer lives."

—— Linda J. Waite and Maggie Gallagher

CHAPTER THIRTEEN

CHRISTOPHER LOVE'S LOVE
(Song of Solomon 8:1-6)

Christopher Love is aptly named. He was a Welsh Presbyterian minister during the English Civil War. In 1651, he was executed by the English government because of his stance as a Puritan pastor against the Church of England. The day he was executed, his wife was allowed to pray with him in the London Tower.

As he rose from his knees after praying, he said to his wife,

"I beg of thee, when I am gone to heaven tomorrow, not to be troubled to hear that I shall not make mention of thee or thine in my prayers when I am upon the scaffold, for I cannot do it but natural affections do arise that will not be suitable for

225

the place, but be assured that the last words that I shall speak in this room shall be to God for those and thine."[93]

You're probably not facing martyrdom, but the love shared by Christopher Love and his wife is the kind of love everyone wants in marriage. In the next two chapters we will listen in as Mr. and Mrs. Solomon reflect on the nature of marriage that fosters that kind of love.

PUBLIC EXPECTATIONS

Shulammite picks up Solomon's poetic flare in Song of Solomon 8:1 by declaring, "Oh that you were like a brother to me who nursed at my mother's breasts. If I found you outdoors, I would kiss you; no one would despise me, either." Most likely this refers to the custom that the only men a woman could touch in public were her father or brothers. Touching your husband in public was viewed as an improper sexual display.

Personal practice

Shulammite was willing to defer to the expectations of her world regarding a woman touching her husband in public. That is not a biblical mandate. But it was still an honorable act on her part. And Solomon didn't force the issue because

---

[93] Don Kistler, *A Spectacle Unto God: The Life and Death of Christopher Love* (Grand Rapids, MI: Soli Deo Gloria Publications, 1994), 94.

he too was willing to place the importance of social expectations over his personal desires.

We see this principle of meeting public expectations a number of times in the Bible:

1. In Genesis 30, Jacob honored his father-in-law by working another seven years for Rachel even after Laban had deceived him.
2. In Ruth 2:5, when Ruth was presented to Boaz, he asked "Whose young woman is this?" They didn't just run off and get married. Boaz had to honor the legal right of redemption before he could marry Ruth.
3. In 1 Corinthians 7:36-38, the father is seen as the one who gives permission for his daughter to get married. This isn't a biblical command but was widely observed. Obtaining this family blessing is still important if a couple wants to share birthdays, holidays, and special events with extended family.

Of course, the proprieties of public perception change from time to time. They were not the same in Solomon's time or even in the New Testament era when Jesus walked the earth. Jewish culture and expectations were much different then.

Jewish weddings were always very public affairs during Bible times. They were usually arranged by the fathers and the young couple then became "betrothed," or engaged. During that time, they hardly saw each other let alone had a chance to touch. At the wedding the whole town joined in the weeklong celebration that included the family and friends waiting outside while the couple consummated their vows.

At various times public expectations of married couples have included such things as buying boxes of seats at churches for the family, men and women being seated on the opposite side of the church building during public services, and women wearing dresses and hats and men wearing suits to church.

In our "anything goes" culture, there are few cultural expectations that impinge on the freedom of couples. But there may be isolated family or cultural taboos that a mature couple will honor as long as they don't have harmful implications.

Personal expression

But her cultural awareness didn't prevent Shulammite from expressing her desire. She might have been proper on the outside but on the inside, she was saying, "I wish that you were like my brother so that I could display my love for you in public as well as privately." We're not quite as offended about this in our culture though "pretzel people" wrapped around each other in public still make most people say, "Get a room!"

Her expression expands her definition of love beyond the physical intimacy seen in the previous chapter. Every married couple realizes that marriage is not filled with sexually tinged moments. The routine of life dominates. We all have to work, raise our kids, pay the bills, maintain the house – and find time for each other.

But this doesn't mean that certain public expressions of love are improper for us today. Who cares if the kids are embarrassed by seeing Mom and Dad kiss or hug in public? So what! They may not admit it, but it provides security and teaches them about marital love. It's what makes kids grow up and say, "I want a marriage just like mom and dad's."

Though not allowed in Solomon's time, non-sexual touching is also a foundational means of expression. This is especially important for a woman to know that every touch doesn't lead to the bedroom. A woman in counseling once told me that her husband never told her he loved her, and never touched her unless he wanted sex, leaving her feeling like nothing more than a five-cent slot machine. He was sitting right beside her and didn't even blink. What a guy!

Even non-verbal touching communicates deeply. It speaks of companionship, understanding, partnership, solidarity, and respect. When I reach for Anne's hand as we walk by the touristy gift shops in Carmel I'm telling her, "I can't stand to rummage through one more store filled with trinkets and junk, but I love you and I'm willing to do it with a smile because I enjoy just walking through life with you."

And I love the "worship touch." Singing at church is greatly enhanced for me when I'm standing with my hands firmly planted in my pockets (my preferred position) and she slips her arm through mine as we sing together. As I put my arm around her as we sing, it reminds me of the most important things in life that touch both of us deeply.

Private intimacy

But Shulammite also expresses the private side of the institution of marriage in Song of Solomon 8:2 when she states, "I would lead you and bring you into the house of my mother, who used to instruct me; I would give you spiced wine to drink from the juice of my pomegranates." We are left again with interpreting the poetic picture she presents but it continues to use her brother as an example.

Her word pictures allude to the privacy of a sexual rendezvous. If Solomon were her brother, she could take him into her mother's house without anyone saying anything. But the "house of my mother" is not the perfect place for sexual passion. That's a little weird actually. Sort of like kissing your sister. But her intentions are clear. She said, "I want to 'lead you and bring you ...and give you spiced wine to drink.'"

But think about her timing. In Song of Solomon 7:12 she suggested they go to the country and "there I will give you my love." So here they are at mom's house near Galilee and she wants to make love to him, but obviously, without public scrutiny. These are all clear messages from her that revealed her desire and intent to make love to her husband. Being at mom's house didn't diminish her sexual appetite one bit. I'm sure Solomon agreed.

MARRIAGE IS TAUGHT AT HOME

Shulammite also noted the instruction from her mother. For most people, advice from mom and dad on sex is about as welcome as the mumps. Unfortunately, our culture has created such a self-obsessed youth culture that most young people think of their parents as buffoons and idiots on almost every issue. Asking parents for advice is like asking Fred and Wilma Flintstone.

That might be true for most kids because the vast majority of parents aren't capable of giving solid, biblically centered advice on love and marriage because they wouldn't know where to start. But that's not the case with Shulammite and Solomon.

Shulammite exhibits a healthy trust in the instruction she received from her mother on the subject. Her reference to "my mother, who used to instruct me" in Song of Solomon 8:2 probably referred specifically to sexual instruction from mom since this was her line of her thinking at the moment. Nothing wrong with that. That's where sexual instruction should take place.

Moms need to take their daughters aside and teach them about how their bodies function. They need to tell them what a boy will want to do but that sex is for their husbands. Daughters need to know that at some time sex will be one of the prime sources of enjoyment in her life.

Dads aren't off the hook either. Dads need to teach boys what will happen to their bodies. They need to tell them what the slang terms about sex mean. Boys need to learn about what their sexual energy will feel like and how to properly channel that into creating a family with a wife. Unfortunately, boys need to know about pornography and how it can damage an accurate perception of women and sex. This means helping them set protocols for their digital devices to handle temptation.

A couple words of advice on having these discussions with your kids may be helpful. Do it before they reach puberty and before they hear about it from their friends or in school. Control sleepovers and monitor all access to your kid's minds through friends, media, and other adults, especially those you don't know well.

Don't expect a "discussion" about sex. Your talk will probably be a one way street. Before puberty it's probable that they won't have any idea about what you're talking about or even have any interest in it. To them it's kind of like having a discussion about potty training. But at some point, they will want to know all about it so don't be surprised if the timing takes you by surprise.

That happened to me. Years ago, a friend called Anne and asked if she would take her to the hospital. I was watching TV and our daughter asked me where mom had gone.

"She went to the hospital with Susan."

"Why? What's wrong with her?"

"She's having some problems."

"What kind of problems?"

"Female problems."

"What kind of female problems?

"Well, she's bleeding."

"Bleeding! Where is she bleeding?"

"Down there."

"Why is she bleeding from down there!?"

"It's because of her period."

"What's a period?"

So, I turned off Magnum P.I. and had "the talk" with my seven-year old daughter. Talk about surprised! Like

Shulammite, I thought that was the mom's job, but there I was. I went into as much detail as I thought she could absorb. I explained ovaries, eggs (no, not scrambled), sperm, the placenta, and the growth of babies.

When I explained the initial fertilization process, she looked at me quizzically like she wanted to ask, "How did they get in there?" So I told her. At the end I tried to explain the birth process in a way that wouldn't give her nightmares. When I got done, she said, "Oh," and went to bed. End of discussion. No more questions. Good job dad, and her mom owed me big time!

Shulammite seems to be suggesting that her mother's instruction was not enough. In Song of Solomon 8:2 she said, "my mother who used to instruct me," implying "but not anymore." She is thinking "if I could be alone with you 'I would give you spiced wine to drink from the juice of my pomegranates.'"

This is a clear reference to sexual pleasures. Mom gave the textbook instruction and now she wanted to give him the practical application. In v. 3 she even expresses her desire to "Let his left hand be under my head and his right hand embrace me." She has used this before as a description of his embrace when she was overcome with emotion, but this time it seems like a clear picture of sexual embrace.

And then in v. 4 the daughters of Jerusalem pop up for the last time as she implores, "I want you to swear, O daughters of Jerusalem, do not arouse or awaken my love until she pleases." This is the third time this phrase has been used. In Song of Solomon 2:7 it referenced not giving in to sexual passion in the dating relationship. In Song of Solomon 3:5 it is used to check her pre-marital jitters.

But this time is different. Given the way she locked him out of the bedroom in Chapter 5, it's probable that she didn't want to use sex in that way again. She also didn't want to seduce her husband in a way that ignored the reconciliation process. She wanted her friends to hold her accountable for the right usage of sex in her marriage.

The privacy of a vibrant sex life must be preserved, or it can become weaponized or misused by both parties. A wife can withhold sex or use it seductively to get what she wants. The husband can demand sex without love and under-standing in a way that humiliates his wife.

These issues must be resolved privately because marriage is the only place where sex works the way God intended. Authors Sean McDowell and John Stonestreet make the same argument in pointing out the consequences of private and public sex:

> Marriage marks two people as sexual partners and makes them publicly responsible for their sexual behavior. This is important because sex, though (hopefully) done in private, has very public consequences. Forced sex brings fear to an entire community. Procreative sex creates new life that must be cared for and integrated into the community. Promiscuous sex risks the mental and physical health of many in the community. Underage

> sex jeopardizes the potential of the community.
> Marital sex secures the future of the community"[94]

The marital boundaries for sex are there for a reason. Any child who doesn't learn this at home is open to all kinds of temptation that they are not able to handle. Parents can provide needed guidance and assistance in several ways.

First, your personal example is paramount. For the most part, kids end up emulating their parents. If you teach and model the gospel values of truth, repentance, confession, and forgiveness in your life and marriage, your children will be inclined to want the same kind of marriage you have. Of course, if your marriage is all show and no go, they will read you like a book and reject what you teach them about marriage.

Second, your relationship to a strong Bible teaching church will do more for your child's development than anything they get at school or their friends. A solid church will exalt Christ-honoring worship, biblically based expository (verse by verse) preaching, biblical counseling, the observance of believer's baptism and communion, strong discipleship, and the exercise of church discipline for unrepentant sin in professing believers.

Caution, most megachurches in America today aren't characterized by these elements. Many churches that are more concerned with concert style music complete with smoke and lighting, and shallow "feel good" messages with little or no biblical teaching. They are more interested in

---

[94] Sean McDowell and John Stonestreet, *Same Sex Marriage: A Thoughtful Approach to God's Design for Marriage* (Grand Rapids, MI: Baker Books, 2014), 47.

getting the "unchurched" into their building than getting God's Word into the hearts of God's people.

Third, parents must teach their kids how to tame social media. Jean Twenge, professor of psychology at San Diego State University, explains:

> Rates of teen depression and suicide have sky-rocketed since 2011. It's not an exaggeration to describe iGen as being on the brink of the worst mental-health crisis in decades. Much of this deterioration can be traced to their phones ... There's not a single exception. All screen activities are linked to less happiness, and all nonscreen activities are linked to more happiness. Eighth-graders who spend 10 or more hours a week on social media are 56 percent more likely to say they're unhappy than those who devote less time to social media. Admittedly, 10 hours a week is a lot. But those who spend six to nine hours a week on social media are still 47 percent more likely to say they are unhappy than those who use social media even less. The opposite is true of in-person interactions. Those who spend an above-average amount of time with their friends in person are 20 percent less likely to say they're unhappy than those who hang out for a below-average amount of time.[95]

---

[95] Jean Twenge, "Have Smartphones Destroyed a Generation?" www.theatlantic.com, September 2017, accessed on June 6, 2020.

The wise parent knows that they especially need to help their kids navigate the murky waters of the tech world. Books like *Irresistible: The Rise of Addictive Technology and the Business of Keeping Us Hooked* by Adan Alter, and *The Shallows: What the Internet is Doing to Our Brains* by Nicholas Carr, are indispensable tools for modern parents. The sexual images and addictive messages on the Internet will destroy your child's ability to discern truth if you don't help them manage their digital devices. The purveyors of porn don't respect privacy or propriety in any way. Parents must beware. If you don't teach your children well, they will.

MARRIAGE IS PERMANENT

Shulammite exhibits a flair for the dramatic as her thoughts move to the permanency of marriage. When her hometown crowd came out to see the king's entourage approaching their little village in v. 5, they asked, "Who is this coming up from the wilderness leaning on her beloved?" Their journey to the country traveled down the same road skirting the town of Beth Shean that she took on her way to Jerusalem to marry Solomon. But on her return, she is leaning regally on the arm of her husband the king.

This isn't a case of "How do you like me now?" pride. The word "leaning" depicts being on his elbow, having her arm through his as they enter the village. This is a public declaration of their union as a married couple. We might take this for granted but it is growing increasingly important in our day when so many denigrate marriage.

There are many reasons given for the demise of marriage. Pastor and author Timothy Keller comments that this leads to a discussion where,

> we began to hear all the now society-wide objections—marriage was originally about property and is now in flux, marriage crushes individual identity and has been oppressive for women, marriage stifles passion and is ill-fitted to psychological reality, marriage is "just a piece of paper" that only serves to complicate love, and so on.[96]

Many of these modern deluded gurus of destruction would have us believe that nirvana is just around the corner when we abolish marriage. But they are trading their diamond ring for a fake one in a box of Cracker Jack. Amazingly they can't even see it when the debris of their deluded dictates washes up downstream. When you see physical and sexual abuse, isolation, disappointment, depression, loneliness, sexual perversions, stress, rebellion, anger, sadness, and economic depravity, you can usually draw a straight line back to a broken marriage.

God intended marriage to be permanent. The permanency of the command to "leave and cleave" that was first given in Genesis 2:24 was never revoked or modified even though most Old Testament characters had multiple wives. Jesus reaffirmed this doctrine in Matthew 19:5 and doubled down by saying that no man could break that bond. The

---

[96] Timothy Keller, *The Meaning of Marriage*, (New York, New York: Riverhead Books, 2011), 4.

Apostle Paul also quoted the Genesis standard in Ephesians 5:31, adding that the covenant of marriage was a great and holy mystery because it was a direct picture of Christ and the church.

Christians lived out these values in the first three hundred years of the Christian era, even in the face of political persecution. Christian marriage defied the culture that saw women as chattel and men as sexual animals free to exercise their sexual tastes wherever they could. But this model for Christian marriage didn't hold.

From the fourth century until the time of the Reformation in the sixteenth century, marriage was the domain of the Roman Catholic Church. The Catholic Church taught (and still does) that if you're not married in the Church you can't get to heaven. Being married in the Catholic Church is still one of the seven sacraments of the Church which are necessary to get to heaven.

Modern marriage in the Western world was formed by biblically based Reformed theologians like Martin Luther and John Calvin in the sixteenth century after a thousand years of perverted teaching under the domination of the Catholic Church. Even our contemporary wedding vows were taken from the Anglican *Book of Common Prayer* published in 1549 during the time of Edward VI of England.

Some of the words are outmoded, but the content is solid and has been used in millions of weddings. This is a public declaration of an exclusive, lifelong, marital partnership. Think of the implication of these words: "I,_____, take thee,_____, to be my wedded Wife, to have and to hold from this day forward, for better for worse, for richer for poorer, in sickness and in health, to love and to cherish, till death us do part, according to God's holy ordinance; and thereto I plight thee my troth."[97]

I understand we no longer use words like "plight" and "troth", but you get the idea. The concept of mutual possession and submission weld the couple together in a permanent bond. The commitment to walk through the sunshine and darkness of life is expressed publicly before family and friends. And it's for a lifetime in obedience to the biblical pattern of Christ's love for the church.

The laws of our nation today don't change God's law by declaring marriage can apply to same-sex couples. Nor do those who refuse to be bound by God's law improve their status or the benefits to society by living together outside of marriage. Furthermore, those who say marriage is outmoded or the remnant of a bygone patriarchal era don't remove the blessings and benefits of marriage even for non-Christians.

As Shulammite came into town on the arm of her husband, she was making a public declaration of their marriage. Anyone who would detract from the permanence of marriage is advocating the demise of their society. Taken with vv. 1-4 it's as if she is declaring, "We are one in the flesh, and we are one in marriage. Nothing can tear us apart!"

MARRIAGE IS PRODUCTIVE

There is another observation we need to make regarding v. 5. The picture of unity in marriage seems as if it is stuck

---

[97] *The Book of Common Prayer: 350th Anniversary Edition* (1662; repr., New York, NY: The Penguin Group, 2012), 313.

in the middle of a section on their private sexual encounter. The first four verses describe their private sexual encounter and she returns to this theme in the second half of v. 5.

But this declaration of "leaning on her beloved" is not merely stuck there like an orphan at a family reunion. The public declaration of unity is a fulfillment of their private sexual encounter. The private provides credibility for the public. Without the private encounter there is no public declaration. The permanence of marriage is due to the productivity that comes from the sexual union of a man and his wife. This leads her to the picture of the apple tree in the last part of the verse.

The apple tree

The images of vv. 1-4 all point to sexual arousal. After beginning v. 5 with her statement on their public unity, she refers to the apple tree in the latter part of v. 5, "Beneath the apple tree I awakened you; there your mother was in labor with you, there she was in labor and gave you birth." All three references to "you" are masculine, so we know this is Shulammite speaking to Solomon.

The apple tree is strong and sturdy. It provides ample shade and produces beautiful, tasty fruit. Apples are plentiful and delicious, providing a picture of productivity.

We used to have a company near us who sold big fat juicy Fuji apples at Christmas that were almost as big as a cantaloupe. They were dipped in caramel and chocolate, then smothered in chopped almonds to form the biggest caramel apple you could imagine. They made a wonderful holiday treat and gift.

In Song of Solomon 2:3 the apple tree was used as a symbol of Solomon's life and Shulammite delighted in basking in the shade of his provision. But here in Song of Solomon 8:5 Solomon is the one under the apple tree, where his wife awakens him. And who else is there? Mom, of course. So, what's up with that?

This speaks of Solomon's sexual impulse being awakened in the same place where his mother gave birth to him as a result of the same sexual impulse. This is not referring to a house but to a home. The apple tree is a picture of the loving home where the sexual union between Solomon's father and mother brought him into the world.

The wonder of bearing children is depicted as the fruit of God's provision under the shade of the tree of marriage. Proverbs 127:3-5 assures us that, "children are a gift of the LORD, the fruit of the womb is a reward. Like arrows in the hand of a warrior, so are the children of one's youth. How blessed is the man whose quiver is full of them.'" Shulammite is standing in awe of the magnificent picture that something as enjoyable as sex is actually the means God uses to continue to propogate a healthy society.

Awakening Solomon's sexual impulse isn't voyeuristic, it's eye opening. The sexual union of a husband and wife is the cornerstone of society. God has placed the very continuation of our existence as a human race in the context of the most beautiful and pleasurable activity men and women can enjoy.

This is what Solomon was talking about in Proverbs 5:18-19 when he said, "Let your fountain be blessed, and rejoice in the wife of your youth. As a loving hind and a graceful doe, let her breasts satisfy you at all times; be exhilarated always with her love." What a wonderful gift God has given us in the sexual union of husband and wife.

Marital sex isn't like two animals in heat. Sex is more than an animal instinct. It's the desire to share the legacy of life with someone who knows you at the deepest level and cares for you like no one else. This is the provision and protection of marriage.

When this private encounter in marriage is broken, the pillars of society shake and begin to crumble. It is even more incredible when we see people actually trying to destroy the family on purpose.

Annie Gottlieb is one of many 60s activists who prided themselves in being the generation that destroyed the American family. She writes,

> We might not have been able to tear down the state, but the family was closer. We could get our hands on it. And...we believed that the family was the foundation of the state, as well as the collective state of mind...We truly believed that the family had to be torn apart to free love, which alone could heal the damage done when the atom was split to release energy. And the first step was to tear ourselves free from our parents.[98]

---

[98] Philip Graham Ryken, *Written in Stone: The Ten Commandments and Today's Moral Crisis* (Wheaton, Illinois: Crossway Books, 2003), 117.

Despite these attempts to destroy the family, logic dictates that these sentiments are ill-advised. Any clear thinking person would affirm the importance of the family in creating stable social order.

A dramatic picture of this truth can be seen in two studies done on families in the late 19th century. In 1874 Richard L. Dugdale was employed by the New York Prison Commission to visit the prisons of the state. He found criminals in six different prisons, under four different family names, were all descended from the same family. This led to deeper investigation where he visited courts, prisons, neighbors, and employers. He found 42 different family names of 504 descendants over five generations who all came from one man. When adding in 169 who married into the family, the total number studied was 1200 in the same family.

Since he couldn't find the name of the one man who spawned this group, he called the whole family the "Jukes" family. "Jukes" is a word that means "to roost." It refers to birds who have no home or nest who fly into trees to roost. It came to refer to people too lazy to "stand up or sit up but sprawl out anywhere."

Dugdale gave the man the first name of Max. He was born in 1720. He didn't go to school or work because he didn't want to do either, so he hung out in bars at night. Though he was vulgar, funny, and fond of talking, he took to living in the woods away from people because he loved to hunt and fish. He built a shanty around 1750 that became a "notorious cradle of crime."

In 1874 Dugdale wrote a report to the New York Prison Commission called "Jukes." His findings about the family that came from this one man were astounding:

*310 were "professional" paupers who lived in public "poor houses" a total of 2300years!

*300 of the 1200 total family members died as babies from lack of care

*50 women lived lives of "notorious debauchery"

*400 wrecked their lives physically early

*60 lived lives as thieves

*130 were habitual criminals

*7 were murderers

*They cost the state over $1,250,000[99]

In 1897 another study was initiated that intersected with the Dugdale study. A professional scholarly organization assigned Albert Winship to prepare an essay on Jonathan Edwards for a May meeting in 1898. Edwards is one of the most profound theologians and intellectuals America has ever produced. He was a pastor, missionary to the Indians in Colonial America, and the 2nd President of Princeton University. He died of a smallpox vaccination six weeks after taking the position at Princeton in 1758.

Winship found out that one of Edwards' descendants was head of the New York Prison Commission when Dugdale made his report. Since Edwards (born in 1703) and Jukes (born in 1720) were contemporaries who both lived in

---

[99] A. E. Winship, *Jukes-Edwards: A Study in Education and Heredity* (Harrisburg, PA: R. L. Myers and Co., 1900), n.a.

Connecticut, the comparison of their families was enticing for Winship.

Shortly after Edwards died, his wife and oldest daughter, who took care of him when he was at Princeton, both died, also of smallpox. His 10 surviving children were left with very little wealth, yet the legacy and achievements of his family are quite remarkable. When he died his sons were 20, 11, and 8. All of daughters except one were under 20. They were left in their pioneer missionary home with the Indians he served before becoming President of Princeton.

And yet all his sons and his sons-in-law graduated from college. Of this group, one became president of Princeton, another the President of Union College. The group included four judges, two members of the Continental Congress, a member of the governor's council of Massachusetts, a member of the Massachusetts war commission in the Revolutionary war, a state senator, a president of the Connecticut House of Representatives, three officers in the Revolutionary war, one member of the famous constitutional convention out of which the United States was born, and a pastor of the historic North church of New Haven, Connecticut.

Edwards had 75 grandchildren. In all, 1400 descendants have been traced, roughly the same number traced in the Jukes family tree. The results of the study of Edwards' grandchildren show they included:

*1 U.S. Vice-President
*3 U.S. Senators
*3 governors
*3 mayors
*13 college presidents

*30 judges
*65 professors
*80 public office holders
*100 lawyers
*100 missionaries
*His descendants never cost the state a dime[100]

Given this comparison, why would anyone think that destroying the family makes sense. There are obvious failures in family life when people don't live up to expectations. But you don't sell a car just because you get a flat tire. And you don't advocate for the demise of marriage given the benefits.

It's tragic when we see so many moving away from this bountiful provision today. And yet our culture seems to be moving away from God's provision of marriage.

Sociologist Mark Regnerus confirms this. He and his global research team recently compiled a study of the attitudes of almost 200 young, mostly single, adult Christians from Mexico, Spain, Poland, Russia, Lebanon, Nigeria, and the United States. Their research indicates that skepticism about marriage is not confined to the West.

The conclusion of their study is that marriage as we know it is under renewed scrutiny. Regnerus notes, "Marriage isn't changing. It's receding. In an era of increasing options, technology, gender equality, 'cheap' sex, and secularization, fewer people – including fewer practicing Christians – actually want what marriage is. That's the bottom line."[101]

---

[100]Ibid.

[101]Mark Regnerus, "Can the Church Save Marriage?" www.christianitytoday. com, June 22, 2020, accessed on July 5, 2020.

Regnerus continues, "But we've lost sight of the fact that marriage is in many ways a corporeal (and spiritual) act of mercy not just to our own spouse and children but to the world beyond our household. The West's successes have been built upon this family social structure and dismantling it will leave us far more vulnerable and psychologically unmoored than we realize.[102]

If our culture continues to retreat from marriage, "millions of Americans will be what the Chinese call 'bare branches'—that is, men and women without kin. Many of these bare branches will not be prepared for the storms brewing on the horizon, be they recurring pandemics, social unrest, a sovereign debt reckoning, or additional economic crises."[103]

The shade of the apple tree isn't fading. People are just moving out from under it to find themselves exposed to the scorching sun of godless secularization that cares nothing for their souls or well-being. We desperately need the affirmation of marriage modeled by Solomon and Shulammite. Otherwise, we will become "bare branches," bereft of fruit with no one to turn to in troubled times.

A seal over your heart

Shulammite's words turn from a description to a plea in Song of Solomon 8:6 when she asks Solomon to "Put me like a seal over your heart, like a seal on your arm. For love is as strong as death, jealousy is as severe as Sheol; its flashes

---

[102]Ibid.

[103]W. Bradford Wilcox and Alysse Elhage, "COVID-19 is Killing the Soulmate Model of Marriage. Good," *Christianity Today*, June 22, 2020, accessed July 10, 2020.

are flashes of fire, the very flame of the Lord." A "seal" is a stamp or signet ring. It's a sign of ownership that denotes value. You don't put a burglar alarm on the outhouse, you put it on the penthouse.

She wants to own his heart! I realize many reject marriage because they don't like the idea of being owned. But, why not? Our rebellious individualism fosters "bare branches" people who go through life disconnected and lonely.

On the other hand, the "seal over your heart" depicts mutual ownership born of love and devotion. And "a seal on your arm" depicts outer security and union for everyone to see. It says, "You belong to me and I belong to you."

This is the symbol of the wedding ring. It depicts value and unending love. My ring reminds me of my wife and the commitment I made to her every time I feel it. Unfortunately, it doesn't mean the same thing to some people.

I worked at Disneyland in college and saw my boss quickly slip his wedding ring off when the "scenery" looked promising at the after-work party. I was naïve and stunned when he told me to find another ride home as he walked off with his latest conquest.

Fast forward twenty-five years when my wedding ring slipped off my finger while water skiing. I felt like I had lost my best friend. Though it wasn't the same ring, I couldn't wait to buy a new one and I still wear it as a "seal on my arm" because my wife is a "seal over my heart."

As strong as death

Why do we feel this way about marriage? Because "love is as strong as death." There is no other force on earth that is stronger than love. And don't be fooled about generic "love" for mankind as a whole. People won't kill to protect that. But husbands and wives will kill to protect the one they love.

This feeling explains marital jealousy. Ask any cop what the most prevalent call outside of traffic stops is. They will tell you "domestic violence." If we're designed to be alone, or if we're mere protoplasm, then why do we so easily become insanely jealous when the marital bonds are broken? It's because we've lost something of the very core of who we are. People go into a murderous rage when someone "steals" their wife or husband.

Years ago, I connected with a cousin I hadn't seen in years who was a long-haul trucker. For over a hundred miles I listened as he poured out the story of his wife's affair. One night he dropped by the house that he had built to see the "other man" sitting in *his* easy chair in *his* house with *his* wife and *his* kids watching *his* TV. It was heartbreaking. That's what happens to the innocent party when the seal of love is broken.

This is not the kind of love Shulammite is talking about. The love in v. 6 is "as strong as death" and it produces security, commitment, and joy. As a pastor I've performed dozens of funerals. One of the most touching scenes I encounter is when someone has lost their husband or wife of 50 years or more. After everyone has passed by the casket to pay their respects the surviving spouse steps forward slowly, usually with a son or daughter at their side. They touch the casket gingerly and with tears running down their cheeks through the smile on their face they say, "Bye honey. Love you. See you in the morning."

Thank God they will if they know Christ. What a joy to know that the life-filling joy of marriage can carry someone all the way through life to their grave. That's the best it gets in this life.

We take great pains to care for every part of our life, our body, our job, our car, and our kids. How many take the greatest care with their marriage? Everything good in life flows out of that, but your marriage doesn't exist in a vacuum. If your marriage prospers, you prosper. If your marriage hurts, you hurt. If your marriage fails, a piece of you dies, and with it a picture of the gospel dies.

SOME PRACTICAL HELP

Let me take a stab at offering some practical help. This can't be reduced to a simplistic list or magic pills, but these quick reminders on how to nurture your marriage might help. Carefully applied, they can help make your love *"stronger than death."*

1. Focus on the gospel in your marriage. You will have plenty of opportunity to confess, repent, and forgive in your marriage. With the gospel as your template you will learn this is a two-way street.
2. Study the Bible together. Take turns reading a passage. Use a good study Bible. Talk about it together.

3. Obey God's instructions. Husbands are to lead and love their wives in a sacrificial way. Wives are to submit and respect their husbands. This is not possible on your own. You must depend on Him to give you the grace to do what you cannot do on your own.

4. Worship together. Pray out loud with each other at home. Find a good church that will teach the Bible accurately and consistently to you and your family.

5. Recognize the traits of your personality. Differences most often attract. One may be talkative, the other one is quiet. One reads a lot, the other one doesn't. One wears their emotions on their sleeve, the other one is subdued. Don't expect your spouse to mirror your personality. You married them because they were different than you. Now let them be that way.

6. Lower your expectations. You are married to a real person, not a saint. Expect imperfection!

7. Nurture friendship. Enter the world of your spouse. You will have different hobbies and interests but find things you can do together. Encourage them by your words, your attention and your presence.

8. Work at your marriage. Read books together a chapter at a time. Talk about what is going on in your family. Write your feelings down. Learn to forgive!

9. Protect your marriage. Your flirting days are over! So are the days of meeting alone with someone of the opposite sex, even at work. Don't listen to anyone else's marriage problems. Don't confide your disappointments or your hopes and dreams to anyone other than you spouse. Never demean your spouse to anyone.

10. Have fun together. Take family vacations and romantic getaways. Play games and sports together. Build fun holiday traditions. Do remodeling projects together. Develop a joint hobby. Travel together. Laugh at yourself.

Remember Christopher Love? You may not have his name, but you can have the kind of loving relationship he had with his wife. Your marriage has all the potential to be what you desire because God invented it. If you protect it, you can expect a lifetime of fulfillment. But it is your marriage. No one else can build into it but you.

"Under love all other duties are comprised: for without it no duty can be well performed ...It is like fire, which is not only hot in itself, but also conveyeth heat into that which is near it."

— William Gouge

CHAPTER FOURTEEN

YOU CAN'T KILL LOVE
(Song of Solomon 8:7-10)

My Dad was thirty years old when he got married. Mom was eighteen. Over the next seventeen years they had eleven kids. The backstory to those statements provides a dramatic picture of the strength of the love they had for one another.

Dad was a small farmer in Nebraska in the 1940s and 50s. He and his younger brother had watched their Dad sell his farm for $1.00 when he lost it during the Depression. When my uncle got married, Dad became a sharecropper, farming land owned by someone else for a share of the profits. This was hard work and left little time for social pursuits. This partially explains his delayed marriage.

According to Dad, the rest of the explanation is that there were very few "worthy" girls around. Dad had a strong conversion experience when he was twenty-one and wanted a girl who would love and honor the Lord as he did. One day at church he met the oldest daughter of a local farmer. She was fourteen. He was twenty-six. Yes, Grandpa wasn't thrilled!

But Dad persevered and courted Mom with honor and tenacity. They were married as soon as she graduated from high school. Eleven months later my older brother was born, followed regularly with another child approximately every other year for the next seventeen years.

But their love never wavered. When my kids were young, we had the opportunity to spend the night at my parent's house. We ended up reminiscing about their marriage and Mom brought out a stack of letters Dad had written to her over the years. Dad was a man of few words, but he often expressed his love for Mom in letters he wrote when he was away.

At one point he worked on a road construction crew and had to be gone for several days at a time. He wrote,

> "Oh, my darling. How I miss you sweetheart. I love you and long to be home with you. I know it's hard when we are separated but I hope and pray that you and the boys are all right. The sweet companionship of Jesus, isn't it wonderful? Your smile, sweetheart. Thank you for every one of them."

If you had known my Dad you would not have thought words like that could come out of his mouth. After reading that letter I told Anne it was too bad she didn't have a husband who expressed himself like that! Mom kept all those letters until the day she died.

Like most of us, Mom and Dad had their share of ups and downs. The years of hard work (sometimes working two jobs) to keep food on the table for eleven kids wasn't easy. They also took in a disabled lady in her old age who had helped raise my Mom, and my Dad's parents either lived with us or next door during my childhood. With this full house they certainly experienced their share of hard work, financial stress, disappointments, and trouble.

But I never saw them waver in their commitment to God or their love for each other. They rose before dawn to read the Bible and pray together every day. They took us to church every time it was open. We didn't have a lot of money but they kept food on the table and clean clothes on our backs. I don't ever remember a cross or demeaning word between them or to anyone else. I never heard my Dad swear or use any kind of profane, crude word. Not once. My Mom had a beautiful voice and would often sing her favorite hymns as she worked her way through the mountains of laundry she did every day. They lived their faith.

My sister Debi wrote a poem expressing her admiration for the impact Mom had on her. One day when she was fifteen she watched Mom knead bread dough for another batch of home-made bread. She noticed her wedding ring was covered in yeast and flour and wrote the following words.

DULLEN GOLD

Two small bands
Worn thin from age
Still decorate the hand
That brushed my hair
And dried my tears
And taught me how to stand;
Atop the dullen gold
Lies solitaire a stone
How proud it seems to sit
Upon its aged throne;
And look within her eyes
You'll see a sparkle there
The finest gemstone in the world
Shan't cast a brighter glare;
And how it warms my heart
To see such simple style
Bring joy into her life
And contentment to her smile;
So if the day should come
For me to have and hold
I hope I get a ring
That shines like dullen gold![104]

My Mom and Dad will never be famous or noted in the eyes of the world. But their marriage was one of thousands that build strong churches and a vibrant society. Marriages like this give evidence of God's common grace to mankind

---

[104]Debi Gallarda, used by permission.

through the institution of marriage. Even more importantly, marriages like this give visible evidence of the impact of the gospel in the everyday lives of men and women.

When my Dad died at eighty-nine, he and Mom had been married for almost sixty years. Their road wasn't always easy, but their commitment to the Lord and to each other smoothed the path immensely and left a legacy for their family to follow.

This chapter speaks about the enduring nature of marital love. We continue to listen in on the conversation of Solomon and Shulammite as they reflect on what makes marital love last in a way that touches us so deeply.

Love Is Persistent

Where does love come from? In 1 John 4:7-8 the apostle John tells us "Beloved, let us love one another, for love is from God; and everyone who loves is born of God and knows God. The one who does not love does not know God, for God is love." To ignore the true source of love is to ignore love. If you want to do away with love, you would have to do away with God.

Shulammite agrees. In Song of Solomon 8:6 she recognizes, "For love is as strong as death, Jealousy is as severe as Sheol; its flashes are flashes of fire, the very flame of the Lord." This is the only time God is mentioned in the Song of Solomon and it's at this critical point. Love is "the flame of the Lord." It's the very essence of God Himself.

That's why the pictures in this chapter are so strong. You can't kill love because you can't kill God. We see two pictures of this in this passage.

It can't be quenched

The first picture is water. In v. 7 Shulammite states, "Many waters cannot quench love, nor will rivers overflow it." This alludes to the fiery spark of love. When love has caught fire there is no amount of water that can put it out. The word "waters" is plural. It's used 580 times in the Old Testament. It's the word that describes the "waters" that covered the earth before land was created in Genesis 1:2, the "upper chambers in the waters" that contain rain in Psalm 104:3, and the "flood of water" during the flood that covered the earth during the time of Noah in Genesis 6:17.

The meaning is clear. Once love is fired up nothing can quench it. A man would stand underneath the deluge of Niagara Falls and sacrifice his life to save his wife and kids. This love is the most powerful force on earth.

But let me remind you. This is speaking of marital love. This is not the emotional, gushy, puppy love of your youth. You could blow that love out like a flickering candle on a birthday cake. But God places an inextinguishable, burning love between a husband and wife that may flicker at times, but it cannot be put out. Married couples may face adversity, sickness and disease, financial stress, loss of a job, sick kids, and eventually, even death. But their love will not be put out. It will only be strengthened, not extinguished.

Shulammite extends the picture of water as she reminds us in Song of Solomon 8:7, "nor will waters overflow it." Water can't put out the flame of love and it can't drown the presence of love. Job 14:19 reminds us, "Water wears away stones, its torrents wash away the dust of the earth." Water can wear away even the hard rough edges of stone and turn them into smooth river rocks, but it can't wear love down.

It can't be bought

The second picture she gives about the persistence of love is money. In the last half of v. 7 she said, "if a man were to give all the riches of his house for love, it would be utterly despised." The Beatles sang, "Can't buy me love" and they were right. You can buy sex, but you can't buy love. Love has to be given.

Why is this true? What makes love so powerful? Is this a function of biology, or our environment, or education? No, it's none of these. The existence of love is a proof of the existence of God. Animals express a type of familial recognition and affinity, but they don't "love" you. Sorry dog lovers, but when Fido responds to those who feed him and scratch his tummy, it's not love, it's a conditioned response.

Benjamin B. Warfield was a renowned scholar and theologian at Princeton Seminary in the late nineteenth and early twentieth century. His book *"The Inspiration and Authority of the Bible"* is a classic that I studied in seminary and still refer to often. Few people realize he spent most of his adult life caring for his paralyzed wife.

They were married in 1876 when he was 25. On their honeymoon in Germany she was struck by lightning and permanently paralyzed. Despite the fact that he was an astute scholar and author, and could have traveled widely, he rarely left their home for more than two hours as he cared for her the next thirty-nine years until she died.[105]

What makes a man do that? Warfield's wife could not have paid for the kind of care she received from her loving husband, no matter how much it cost. Warfield, like Shulammite, understood that all the riches of the world couldn't compare to the love he had for his wife.

LOVE IS PURE

We've seen that love is powerful, but what causes this love to prosper? It is the development of character. Shulammite takes on a reflective mood as she looks into her past to answer this question. She comments in v. 8, "We have a little sister, and she has no breasts." Since Shulammite has been speaking, it's best to view this as her voice, not that of her brothers who haven't been heard from since Chapter 1.

But "we" probably refers to her brothers and her since she is describing the protective and nurturing role older siblings often assume. Their "little sister... has no breasts" indicates pre-puberty. Their concern is clear in asking, "What shall we do for our sister on the day when she is spoken for?" Their concern is how to protect her purity and prepare her for marriage. Unfortunately, purity is not important to many today.

In our culture, specific training on sexual purity is increasingly marginalized as people redefine "truth" that is based on feelings, not facts or tradition. In 2016 the Oxford English Dictionary's word of the year was *post-truth*. It means: "relating

---

[105]John Piper, *Future Grace: The Purifying Power of the Grace of God* (Colorado Springs, Colorado: Multnomah Books, 2012), 172.

to or denoting circumstances in which objective facts are less influential in shaping public opinion than appeals to emotion and personal belief."[106]

Purity is up for grabs because truth is up for grabs. Many in our culture are making up their own "truth" as they go along. This is especially true in regard to marriage where emotion and feelings increasingly rule the day.

Glennon Doyle Melton, a popular women's blogger and author left her husband Craig, and three kids and married lesbian soccer player Abby Wambach a few years ago. Melton described her new lover by noting, "She is committed to her friends and family. She has this sense of country and honor and chivalry that feels beautiful to me. She cares about the vulnerable – children and animals especially. She's unwaveringly good to Craig, to the kids, to Sister and to all my people."[107]

Wow! That's nice. Wambach is "unwaveringly good" to the man who lost his wife to her. And she "cares about the vulnerable – children and animals especially," except the children who lost their mom because she is "in love" and "really, deeply happy," who feels that "the most revolutionary thing a woman can do is not explain herself."[108] In telling her three kids about her newfound joy in lesbian love, Melton told them, "Now it is my job as a leader not to concern myself

[106]https://en.oxforddictionaries.com/definition/post-truth

[107]Jen Pollock Michel, "Glennon Doyle Melton's Gospel of Self-Fulfillment," www.christianitytoday.com, accessed on 5/28/20.

[108]Ibid.

too deeply about what you think and feel about me – about the way I live my life."[109]

What incredible self-centered hubris! This is what respected philosopher Charles Taylor, in his monumental work, *A Secular Age,* described as the one who "accept[s] no final goals beyond human flourishing, nor any allegiance to anything else beyond this flourishing. Of no previous society was this true."[110] He's right. No previous society has been so collectively self-obsessed as ours is today.

We've changed the rules *and* the game today in a way that's never been done before. In Wambach's game of soccer, they have side boundaries, rules for playing, and referees in striped shirts to enforce them. But if the game is marriage, we make up our own rules.

The lesson of Shulammite's "little sister" is that someone must instruct the next generation in the rules of life and protect their purity along their way to marriage. Shulammite mentions two pictures that portrays our responsibilities to the younger generation.

A wall

The first one is a wall. Verse 9 reads, "If she is a wall, we will build on her a battlement of silver." The picture is the solid wall of a fortress, not the wall of a house. This wall is defensive, it defines boundaries and keeps marauders out.

[109]https://nl-nl.facebook.com/glennondoyle/photos/feels-like-the-world-could-use-all-the-love-it-can-get-right-now-so-today-im-goi/10154703803624710, accessed on 6/5/20

[110]Charles Taylor, *A Secular Age* (Cambridge, Massachusetts: Belknap Press, 2007), 18.

Before marriage, a "little sister" who "has no breasts" is a virgin. Metaphorically, the wall pictures chastity, unavailability, and protection. She can't be touched because she is behind the wall of her family. She is protected and her virginity is intact. This is universal. No thinking, loving parent wants their daughter to lose her virginity before she is married, let alone before puberty. This is God's provision and intent.

The Apostle Paul in 1 Thessalonians 4:3-6 expresses it this way, "For this is the will of God, your sanctification; that is, that you abstain from sexual immorality; that each of you know how to possess his own vessel in sanctification and honor, not in lustful passion, like the Gentiles who do not know God; and that no man transgress and defraud his brother in the matter because the Lord is the avenger in all these things, just as we also told you before and solemnly warned you."

This passage answers the question, "Why is sexual purity so critical?" The answers may be summarized this way:

1. It's God's will. This is rooted in His design in Genesis 2. From the very beginning God created the pattern for human relationships to be one man and one woman in a marital relationship. He knows the purpose of His own creation.

2. Abstinence leads to spiritual maturity. Sexual purity is part of the process of becoming holy through the sanctification process.

3. Abstinence brings "honor." Despite what pop culture says, family, friends, and most of our society respects and honors one who remains abstinent.

4. Abstinence is the opposite of "lustful passion" which is fueled by emotion and impulse, not by reason.

5. Immorality "defrauds" your "brother." This refers to the sexual partner. It means, to "take advantage of, outwit, or cheat."[111] A sexually willing person takes advantage of their partner and cheats them out of their virginity.

6. Immorality will be "avenged" by the Lord.

7. God has called us to be pure as a picture of His holiness.

This is consistent with what we've seen before. Immorality destroys the picture of Christ's love for the church. We also know that sexual immorality damages your soul. In 1 Corinthians 6:18 Paul instructs us to "Flee immorality. Every other sin that a man commits is outside the body, but the immoral man sins against his own body."

Sins other than sexual sins are committed outside the body. But sexual sin is a sin "against his own body" because he or she is violating the power and presence of the reproductive capability God has given people in their own body. This ability to reproduce is the closest thing humans have to participation in a miracle.

There is a reward for building a wall. In Song of Solomon 8:9 Shulammite said, "We will build on her a battlement of silver." This was a sign of honor and value. Those who see a virgin's commitment to be a wall will trust and honor her.

How do you build a wall? A young woman (or man) needs to think of this *before* they place themselves in any kind of

---

[111]Colin Brown, general editor, *New International Dictionary of New Testament Theology*, vol. 1, (Grand Rapids, MI: Zondervan Publishing House, 1986), 137.

potentially compromising situation where two people are alone and sexual passion could cause them to get carried away. There is a word for a young woman who doesn't think this through in advance – it's "mother."

The following are some guidelines for parents to work through with their sons and daughters. I will address the comments to sons and daughters, but it's the parent's job to nurture them through this process. To the young man or woman who wants to be a "wall," here are some things to remember.

First, you must decide beforehand whether you want to honor God or follow your emotions. One or the other will win out. Will you ever regret honoring God and being a "wall?" No. Will you regret losing your virginity before you get married? Most likely.

Every young person needs to decide in advance what they want to do before they find themselves in a compromising situation. Know what you are going to say *before* a manipulative guy says, "If you loved me, you'll have sex with me." Plan in advance ways to avoid any place where you will be alone with your boyfriend or girlfriend where your passions could get carried away.

Second, focus on your own growth, not finding a spouse. A wise person once told me that *you need to be the kind of person that the kind of person you want, would want.* Grow in your knowledge of the Bible and serve God in your church. Do your best in your school or job. Hang out with a group of friends who are going in the same direction that you are. Let God take care of the results.

Next, you might also consider making a "dating pact" with your parents, or a trusted sibling or friend, depending on their spiritual commitments. This could include making a list of your top requirements in a husband or wife. These should be character qualities, not what they own or where they work. When someone comes into your life ask your team if the person seems to possess the qualifications on your list.

One last thing. Decide if you want to date as recreation, or if you are dating to find a husband or wife. If you're dating recreationally, be very careful. It's not wise to play with the emotions of someone you would not seriously pursue, and you can't guarantee that you won't get caught in an emotional trap too.

Here is a guideline for dating: *Until you are ready to be physically, emotionally, socially, spiritually, and financially committed to a person, you're not ready for marriage.* Until then, any dating you do should be focused on identifying the person's suitability in each one of those areas. Talking about this as early as you can in the dating relationship will let the person you are dating know that you are not out just for a fling. People get hurt that way.

A door

The other picture Shulammite uses is a door. She continues in v. 9, "But if she is a door, we will barricade her with planks of cedar." A door is different than a wall. A door can be opened to let people in and out. That's the way it is with our hearts. We can let people in or keep them out.

In this context a door symbolizes an immature, petulant, self-centered girl who wants her own way. Her door swings wide open to invite everyone in. She's "boy crazy." If a guy is a door, he becomes a sexual predator. He sees every girl as a potential conquest. Whether a guy or a girl, the "door" type of person does everything they can to invite the attention of the opposite sex.

You really don't have to "choose" to be a door. It's easy. Just follow your own emotions and listen to your friends. Focus on a boy – any boy! Show as much skin as you can, and you can get the boys to look at you. But I guarantee that they won't be looking at your character. "Follow your heart," and you can get the boy of your nightmares! And if you open the door to that kind of life, you will end up as pure as the driven slush.

The Apostle Paul explains what it means to be a door. In 1 Corinthians 6:16 he warns, "do you not know that the one who joins himself to a prostitute is one body with her?" He is referring to Genesis 2 where God says a husband and wife are to be one flesh.

But when a Christian is a door with someone who is not his wife it is not merely him doing it. This is Paul's point later in vv. 19-20 when he says, "Or do you not know that your body is a temple of the Holy Spirit who is in you, whom you have from God, and that you are not your own? For you have been bought with a price: therefore glorify God in your body."

When a Christian has sex outside of marriage, they take the Holy Spirit with them into the bedroom to watch. In the Old Testament the Holy Spirit resided in the innermost part of the Temple called the Holy of Holies. Today there is no Temple. We are the Temple of God. Our bodies are the holy habitation of God on earth.

Love Is Peaceful

Shulammite was a wall. She was confident and committed in her character. In v. 10 she states, "I was a wall, and my breasts were like towers." This is not an allusion to the size of her breasts by saying her breasts *were* towers. This is a classic use of a simile in English. She said her breasts were *like* towers. Towers were placed at regular intervals on the wall of a city for security. Since she was no longer a little girl, her developed breasts were reminders that she had protected her purity.

This is an allusion to her character. We saw in Chapter 1 that she refused to be mistaken as a prostitute by chasing Solomon and the rest of the shepherds. She was not a door, allowing access to her feminine charms to every guy who came along. She lived her life in defiance of those who would destroy her honor. That's hard for a young woman to do in any age. But it brings great satisfaction when a woman presents herself to her husband on their wedding night as a virgin.

Ancient Jewish culture placed great value in this. At the culmination of the week-long wedding celebration, the bride and groom would leave their family and friends and enter their bedroom. The crowd would wait outside while the couple consummated their wedding vows. Afterward they were required to show the sheet they laid on to see if it had any blood on it. This verified that they indeed had intercourse, and the wedding was indeed consummated, and that the woman was in fact a virgin, verified by the blood on the sheet that showed her hymen had been broken.

The result of being a wall is clear. Song of Solomon 8:10 promises, "Then I became in his eyes as one who finds peace." There's a play on words here. The word "peace" is *shalom*, the same word as "Solomon." *Shalom* refers to balance and well-being in all areas of life. The general meaning of the word points to "completion and fulfillment—of entering into a state of wholeness and unity, a restored relationship."[112]

This is what everyone wants in a marital relationship. No one gets married wanting disappointment, division, and a broken relationship. They want peace – *shalom*. The promise of peace is the result of maintaining purity before marriage.

When two people meet who have kept themselves pure, they complement each other. They make each other whole. Peace is the result. It comes from trust. When you marry a virgin you trust them, and they trust you.

If your husband asks on your wedding night if you're a virgin what will you say? "Well, there was that guy on prom night, and my boyfriend in college." Guys, how will you answer? "Well, there was the girl I met at the beach, and the one-nighter with my neighbor, and the 'thing' I had with a girl in the office." How much more fulfilling to be able to honestly say, "Yes."

Pastor Tommy Nelson comments:

> The man who marries a virgin goes into marriage
> with the significant trust and faith in his wife. The
> husband of a virgin can't help reasoning, even
> sub-consciously, 'She saved herself for me. If she

---

[112]G. Lloyd Carr, "2401 פְלֹם," ed. R. Laird Harris, Gleason L. Archer Jr., and Bruce K. Waltke, *Theological Wordbook of the Old Testament* (Chicago: Moody Press, 1999), 930.

has that kind of personal discipline and righteousness before marriage, she no doubt will have that
kind of personal discipline and righteousness after
the wedding is over. She is a woman who will stay
faithful to me.[113]

LOVE IS A STRUGGLE

If you're thinking that this kind of love is a struggle, you're
right. Maintaining your virginity in our world is like trying to
tread water in fishing waders. And when you meet the one
you love and intend to marry; it doesn't get any easier. Don't
be discouraged because you're not alone. Consider the story
of one of the most respected theologians in the history of
the church.

Augustine was a great church scholar of the 4th century. In his younger years he lived a life of profligate sexual
immorality. But he had a praying mother and he became a
Christian in his early 30s and devoted himself to scholar-
ship and the church. In *The Confessions* he wrote about his
insatiable sexual desire, amazed to find he could write great
theological truth and still be sexually tempted. He describes
the torment of his struggle:

> My old loves held me back. They tugged at the gar-
> ment of my flesh and whispered, 'Are you going to
> part with us? And from that moment will we never
> be with you anymore?' ...Let thy mercy guard the

[113]Tommy Nelson, *The Book of Romance: What Solomon Says About Love, Sex, and Intimacy* (Nashville, Tennessee: Thomas Nelson, 1998), 147.

soul of thy servant from the vileness and the shame they did suggest! And now I scarcely heard them, for they were not openly showing themselves and opposing me face to face; but muttering, as it were behind my back; and furtively plucking at me as I was leaving, trying to make me look back at them. Still they delayed me, so that I hesitated to break loose and shake myself free of them and leap over to the places to which I was being called – for unruly habit kept saying to me, 'Do you think you can live without them?'[114]

One night he had a vision of a woman he called, "Lady Continence." In his despair, she said to him, "Why are you relying on yourself, only to find yourself unreliable? Cast yourself upon [Christ], do not be afraid. He will not withdraw himself so that you fall. Make the leap without anxiety; he will catch you and heal you."[115]

He continued in deep turmoil over his struggle with sexual temptation. "Now when deep reflection had drawn up out of the secret depths of my soul all my misery and had heaped it up before the sight of my heart, there arose a mighty storm, accompanied by a mighty rain of tears."[116] His friend Alypius was with him but Augustine moved away from him so he wouldn't be heard weeping as he asked God to deliver him.

---

[114]St. Augustine, *Confessions*, Oxford World's Classics (1992; repr., Oxford: Oxford University Press, 2008), 151.

[115]Ibid., 158.

[116]Ibid., 159.

His grief finally overwhelmed him, saying, "I flung myself down under a fig tree – how I know not – and gave free course to my tears. The streams of my eyes gushed out an acceptable sacrifice to thee... "How long, O Lord? Wilt thou be angry forever? Oh, remember not against us our former iniquities."

As he was weeping "suddenly I heard the voice of a boy or a girl – I know not which – coming from the neighboring house, chanting over and over again, 'Pick it up, read it; pick it up, read it." Annoyed with the meaning of the words, he returned to where Alypius was sitting and took a Bible and opened it. It fell open to Romans 13:13–14: "Let us walk properly as in the daytime, not in orgies and drunkenness, not in sexual immorality and sensuality, not in quarreling and jealousy. But put on the Lord Jesus Christ, and make no provision for the flesh, to gratify its desires."

God gave him great contentment from this verse. Immediately he told Alypius what had happened to him and they both ran to tell his mother of the deliverance he felt from this spiritual battle.[117]

It may not happen to you like this, but if you ask God to deliver you from sexual temptation, He will. If you don't want to be a door, Romans 13:14 tells us to "put on the Lord Jesus Christ, and make no provision for the flesh in regard to its lusts."

That means you deny your fleshly desires. You don't go to places that provide opportunity for sexual indulgence. You don't hang with loose people. You don't fill your mind with false media representations of "true love." Like Joseph in the Old Testament, when confronted with sexual opportunity

---

[117]Ibid., 160.

you exit stage left as fast as you can, even if it means leaving your coat behind (Genesis 39:6-12).

That's why the phrase "follow your heart" is directly contradicted by Scripture. If you follow your heart, it will lead you into trouble almost every time. The heart of an alcoholic tells them they can have "one more beer," but they can't. Someone struggling with sexual temptation follows their heart until they see how destructive that can be.

Ladies, start praying for your future husband. Visualize him. Ask God to protect you until he arrives. Don't waste time dating guys who are only playing religion. Trust that God will provide the right man for you if you are a wall and not a door.

Men, pray for the woman you want to marry. Treat every girl with the same respect you'd like men to be treating your future wife. Hold fast to the kind of woman you want. Ask God for someone who is growing in their Christian life and don't feel fooled with casual religious talk. Look for someone who is emotionally stable and "low maintenance." Be accountable in your dating with someone you trust.

If you have failed sexually please know that it is never too late to start over. The Apostle Paul listed a number of types of sexual sin in 1 Corinthians 6:11. But then he said, "Such *were* some of you; but you *were* washed, but you *were* sanctified, but you *were* justified in the name of the Lord Jesus Christ and in the Spirit of our God." (emphasis mine) That's past tense. The wonderful thing about confessing to God is that He hears – and forgives.

Don't you think that's cause for a little celebration?

"Every time a wedding takes place, the highest hopes and ideals of the whole community are rekindled. A wedding is the keynote address to the convention of human brotherhood."

— Mike Mason

CHAPTER FIFTEEN

SHOUT IT OUT!

(Song of Solomon 8:11-14)

John Wooden is one of the most beloved and respected college basketball coaches of all time. His run of ten national championships at UCLA from 1964 to 1975 will possibly never be eclipsed. Wooden was also a fine Christian gentleman. Pat Williams, former senior vice president of the Orlando Magic basketball team, wrote a book about his friend John Wooden called, *Coach Wooden: The 7 Principles That Shaped His Life and Will Change Yours.* I commend it for anyone who wants a solid description of character and virtue. I keep copies to give to every man I come in contact with.

Williams relates a time when Wooden had an argument with his wife, Nell that got heated. It was one of the few times in Coach's life that he got so angry he actually had to leave the house to cool off. "When I got home," he recalled, "there was a card on my pillow. On the card Nellie had written:

'Don't try to understand me, just love me.' It was a lesson I needed to learn."[118]

The account of Wooden's devotion to his wife is moving. Williams provides a glimpse of a man who was much more than a basketball coach:

> Ever since Nell passed away, Coach Wooden has observed the twenty-first day of every month by sitting down at his desk and writing a love letter to her. He tells her how much he loves her, misses her, and looks forward to seeing her again. He puts each letter in an envelope and places it on a stack of love letters that sits on the pillow on her side of the bed. Coach took me into that bedroom one time, and I got a lump in my throat when I saw that enormous yet neat bundle of love letters, tied with a yellow ribbon. Coach sleeps only on his side of the bed and leaves her side undisturbed. Next to Nell's pillow lies the packet of love letters, plus one other thing: the card that Nell wrote to him so many years ago after their argument, the card that reads, "Don't try to understand me, just love me."[119]

What an example. But it's not the laying of the letters on her pillow at night. It's the devotion that prompted the action. This was long term through their marriage. I recall watching UCLA games as a teenager. Right before the tip-off,

---

[118]Pat Williams, with James Denney, *Coach Wooden: The 7 Principles That Shaped His Life and Will Change Yours* (Grand Rapids, MI: Revell, 2011), 128-129.

[119]Ibid.

Wooden would always turn around, seek out Nellie in the crowd, and wave a rolled-up copy of the program at her as if to gain confidence from her and say, "Thanks for being here to share this moment with me." That mutual devotion lasted through a lifetime.

TOTALLY YOURS!

The last four verses of the Song of Solomon contain Solomon and Shulammite's final thoughts on marriage. She speaks for two verses then he speaks for one, and she ends it all with one final shout out for marriage – one final hurrah!

Solomon was an accomplished man. Song of Solomon 8:11 tells us he "had a vineyard at Baal-hamon; He entrusted the vineyard to caretakers. Each one was to bring a thousand shekels of silver for its fruit." That's pretty straightforward. Solomon actually had a number of vineyards. He leased them out to caretakers for the going rate of a "thousand shekels of silver" (Isaiah 7:23). Verse 12 indicates he then paid them two hundred shekels "to those who care for its fruit." So his net profit was eight hundred shekels of silver. The bottom line is that Solomon profited from renting out his vineyards.

In contrast, Shulammite spoke of "my own vineyard." But she didn't have any vineyards. As she has done before, she is speaking of her own body.

The theme that ties these vineyards together is the right of ownership. Solomon had a right to his vineyards. He could rent them out and receive the profit if he wanted, and he could give away the produce if he wanted. Such are the rights of ownership.

The same is true of Shulammite. She had the rights over her own body. The Hebrew language is emphatically possessive here. Literally, v. 12 reads, "My vineyard which is mine is before me." This emphasized her complete autocratic rights to govern her body. She could "rent" it out or give it to whomever she wanted. Her body was "at my disposal."

This is not an Old Testament version of "I am woman, hear me roar!" This is not early feminism. Her body is completely at her disposal but v. 12 said "the thousand shekels are for you, Solomon." There's a mixed message here. If her vineyard is her body then she should be receiving one thousand shekels in keeping with the illustration. But she is *giving* one thousand shekels to Solomon thus, she is the equivalent of the lender *and* the caretaker. She owns the vineyard, but she is giving it up to her caretaker – her husband.

But who does the "two hundred are for those who take care of its fruit" in v. 12 refer to? If the garden is her body, then the ones who took care of her fruit are likely her mother and brothers, the ones who raised her and protected her. This refers to a dowry which was very important in a patriarchal society. A son would work with his father in the family business. A daughter would be married off and a dowry paid to the father for the lost revenue of a daughter leaving the family.

The point of her illustration is that she was giving herself to Solomon out of love. Love is not a business transaction. Her point is that she was giving Solomon something that he could never buy, even with his wealth. A man who buys a woman expensive gifts thinking he can buy her love is a pathetic figure. And a woman who gives her body to a man thinking that will make him love her is also sadly mistaken. Neither can buy love!

Individuals and society prosper by encouraging marriage. At its best, it funnels sexual energy into emotional stability, keeps crime down, maintains physical health, and increases productivity and financial prosperity. Marriages like this produce happy, balanced kids and the process starts all over again.

Shulammite is a savvy lady. Her comments are *not* mere cultural preferences. Couples who give themselves willingly to each other in mutual ownership live happier and more productive lives. This isn't bondage – it's freedom to enjoy the benefits God has provided in marriage.

SOLOMON'S GARDEN

After twelve verses of Shulammite's wisdom on marriage, Solomon gives us his parting words in Song of Solomon 8:13-14. He addresses his comments to "you who sit in the gardens." So, who is he speaking to and what is he saying?

He is speaking to Shulammite regarding her sexual receptivity. The "you" is feminine singular, indicating he is speaking to his bride, Shulammite. The "gardens" he refers to is the same language he used in Song of Solomon 4:12 on their wedding night when he said, "A garden locked is my sister, my bride, a rock garden locked, a spring sealed up." Three verses later he speaks of Shulammite as a "garden spring."

Shulammite continues the word picture in Song of Solomon 4:16 (the exact middle verse of the book) with her invitation, "May my beloved come into his garden and eat its choice fruits!" This clearly indicates her invitation to enjoy her sexually.

In Song of Solomon 5:1 he responds, "I have come into my garden, my sister, my bride; I have gathered my myrrh along with my balsam. I have eaten my honeycomb and my honey; I have drunk my wine and my milk." Their marital union was sweet and satisfying for both of them.

Their personal enjoyment was recognized and blessed by the cheering crowd of family and friends at their wedding. Couples didn't get in their chariots and race off to their honeymoon hotel in those days. We're not told much about Solomon's wedding ceremony, but the custom was for the couple to retreat to their bedroom while the crowd was still enjoying the festivities which often went on for a week.

Solomon caps this exact middle verse of the whole book by interjecting a statement of blessing for everyone in Song of Solomon 5:11, "Eat, friends; drink and imbibe deeply, O lovers." He was saying, "Enjoy the party while I enjoy my bride!"

This is the sentiment he's repeating in Chapter 8. He wants to repeat their wedding night. Not just the vows, the whole night. They have been married for a while, they've had their first fight, and now they've gone on a little vacation back to her hometown. They've talked about what marriage means for a man and his wife and expressed mutual love to each other again in very clear terms.

Why does Solomon include these verses as his last recorded thought on the subject? It's because he wants to make sure they have completely resolved the incident at their bedroom door when Shulammite locked him out and refused his sexual advances. He wants to revisit the passion of his wedding night and make sure there are no inhibitions or roadblocks between them.

Every couple needs this. Anne and I spent part of our honeymoon at the iconic Del Coronado Hotel right on the beach on Coronado Island just south of San Diego, CA. The hotel is a majestic white 19th century building with a red roof that has been a symbol of an aristocratic past for over one hundred years. The setting of white sand beaches lining the blue Pacific Ocean provides an elegant experience for all visitors.

LET ME HEAR IT!

Every marriage needs this type of refreshment from time to time. But Solomon is not thinking of personal enjoyment only. In v. 13 he adds, "My companions are listening for your voice." The word "my" is not in the original language, so it's probable that he is not speaking about his personal friends. It's more likely he is speaking about her friends, the "daughters of Jerusalem," who were mentioned in v. 4.

We also know that she woke them up when she found out that he had gone out into the night after she turned him away at their bedroom door. When he returned, they were standing there until she dismissed them.

In saying, "companions are listening for your voice," it's probable that he wants her to make some kind of reaffirmation of her love for him. We don't know how much time has passed but it's probably been at least a couple of weeks since their fight. They have made up, but Solomon sees the importance in making a public statement of their love.

I love Solomon's next statement in v. 13 when he says, "Let me hear it!" The mention of *"the gardens"* in the first line references her sexual invitation. This is the subject matter he wants her friends to hear. He wants a strong, public affirmation of her desire for him to come and enjoy the garden of her sexual pleasures.

Since they knew all about their earlier spat, it's possible that Solomon wants to set the record straight. He's not trying to belittle her or demand a public apology. He wants people to know that he doesn't have to pound on the door to gain entrance to her heart. He's doing this as much for her as it is for him. He wants to make sure they are okay and that everyone knows it.

Solomon's cry is an invitation to his wife to stand with him in a public declaration of the joy and strength of their marriage. He's calling for an affirmation that his clueless ignorance of his wife's feelings and expectations, and her withholding sexual intimacy from him as a weapon, is not enough to damage their relationship. He's saying, "Let me hear that you desire me as much as I desire you. Let me hear that *we* still matter, that *we* are stronger than we were before, and that *we* will continue to affirm our love for each other."

It would be the same if the family or friends of a couple today had witnessed a dispute between a husband and wife. They would want everyone to know that the dispute was over and done with. It was a minor blip on the screen. They would want everyone to know, "We still love each other, and we are OK!"

But the application of Solomon's statement doesn't have to be limited to the response from a fight. We could use more public affirmations of post-marital love and commitment. We don't do this enough in our culture. We don't have ceremonies that publicly declare that we still love each other like the day we were married. But it's not a bad idea.

The closest my wife Anne and I have come is a surprise I arranged for her on our 25th anniversary. I invited some of our family who live in Southern California to meet us at the church where Anne and I were married in Anaheim. We drove all day and when we got to Anaheim I suggested that we stop by the church – just for old time's sake. As we walked in everyone surprised her and I had my brother (who is a pastor) "officiate" our anniversary service. There on the same stage where we had been married 25 years before, we repeated the same vows we said then.

This was especially meaningful because our kids were there. None of them were married at the time, but I wanted them to know how much I still loved their mom and what our hopes were for their marriages. Today they are all married to wonderful Christian mates and have blessed us with ten grandkids.

God wants us to say, "Let me hear it!" Why would anyone want anything less in marriage? G.K. Chesterton contemplated Christian marriage and spoke accurately when he said,

> The more I considered Christianity, the more I found that while it had established a rule and order, the chief aim of that order was to give room for good things to run wild.' He used the example of sex: 'I could never mix in the common murmur of that rising generation against monogamy, because

no restriction on sex seemed so odd and unexpected as sex itself...Keeping to one woman is a small price for so much as seeing one woman. To complain that I could only be married once was like complaining that I had only been born once. It was incommensurate with the terrible excitement of which one was talking. It showed, not an exaggerated sensibility to sex, but a curious insensibility to it. A man is a fool who complains that he cannot enter Eden by five gates at once. Polygamy is a lack of the realization of sex; it is like a man plucking five pears in mere absence of mind.'[120]

HURRY HOME!

Shulammite responds with the last word that's every bit as enthusiastic as Solomon's call to her. The last verse in the book is especially poignant, "Hurry, my beloved, and be like a gazelle or a young stag on the mountains of spices." In case the daughters of Jerusalem or anyone else in the court missed it, this woman wants her man to come home. She wants him and anyone else who might be listening to understand her clear desire to have him back in her arms again.

You can't miss the urgency of these words. In v. 14 she said, "Hurry." The word means, to "flee, run away, chase, drive

---

[120]G. K. Chesterton, *Orthodoxy* (1908; repr., Peabody, Massachusetts: Hendrickson Publishers, 2008), 103.

away, put to flight." [121] Most of the time it depicts fleeing or running away from something.

But Shulammite is asking her husband to flee to her. She compared him to a "gazelle or a young stag" as she did in their first encounter. There is a definite tinge of urgent sexual invitation in her voice. She wanted to share her time, her bed, her thoughts and dreams, and her life with him.

Young couples seldom comprehend this. When love is young most people have a sense that life will always be like this. But the longer you live, the more precious life becomes. It's the same with marriage. The longer you live the more you realize how precious marriage is.

Years ago, I read a poignant account of this in a newspaper advice column written by columnist Ann Landers:

> 'Please come home early.' This was the most unreasonable request ever made by my wife of almost 40 years. She didn't make this request often. It came mostly on Saturdays, Sundays, and holidays, but it seemed that I always had so many things to do that in spite of her gentle urging, I rarely came home early. I don't want to give the impression that I was never at home. I was at home a lot. We rarely did anything out of the ordinary. We enjoyed the kids and the grandchildren. We listened to music, read the paper, and had meals together. Sometimes we would just talk about how the day had gone. Now I know why she asked me so often to 'Please come

[121]Earl S. Kalland, "284 חָרַב," ed. R. Laird Harris, Gleason L. Archer Jr., and Bruce K. Waltke, *Theological Wordbook of the Old Testament* (Chicago: Moody Press, 1999), 131.

home early.' She wasn't just lonely; she was lonely for me. When she passed away a short time ago, I learned firsthand what loneliness is all about. I have a supportive family and many good friends. I'm free now to go places and do things, but I'm lonesome. Lonesome for her. Now that she's gone, I've found the time to 'come home early,' but there is nobody to come home to. There is nobody to do those simple little things with, such as watching the evening news, listening to music, and reading the paper. And nobody cares how my day went. If I should get a call from the good Lord to 'Please come home early,' I won't fight it.–Lonesome in K.C.[122]

Someone once said, "Once you're part of a chord in tune, you're never the same again." Being in a loving marriage is being part of a chord in tune. And when part of that chord is removed, you're not the same. Shulammite's last advice is to take full advantage of the time you have with the husband or wife God has given you.

STARTING OVER

I would like to end with one last comment that is not in the Song of Solomon. I've found that often when I speak on a passage of Scripture addressed to a specific group of people that it can cause a fair amount of pushback. I'm thinking of passages like Proverbs 31 that addresses a godly wife, or

---

[122]Ann Landers, *Chicago Tribune*, July 7, 1990, www.chicagotribune.newspapers. com, accessed on May 15, 2020.

Titus 2 that speaks about the role of a woman, or 1 Timothy 3 which outlines the pattern for biblical elders.

The pushback I receive is, "That's hopeless, I could never measure up to that." I hope that you won't feel like this about the Song of Solomon. This is a real book about real people. But, along with all the flowery language, you can see that both Solomon and Shulammite are presented as flawed people. After all, the last half of the book deals with the response to their first fight.

The other response I hear is often, "It's too late. I've already blown it." I want to speak to this issue a bit in closing because I don't want anyone to think that failing to live up to the template of Solomon and Shulammite means they can't start over.

So, if you've failed in some way in your marriage, or maybe if your marriage has completely blown up, I want you to know there is hope. That's the message of the Bible. Every single one of us comes into this world in a sinful condition. In Psalm 58:3, King David said, "The wicked are estranged from the womb; these who speak lies go astray from birth." And, just so we know we are all in the same kayak together, Romans 3:23 reminds us that, "all of us have sinned and fall short of the glory of God."

We're all in this together. God doesn't grade on a curve and no one starts at the head of the class. So please accept these reminders as my sincere desire to offer a way forward for you, no matter where you find yourself.

First, if you are not a Christian, please know that you must start there. My advice to the non-Christian is simple – receive Christ. Confess your sin and believe in the work that

Christ did on the cross for you. Receive His work for you by faith. If you fail to do this, then you will not have His power to confess, repent, and forgive in your marriage because you have never accepted His provision of salvation.

Second, to those living together without being married, my advice is also simple – move out. I realize that if you're not a Christian this will probably seem completely archaic and stupid. Others may say, "I can't afford to live alone." But even sociologists will tell you that human relationships don't flourish when men and women live together without being married. This is especially true if children are involved. Find another arrangement.

Third, a word to the divorced. Before moving on you will need to assess your previous marriage and your role in the divorce. If you were the innocent party (rare, but it does happen), then take some time before you move on. If the divorce was mutual then stop blaming the other person and see what you can do about your own sins and faults that contributed to the break-up. More than anything, you also need to evaluate your relationship to Christ. If you are not a Christian, you need to repent of your sin and receive Him today. If you *are* a Christian, you need to confess any known sin in your life, then recognize that divorce is not the unpardonable sin, and move on in God's grace.

Fourth, to the single person. Though most people marry, there is nothing wrong with being single. God is completely in control and is aware of your needs. The Apostle Paul was single and said that he wished everyone was so that they could serve God with the same abandon he did. Trust God for your future and get busy serving Him.

Fifth, to all married couples. This book has been written to help you understand God's provision for you in your marriage and help you to refresh and renew your commitment to your spouse. Marriage is a paradox of emotion – we crave independence, but we are wired for intimacy. We can't live with our spouse, but we can't live without them. The freedom of the single life beckons us at times, but we can't imagine an empty house and no family.

Sixth, a word to young people who are not yet married. Please understand that there is no more important decision in your life than your decision to get married. If you listen to most of your professors in college, your political leaders, media giants in music and movies, you will develop a very negative attitude toward marriage.

You will be told it is an outmoded model of our patriarchal past that doesn't work anymore. Many of your friends will tell you that it's just not worth it because you will only end up divorced. Others will tell you that the new models of homosexuality and transgendered individuals present a much more viable lifestyle.

But these voices will never bring personal fulfillment let alone advance society. That doesn't mean that marriage, even Christian marriage, will fulfill all of our earthly expectations. Marriage isn't a self-actualization plan. But it is still the best plan available.

Last, to everyone, married or not, remember this. When the glow of your marital expectations fades, remember that you were meant for a greater romance. You were meant to know an eternal love that will never let you down. Marital love at its best points to the cross of Christ. But outside of salvation, the greatest joy we can experience on this earth is the love of a godly husband or wife.

Oh, how we need this. It is beyond breath-taking to consider the storms that assail marriage today. I would have never thought that our culture could descend to this point when I was married years ago. In the time that I've been married our culture has seen the rise of the ungodly feminist movement, the "shack up" culture, the explosion of sexual "freedom," a dramatic rise in "blended" families, the state approval of same-sex marriage, and a wild embrace of people who don't even know what sex they are.

This is beyond throwing the baby out with the bathwater. This is insane. Ryan Anderson, senior research fellow at The Heritage Foundation, encapsulates the problems that occur when God's standards of marriage are abandoned:

> The evidence is simply overwhelming that the marital norms of monogamy, sexual exclusivity, and permanence make a difference for society—and those norms are based on sexual complementarity. If a man does not commit to a woman in a permanent and exclusive relationship, the likelihood of his begetting fatherless children and leaving fragmented families in his wake increases. The more sexual partners a man has and the shorter those relationships are, the more likely he is to have children with multiple women to whom he is not committed. His attention and resources thus

divided, the predictable consequences unfold for
the mothers, the children, and society.[123]

The marriage of Solomon and Shulammite isn't calling us
to a throwback of a better time. This isn't a nostalgic call for
the "good old days." No, this is a higher calling. It's a calling
that casts a vision for marriage as God intended it to be, two
frail human beings living imperfect lives touched by the grace
and truth of our Redeemer, Jesus Christ.

So how do we acquire this? The best way is to write your
own lovesong. It will be different than that of everyone else.
But one by one, when couples commit to loving each other
the way God calls us to, then our world will take note because
that is really what they are looking for too.

A LOVE STORY

Let me close with a love story. It's about a man named
Eric Liddell and his wife Florence. Liddell is known to many
as the hero of the 1981 movie, *Chariots of Fire*. It's the real-life
story of Liddell's rise as an Olympic champion from Great
Britain in the 1924 Olympics. As the son of Scottish missionaries, and a committed Christian, Liddell ran for the
glory of God.

That's the story in the movie. But Eric Liddell's life is much
more than his Olympic fame. Author Duncan Hamilton
wrote about his life in the wonderful book, *For the Glory*. I've
summarized his account below.

---

[123]Ryan T. Anderson, *Truth Overruled: The Future of Marriage and Religious Freedom*
(Washington, DC: Regnery Publishing, 2015), 50.

Several months before the Olympics, Liddell discovered that the 100 meters, his specialty, would be run on a Sunday. On learning this, he refused to run because he felt running on Sunday would dishonor God. He wound up running the 400 meter race, with very little preparation, and won the gold medal, setting a new Olympic and world record.

The rest of his story is not in the movie but is more intriguing. After the Olympics Liddell went to China as a missionary. Following his first furlough home to Scotland he married Florence Mackenzie in Tianjin, China in 1934. Over the next seven years the Liddells threw themselves into their work in China.

In 1941, the winds of war blew stronger. China had become so vulnerable to the Japanese that Great Britain advised all British citizens to leave. Florence and the two oldest daughters, Patricia and Heather, left for Canada to be with her family. Eric never saw them again and never met his youngest daughter, Maureen, who was born in Canada after Florence returned home.

The Japanese took over the mission compound in 1943, and Liddell was captured and imprisoned at the Weihsien Internment Camp. Everyone in the camp regarded him as a model of Christian compassion and mercy. Florence continued to write, trying to be encouraging and hopeful. "Oh Eric, my thoughts and prayers are forever with you and I long for the time when we'll be able to live as a family again... We will appreciate our life together all the more and, in the meantime, we have some wonderful memories to live on

...Yes, I know I have wild hopes ...I know I'm crazy ...Yours forever and a day."[124]

On February 21, 1945 Eric suffered a series of three strokes, the result of an undiagnosed brain tumor. As his friend, fellow Scottish missionary Annie Buchan, leaned over his withered body, he uttered his last words, "It's complete surrender."[125]

The camp was rocked with disbelief and despair. His funeral stopped all activity at the camp. It was called "one of the most moving events in the whole of camp life."[126]

Florence and her daughters faced the daunting task of recovering from the unexpected loss of one they loved so much. Hamilton captured a moment decades later that illustrates the deep love Florence had for Eric:

> One evening Florence sat on the couch at her daughter Heather's home and watched a reel of celluloid she'd never seen before. It was Pathe's black-and-white film of Liddell's 400-meters win in Paris. She saw then what anyone can view now on YouTube. The focus on his twenty-two-year-old face. Those long fingers resting on his hips. That number – 451 – on his shirt front. The crowd massed steeply behind him. That stare down the line and the curve of the Colombes track before the gun releases him on the race of a lifetime. His

---

[124]Duncan Hamilton, *For the Glory: Eric Liddell's Journey from Olympic Champion to Modern Martyr* (New York, New York: Penguin Press, 2016), 306.

[125]Ibid., 325.

[126]Ibid., 326.

fleet feet pounding along the cinder. The spray of that cinder as he runs. His head thrown back. The snap of the tape.

"She couldn't believe what she was seeing," remembers Heather. Florence leaned forward on the very lip of her seat, oblivious for more than a full minute to absolutely everything except the scene played out in front of her on a twenty-one-inch television. "It was as if she was there with him, sitting in the stand," adds Heather. As the race began, Florence was lost in the brightness of it. She even yelled: "Come on honey. You can beat him. You can do it."

The last frame of that film shows Liddell after his triumph. He is accepting a congratulatory handshake. The image lingers, freezing him in that pose for a while – the splendor of the man he'd once been so apparent. Florence stood up and looked at it as though in that moment she was remembering every one of the yesterdays she had spent beside him. She bowed her head, raised her hands to her face, and began to weep ... Florence died in June 1984. She had never stopped loving him.[127]

That's the same kind of love that Solomon and Shulammite enjoyed. It's the kind of love that God designed for those who find their love in Him first, and then for the beloved one God has given them. That's worth shouting about!

---

[127]Ibid., 350-351.

One of the most natural phenomena known to mankind is the mystery of attraction between men and woman. But God is the author of this attraction. And He has designed men and women to be physically, emotionally, intellectually, and spiritually attracted to each other in a way that leads to a life-long commitment in marriage that fulfills their desires and pleases Him.

Outside of salvation, this is the most important decision anyone can ever make. That's why Satan is trying his hardest to destroy it. We can identify his tactics clearly over the past fifty years as we have seen the rise of egalitarianism, divorce rates, co-habitation, same-sex marriage, and now the trans-gendered revolution which tells people they cannot even be sure of their sexual makeup.

These issues have combined to form a massive frontal attack on God's design for human relationships. Left unchallenged and unchecked, they will prove to be more disastrous in each succeeding generation, resulting in pathologies of all kinds, including, loneliness, crime, poverty, lack of education, drug and alcohol abuse, volatile relationships, emotional and behavioral problems, and societal confusion and chaos.

And yet marriage remains our best response to these degrading factors and our best chance for personal fulfillment and societal stability. This is not only because it is designed by God, but because it is the only thing that works. Marriage brings spiritual fulfillment, emotional contentment, personal companionship, marital partnership, and financial stability, in ways that can't be duplicated in any other relationship.

These values can't be faked. If couples don't experience stability in their marriage they can't pass it on to their children.

But that doesn't mean the future is all doom and gloom. Even though parents can fail in passing along the benefits of a vibrant marriage to their children, each child who grows up without these values can discover them for themselves and put a stop to their dysfunctional family life in one generation.

My hope and prayer is that every person who is not married who reads this book will grasp God's pattern for marriage that is laid out in the Song of Solomon. If you had Godly parents praise God for them and duplicate their example in the next generation with your kids.

If your parents were not good examples, you don't have to repeat their mistakes. Ask God to bring someone into your life who will love Him first and then love you in the way God intended for you to be loved in a Christian marriage.

For all of those who are married, my prayer is that you would be encouraged and deepen your walk with God and your marriage as a result of reading this book. I pray that you will learn to rely on Him daily as you walk life together, no matter where you live or how long you've been married.

Marriage is not heaven. But it's a piece of heaven we get to enjoy under the apple tree of God's provision of marriage. Thank God that He has made a way for us to experience life together in this way as we await the greater love-song in heaven with Him some day.

CPSIA information can be obtained
at www.ICGtesting.com
Printed in the USA
BVHW070303030321
601494BV00002B/118